The Alphorn through the Eyes of the Classical Composer

by
Frances Jones

Series in Music

VERNON PRESS

www.vernonpress.com

In the Americas:	*In the rest of the world:*
Vernon Press	Vernon Press
1000 N West Street, Suite 1200,	C/Sancti Espiritu 17,
Wilmington, Delaware 19801	Malaga, 29006
United States	Spain

Series in Music

Library of Congress Control Number: 2020940993

ISBN: 978-1-64889-246-2

Also available:

978-1-64889-060-4 [Hardback, Premium Color]; 978-1-64889-044-4 [Hardback, B&W];

978-1-64889-247-9 [Paperback, Premium Color]; 978-1-64889-136-6 [PDF, E-Book]

Cover design by Vernon Press.
Cover image: Lai da Palpuogna, Canton Graubunden, eastern Switzerland, photo Frances Jones.

Table of Contents

List of Figures and Tables

Figures

Tables

The author with alphorn in context, Männlichen, Bernese Oberland, Switzerland.

Preface

To the modern audience, the visual and aural qualities of the alphorn are quintessentially evocative of the Swiss Alps. A number of nineteenth-century composers quote alphorn music in their symphonic and chamber works, and the power of such a quotation is unspoken but unmistakable. What lies behind this effect?

Why is it, for example, that we expect a reply to the shepherd's call at the end of the *Scène aux Champs* in Berlioz's *Symphonie fantastique*? How is it that Berlioz can convey such a profound sense of unease, and not even by what he has written, but by what he has *not* written? Upon what basis can he assume that we will understand his meaning? Alternatively, how is it that we understand Beethoven's intention when he writes those reassuring horn calls at the beginning of the last movement of his 'Pastoral' Symphony? How can his music convey to us that we can now relax, that all is in fact well? These are not random melodic choices. There is something powerful at work here. Such composers are making use of a rich heritage of extra-musical reference. We, the audience, are led to places of which we may barely be aware, and may indeed have no personal experience, yet the metaphors are so strong that we understand them immediately. The composer is drawing on a particular repertoire of such signifiers to convey the specific moods that he requires.

But why is it that a reference to a sound made on an unsophisticated piece of hollow tree trunk can have such a profound effect on us? That in itself is extraordinary. Who first discovered that the alphorn was the perfect piece of equipment to use in the management of cattle in the mountains, why is it that cows are soothed by the low, rich sound of an alphorn—and what about other animals, and indeed, does this relate to our own natural affinity with the sound?

When we turn to these musical allusions in the hands of the composer, we find that such references penetrate beyond the realm of superficial delight: they communicate with our inner spirit, our unconscious mind.

This book has grown and evolved from material researched for my PhD thesis 'The Alphorn in Western Art Music: a Cultural and Historical Study' (University of Hull, UK, 2015). It explores the use of the musical language of the alphorn call to ascertain why and how such references as those of Berlioz or Beethoven can convey so much meaning. I seek out what it is that a composer brings into the concert hall, the theatre, the opera house, the church or the drawing room by such a quotation, to what heritage he is referring, and upon what basis there are grounds for an assumption that such a reference will be understood by an audience.

There's lots to unravel. The magic of the alphorn will not be spoiled by this voyage of discovery—rather, enhanced, and all the more to be wondered at. It is a fusion between a love of the mountains, of nature, of Swiss people with a passion for their country and their instrument, of gentle Swiss cows, of haunting alphorn music, of the profundity of classical music and of the genius of composition. It is a remarkable synthesis.

All translations are my own unless otherwise acknowledged. All manuscript, illustration and document source and credit details are given in a caption or an endnote. Every effort has been made to contact copyright holders of materials and illustrations. We shall gladly respond to and rectify any substantiated omissions.

I wish to thank all my Swiss alphorn-playing colleagues and friends for their insider information and endless encouragement in the preparation of this book, my Professor Christopher R Wilson at the University of Hull for believing in the project and my husband Martin for lots of technical and moral support, and for buying me a CD of alphorn music at Geneva airport in 2004 which inspired me to set off on this amazing journey. Special thanks are extended to The Delius Trust for a generous grant to help with the costs of reproduction of some of the images included.

I hope that this unique and extraordinary journey brings you as much pleasure and delight as it has brought to me.

Frances Jones. Summer 2020
www.AmazingAlphorn.com

Foreword

This book is one of the most fascinating and thought-provoking musical publications of the decade. Dr Frances Jones is an acknowledged authority on the alphorn, its history and its music; furthermore, she is a highly skilled player of the instrument. Her remarkable achievement in 'The Alphorn through the Eyes of the Classical Composer', as a result of many years of meticulous research and fieldwork, is that she conclusively demonstrates that the alphorn has constantly influenced the music of an enormous number of composers, over a period of more than 400 years.

Dr Jones postulates very convincingly that the plangent sonority of this acoustically primitive instrument is powerfully and imaginatively evoked in the musical creations of Bach, Handel, Haydn, L. and W.A. Mozart, Grétry, Gossec, Viotti, Clementi, Beethoven, Rossini, Schubert, Berlioz, Schumann, Liszt, Wagner, Raff, Brahms, Mendelssohn, Mahler, Elgar, R. Strauss, Delius, Bax, Walton and Britten. I am especially pleased to see the inclusion of the memorable alphorn-like passage in Delius's *A Mass of Life*.

Chapter 6, 'Alphorn for the Modern Composer', is a particularly valuable resource, in that it includes several delightful and highly effective original alphorn works, including an impressive one by the author's husband. Of particular interest are Frances Jones's thoughts in the closing Epilogue at the end of this chapter (pages 288-291). Her concluding evaluation of the alphorn and its place in musical history is enshrined in her final sentence: 'The outstanding beauty and unique voice of the alphorn will ensure that it will continue to be enjoyed long into the future'. I must confess that my own previously rather dormant interest in the alphorn has now been re-kindled to the extent that I am determined to acquire one of these magnificent instruments.

I very much hope that this beautifully written book will be enjoyed by a much wider public than alphorn enthusiasts; indeed, it deserves a place in the library of every brass player.

Anthony Halstead

Chapter 1

The Alphorn

The sound of the alphorn is an unmistakable evocation of the Swiss mountains. That composers should use this sound, either literally or metaphorically, in representation of the Alps, is a remarkable phenomenon. To explore this subject, first of all we need to look at the key ingredients: what is an alphorn, and what is alphorn music.

Terminology

What do we understand by the word 'alphorn'? In fact, what is an 'alp' and what is a 'horn'? Both components have multiple meanings, and many of these are relevant to the instrument.

'Alp' has two meanings, one specific (upper case A) and one general (lower case a). The Romans used the word Alps to describe the mountainous regions of central Europe: these form what is today the major part of the northern border of Italy, part of eastern France, southern Switzerland and western Austria. In more general terms, though, an alp is an area of pasture on a high mountainside, generally above the tree line and below the snow line, used for grazing in the summer months. Both of these meanings have significance in this book.

The word 'horn' in musical terminology can be used in the context of an animal horn that can be blown; the term is also used for an instrument made of another substance that generally has similarities with the shape of a natural horn, in other words, it has a conical bore and is curved. This contrasts with the category of trumpet, which refers to an instrument that is cylindrical and straight or folded.

The word 'alphorn' exists in many versions: in German or English we find alphorn, alp-horn, alp horn or alpenhorn; in addition, its equivalents in the other Swiss national languages are *cor des Alpes* and *corno alpino*. While the use of the word alphorn or its equivalents by the Swiss always refers to a man-made horn, both of the implications of the word alp, as examined above, are relevant; moreover, it can be seen that over time, the usage has changed. In the sixteenth century, the term referred to the horn that was used by the herdsmen in the mountains. The accounts of the monastery of St. Urban in the canton of

Lucerne of 1527 state that two coins were given to a strolling alphorn player from the canton of Valais: '*einem Walliser mit einem Alp horn gen 2 Batzen*'.[1] The word 'alphorn' is today normally reserved for use in conjunction with the Alps, or with the instruments of emigrants from there, while *Hirtenhorn* (herdsman's horn) is generally used to describe similar instruments from other sources.

A number of other names for the instrument are also found, even in Switzerland. In 1555 Conrad Gesner chooses the term *lituu alpinum*,[2] whereas in 1563 a letter from the Governor of the canton of Neuchâtel refers to a mountain herdsman who plays a *cornet* to his cattle.[3] German writer Michael Praetorius uses the term *Hölzern Trummet* (wooden trumpet) in 1619 for his description and engraving of the long wooden horn of the Swiss herdsman,[4] and in 1767 Moritz Capeler describes an '*alp-horn, cornu alpinum vulgit*,' in his volume about Mount Pilatus which overlooks Lucerne.[5]

Other names are given to long wooden horns used in herding communities in other countries, like the *trembita* in Poland and the *tulnic* or *bucium* in Romania. Various names are also used that can be translated into English as herdsman's horn or pastoral trumpet: *Hirten Horn* is a term used by Leopold Mozart, and *tuba pastoralis* is the name used in Christmas music from the eighteenth and nineteenth centuries in the Czech-speaking regions of eastern Europe.

The instrument

Alongside the variety of nomenclature, the term 'alphorn' has been applied to herdsmen's horns in the Alps with a range of different shapes and lengths. Of primary importance, though, is that it was longer than an animal horn. This is for two reasons: in order to communicate with cows, low notes are most effective. Even on the longest animal horns, such as those of the kudu at around three feet long, where one can play five or six different notes, only the lowest one of these is below middle C. Secondly, a key function of the alphorn is to play melodies: substantial tunes can only be played on an instrument long enough to gain access to a number of high notes, and to produce notes that are 'in tune' with each other. An alphorn therefore needs to be both longer than a natural horn, to enable the production of lower and higher notes, and carefully constructed so that it is 'in tune' with itself in order to produce a pleasing melody.

Fig. 1.1. Swiss cows are attracted when low notes are played on an alphorn. The author, canton of Appenzell, Switzerland. Photo: Lina Frischknecht.

Pictorial and written records show that alphorns even within Switzerland used to be of varying length. In 1767, for example, the scientist Moritz Anton Capeler described the instruments he saw on Mount Pilatus, above Lucerne. He states that the instrument can be from four to twelve feet in length. He describes the instrument, the way in which it had been made, the sound it makes and the style of music that it played. Capeler includes both a sketch of an alphorn and notation of a sample of the herdsmen's music:

> The alp-horn, as it is generally known, is a long tube made entirely of wood, the length varying between 4 and 12 feet: the curve follows the exact shape of a geometric cissoidal curve: from the bottom opening of 3 to 5 fingers wide it gradually becomes narrower so that where the mouth is placed there is an opening of 1½ thumb widths, internally it is jointed, with long thin lengths, and for its whole length it is tightly bound together externally with flexible twigs: and so that there are no gaps to let air out it is covered all over with pitch and wax. It gives a very deep, penetrating sound, which though not too powerful close by, can be heard a long distance away, and in order to give all information, I add that it is used for calling by the herdsman, in the herdsman's melody known as the *Kuh-reyen*, and in the various similar rural songs.[6]

Fig. 1.2. Alphorn and melody reproduced in Capeler's *Pilati Montis Historia*, 1767.

Music from the eighteenth and nineteenth centuries explored later is written for an instrument in a specific key: the pitches written for each instrument reflect the length of the instrument for which each work was written.

The shape is also not standardised. Some alphorns are straight, while others have a gradual flare with no further bell expansion beyond that of the cone itself.

Fig. 1.3. A collection of wooden alphorns, between four and six feet in length, undated, at the Museum Regiunal Surselva, Ilanz, in eastern Switzerland. Photo: Frances Jones.

Nowadays, though, the typical alphorn that is depicted on countless Swiss postcards and tourist items has a specific form and dimensions. It appears in the Hornbostel-Sachs system of classification of musical instruments as an end-blown lip-vibrated aerophone, with a conical bore, straight with a flared end, classification number 413.121.[7] A typical alphorn has the following features:

material of construction	wood, bound with rattan
length	11½ feet long (*doh* of its harmonic series is F sharp)
shape	conical; straight apart from a curved flared bell
properties	uninterrupted bore: no valves, no finger holes
mouthpiece	French horn type,[8] separate from the main tube
decoration	typically a painting on the bell that for example shows the canton flag surrounded with mountain flowers
method of playing	lip-vibrated (buzz-blown)
position when played	bell rests on the ground
geographical range	mainly the mountainous regions of Switzerland
played by	alphorn enthusiasts
use	played for tourists, at Swiss events and at alphorn festivals
music played	'traditional' alphorn music that is evocative of the alpine idyll
accompaniment	solo, or up to four players. Not traditionally played with any other instrument.

A tree can provide a readily available source of material from which a long horn can be made: long wooden instruments are found in many regions of the world, from Norway to Ethiopia or the Andes. In the Alps, the horn typically takes the natural shape of a tree that grows on a slope, with a curve at the broad end that can project the sound outwards when the instrument rests on the ground. The traditional Swiss alphorn is made from one pine tree of the required shape, halved lengthways, gouged out and bound together again with softened willow shoots, rushes, strips of bark or something similar.

Fig. 1.4. Trees on mountain slopes naturally grow in the shape required for a typical long alphorn. Photo: Simon Jones.

Fig. 1.5. A postcard of unknown date from the French Alps shows how a tree is sawn to make an alphorn.

There has since 1999 been a type of telescopic alphorn made from carbon-fibre that is popular today both in Switzerland and elsewhere, invented by the late Swiss alphorn enthusiast Roger Zanetti.

In addition, there are other instruments in Switzerland today that could be described as belonging to the alphorn family. These include the *Büchel* which has a folded form like a fanfare trumpet, the *Stockbüchel* which is slender, the *Tiba*, sometimes made of metal, and the shorter *Litu*.

Fig. 1.6. Sami Lörtscher plays a *Büchel*. Photo: Daniel Pfenninger.

For the purposes of this book, the influence of the music of a long wooden herdsman's horn upon the music of classical composers is the subject, irrespective of local nomenclature, shape, length or material of construction. I have chosen six primary criteria:

1. it has a conical bore,
2. it is long enough that it can produce a number of different notes,
3. it is buzz-blown; in other words, there is no reed to activate the sound,
4. it is only open at one end, thus excludes tubes played like a flute,
5. it has no lateral holes for fingers to alter its sounding length, unlike the cornett family,
6. it is not altered in length (as with a trombone) in order to gain access to notes other than those in its natural harmonic series.

Functions

The alphorn evolved primarily as a tool for the herdsman to use for the management of animals in his care. It was also used as a calling instrument. Its use for purely musical enjoyment is a secondary phenomenon: to what extent the alphorn was part of the rustic music-making scene before about the seventeenth century is not known.

There is written and graphic evidence of the sophisticated use of horns for animal husbandry by Roman times. Marcus Terentius Varro (116–27 BC), for example, tells of training young pigs to respond to the horn call. In *De Rerum Rusticum*, three volumes that describe Roman farming methods, one section documents the handling of the sow and her new piglets with the training of the young to come to the call of the horn. Events such as the provision of food were associated with a horn call, so that the animals soon learned to recognise the sounds:

> When the piglets are born, the mothers only go out of the sty for water. After ten days they are allowed out to forage for food, just in the vicinity of the farm, so that they can return frequently to suckle their piglets. As the piglets grow they can go out with the mother, and when they come home they are parted from her and fed separately, so that they get used to the lack of the mother's milk, which happens after ten days. The swineherd should train them to do everything to the sound of the horn. They start off in the pen, and then when the horn sounds, the door is opened so that they can go out to where barley is spread out ... The idea to have them gather at the sound of the horn is that they will not become lost when they spread out in wooded country ...[9]

The technique is explained by Polybius, a Greek chronicler who lived around 203–120 BC. In his *Histories*, he describes how the swineherds of Italy used horns to communicate with pigs on the plains of Tuscany. Families of pigs were taught their own call so that the herdsmen, by blowing their call, could divide up the family groups to take them home at the end of a day, a task that would otherwise be impossible:

> They do not follow close behind the animals but keep some distance in front of them, sounding their horn every now and then, and the animals follow behind and run together at the sound. Indeed, the complete familiarity which the animals show with the particular horn to which they belong seems at first astonishing and almost incredible. For owing to the populousness and wealth of the country, the droves of swine are exceedingly large, especially along the sea coast of the Tuscans: for one

sow will bring up a thousand pigs, or sometimes even more. They drive them out from their night sties to feed, in the order determined by their litters and ages. If several droves are taken to the same place, they cannot preserve these distinction of litters, and of course they get mixed up with each other as they are being driven out, as they feed, and as they are being brought home. Thus horn-blowing is used to separate them when they have got mixed up together, without effort or difficulty. For as they feed, one swineherd goes in one direction sounding his horn, and another in another: and thus the animals sort themselves, and follow their own horns with such eagerness that it is impossible by any means to stop or hinder them.[10]

By the time of the ancient Greeks and Romans, then, the sounding of a horn had acquired comparatively sophisticated use as a piece of equipment essential to rural life. At times the horn blown to attract the attention of people was referred to as a pastoral or herdsman's horn. The Roman poet Virgil (70–19 BC) wrote in his epic poem *Aeneid* of the taking of Italy by the Trojans. They had the assistance of various goddesses and Furies, and in *Aeneid* Book 7, Virgil describes the blowing of a pastoral horn by a goddess to rally the people. The description includes a factor that is a recurring theme in the use of horns for calling: that the horn blower stands on a high vantage point. This may be an outcrop of rock, the roof of a building, a high tower or some other place from which the sound will be thrown to the maximum:

... the goddess, on finding those to be harmed, from her vantage point, in anger seeks out a high stable roof and from the highest point plays a fierce signal on a curved pastoral horn. She directs the infernal sound so that the fields tremble and the deep woods resound. It reverberated in the Trivia Lake for a long time; also in the white sulphurous river of Nar and the fountains of Velinus, and terrified mothers clasped their infants to their bosoms. The horn gave a terrible signal, and at the sound, the farmers quickly and wildly ran away like darts, and indeed the population of Troy poured out of the open camps to Ascanius for help.[11]

There is no record of whether these were natural horns or constructed wooden horns, but there are some visual records that show that probably both kinds were used. A mosaic dating from around the first century at Boscéaz, near Orbe in the canton of Vaud in Switzerland, shows a pastoral scene that includes a man who blows a horn walking ahead of some cattle.

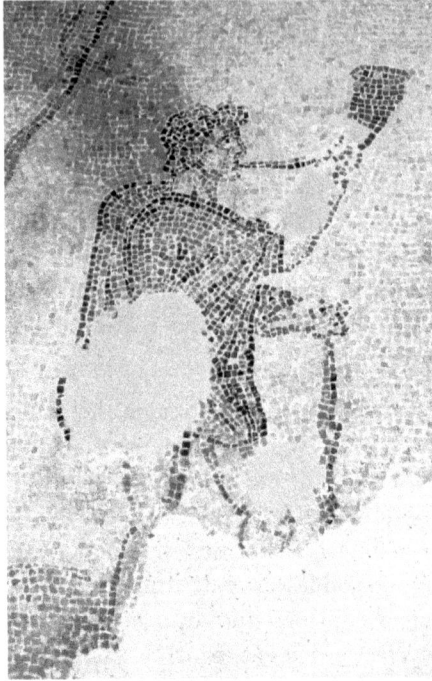

Fig. 1.7. A man plays a horn in one of a series of rural scenes depicted in the Roman mosaics at Boscéaz, Switzerland. Photo: Frances Jones.[12]

An eighth-century English etching shows shepherds with horns that appear to be made of wood, with binding to hold them together.

Fig. 1.8. Shepherds with horns, English, eighth century.[13]

Monasteries in Medieval England owned vast tracts of the countryside, and working with sheep provided a substantial part of monastic income. The number of illustrations in illuminated manuscripts that feature a monk or other herdsman with a horn of this type demonstrates that it was a familiar item both in rural England and across Europe.[14] In an English psalter that dates from the first quarter of the thirteenth century, a monk blows a similarly banded horn:

Fig. 1.9. A monk plays a bound horn, illumination of the letter E, beginning of Psalm 97. *Psalter with Canticles*, English, early thirteenth century.[15]

A later depiction of a herdsman with a horn appears in an illuminated antiphonary, a large format parchment choir book used to lead the singing in a monastic church. This manuscript of around 1750 comes from the Franciscan convent at Horb am Neckar, in southern Germany. The herdsman and his horn, together with a tree behind, form the initial letter K for the word *Kyrie*.

Fig. 1.10. A herdsman, his horn and a tree form the initial letter K for the word *Kyrie*.[16]

There are other references to the use of the horn in animal management. It is the subject of the English children's rhyme that begins:

Little Boy Blue, come blow up your horn:
The sheep's in the meadow, the cow's in the corn ...

The earliest known printed version of this rhyme is found in *The Famous Tommy Thumb's Little Story-book* of 1760, but it was familiar before that: 150 years earlier it is parodied by Edgar in Shakespeare's *King Lear* (Act 3, Scene 6), written around 1604:

Edgar (sings)
Sleepest or wakest thou, jolly shepherd?
Thy sheep be in the corn,
And for one blast of thy minikin mouth
Thy sheep will take no harm.[17]

A description of a long wooden horn, named a *lituü alpinum*, appears in 1555, when the Zürich naturalist Conrad Gesner wrote one of the first detailed descriptions of the Alps, a volume entitled *Commentariolus de raris et admirandis herbis*. In it, he describes a scene on Mount Pilatus, above Lucerne, where his party came across a herdsman in a cow byre high on the mountain. He gave them a drink of milk and invited them to blow his alphorn:

> ... in the highest cow byre, after we had refreshed ourselves with the most delicate and rich milk, we blew an alpine trumpet (nearly eleven feet long, made from two lengths of wood, curved and gouged, and expertly bound with twigs ...)[18]

A common feature of stock management in the mountains is a method known as transhumance. Cattle spend the winter in barns on the lower slopes, valleys or in the villages, and can graze the high pasture-land only during the summer months. The animals are collected from their winter quarters at the end of June, once the grass on the high pastures has started to grow, and returned at the end of the summer when the warmth begins to leave the high pastures. These annual transhumance processions can still be seen every summer in the mountains. From the mid-eighteenth century, there is a pictoral record of these activities.

A Swiss prayer-book compiled by Abraham Kyburz in 1754, *Theologia Naturalis*, contains an engraving (See Fig. 1.11), with the caption: '*Aufarth eines Kühers mit Weib und Kind, Haab und Vieh auf den Berg*' (Ascent of a cowherd with wife and child, belongings and cattle up the mountain. The illustration accompanies the following prayer:

> *Der Bergman führt das Vieh auf hoher Berge Wiesen / O daß der Schöpfer wurd von ihm auch hoch gepriesen / O daß der Höchste stäts behüte Hirt und Herd / Bis einst auf Zions Berg ein Hirt und Herde werd*. (The mountain man leads the cattle to high mountain meadows / Oh that the Creator be highly praised by him / Oh that the Highest always protects the cowherd and herd / Until some day they become herdsman and herd on Mount Sion).

Sometimes stock remains on the pastures for the duration of the summer; in the high villages, the animals can be gathered and returned each day. A description of these journeys widespread throughout the Alps is given by the French writer François-René de Chateaubriand in 1833, when he was staying in Waldmünchen in Bavaria. Every day he witnessed the use of the horn to call the animals:

> At 6am an old, tall, lean herdsman goes around the village to various locations; he sounds a straight horn, six feet long, which from a distance looks like a megaphone or a shepherd's crook. First, he sounds three pleasant bright notes, then he blows short notes in a kind of gallop or

ranz des vaches, imitating the lowing of cattle and the cries of pigs. The fanfare ends on a sustained note that rises in pitch. Suddenly out of every gate come heifers, cows, calves and bulls; they fill the centre of the village with much commotion; they climb or descend from all the surrounding roads, and, lined up in a procession, they take their usual route to the pasture ... in a quarter of an hour, all have vanished.[19]

Fig. 1.11. An etching in a mid-eighteenth-century prayer book shows an alphorn player who leads his animals to the high pastures. The text beneath is a prayer for his safe-keeping. Abraham Kyburz, *Theologia Naturalis*, Bern, 1754.[20]

Chateaubriand continued that in the evening at seven o'clock, the horn was heard again and the animals returned, to musical accompaniment. The order of the procession was altered: the pigs came first, and some ran around randomly or stopped in every corner. The sheep filed by and the cattle ended the procession, while the geese waddled alongside. All the animals returned to their dwellings, each to his own gate, although there were a few who ran around and refused to enter, so the women and children needed to gather the remainder back into their yards.

Transhumance, however, is not only a mountain phenomenon, as was seen in the daily movement of swine in the Roman writings quoted earlier. Well-established cattle-trails in use in Roman times are also mentioned by Varro: he writes of moving his animals along them to the hills for the summer grazing. During the winter they could feed on the fertile coastal plains, but these became infested with malarial mosquitoes when the weather became hotter, so it was necessary to travel inland for the summer months. Alexander Carmichael also describes lowland transhumance in the nineteenth century in the Scottish islands of The Hebrides:

> Throughout Lewis the crofters of the townland go to the shieling [common grazing land] on the same date each year. The sheep and cattle know their day as well as do the men and women, and on that day the scene is striking and touching: all the *ni* (flocks) are astir and restless to be off … should any event, such as a death or burial, cause the people to postpone the migration, the flocks have to be guarded day and night, or they would be off to their summer pastures by themselves.[21]

Documentation and film archive at the Deutsches Hirtenmuseum (German Museum of Herding) in Hersbruck in central Germany, describe the scene whereby a herdsman would gather the villagers' cattle daily in this fashion by blowing a long horn, in order to lead them to pastureland outside the village:

> Until the 1960s the cowherd was employed by the local council. In the 1920s he was paid 26 marks a year which meant that he was very poor indeed. In the alpine regions the cows stayed on the pastures for the whole summer. Here in the lowlands, the herdsman drove the cows to the pastures every morning and brought them back in the evening. … Typical for the region around Hersbruck is the so-called "Franconian Longhorn". This instrument is made of juniper. The shaft is hollowed out and wrapped with cherry tree bark. Every herdsman played his own tune with which he called the herd together in the mornings. The cows recognised the call and ran out of their stalls to gather on the square.

In the museum is the following photograph that shows a herdsman blowing a 'longhorn':

Fig. 1.12. Photograph of the village herdsman with a horn, no date, Deutsches
Hirtenmuseum, Hersbruck.

Thus the alphorn was used to gather the animals together in preparation for
the journey to the pastures, to direct them on the journey and back, and to
attract the attention of the cattle when necessary while grazing. The
observance of such routines in non-mountainous areas is a key factor that
could be relevant to the recognition of alphorn calls in concert repertoire by
audiences who had had no contact with the Alps.

The horn was also played to the cattle during milking and for their relaxation.
It is well-documented and discussed among farmers still today, that soothing
music plays a part in good milk production.

Fig. 1.13. A herdsman plays to cows during milking. One of a set of drawings that depict
activities of herdsmen for heraldic stained glass window panels, by Daniel Lindtmayer, 1601.[22]

In 1563 Prince Léonor of Orléans wrote to J. J. de Bonstetten, the Governor of Neuchâtel, to ask for a Swiss alphorn player to work for him. Bonstetten's reply is preserved in the Neuchâtel Cantonal Archive:

> Sir, further to your request I have found you a horn player from Schwyz … you can get him to play tunes on his horn, and other soothing sounds, which he play to cows to help them digest well.[23]

In the Alps, the alphorn was also a vital tool used to communicate with other herdsmen and with those in the valley below, as the sound of the alphorn can carry over a great distance, especially in the silence of the mountains. A melody was played every evening at sunset in order to let the villagers down in the valleys know that all was well. There is a large number of illustrations of such scenes, particularly in the nineteenth century when the romanticism of this daily event was not lost on poets, artists and composers.

Fig. 1.14. A herdsman plays his alphorn across the valley at sunset. Engraving by Gabriel Lory, 1818.[24]

Once the cattle were returned to the safety of the villages for the winter months, the herdsmen found other work to do in the villages or on the farms. They would also play for weddings and celebrations, and street musicians were common in the towns. The German musician and scholar Michael Praetorius compiled the first substantial encyclopaedia of music, *Syntagma Musicum*, in 1619. Under the section concerning the trumpet family, he describes long wooden herding horns and the activity of some of the herdsmen during the winter months:

> You also find long trumpets bound firmly together with bark, with which the shepherds from the Vosges and Switzerland (those known as the Western Forest people) wander around the cities in search of food'. [The three original cantons of Switzerland, Uri, Schwyz (normal modern spelling) and Unterwalden, were known as the 'Forest Cantons'].[25]

Alphorns were sometimes used for other signalling, as recorded in the writing of Virgil, quoted earlier. Swiss documentation notes that in 1212 a herdsman played on his alphorn in the Baldschiedertal in Wallis to warn of the approaching men of Unterwalden, thus alerting his people to resist the enemy. In 1653 during an uprising in the Entlebuch region, people were summoned to fight with the sound of an alphorn.[26] A more specialised use for the alphorn was to place players at pre-arranged places to relay messages over considerable distances. One such network in the Bernese Oberland in use as late as 1855 is described by Heinrich Szadrowsky in the *Jahrbuch des Schweizer Alpenclubs*:

> In the Bernese Oberland there are 12 to 14 stations for alphorn players: near Staubach; above the village of Wengen, near Mettenberg, up on Reichenbach; up on Alpbigel [otherwise known as Alpiglen], opposite the Eiger, on the road between Wengen and Scheidegg, outside Grindelwald; on the road to Grindelwald, on the bank of the Lütschine; between Rosenlaui and Scheidegg; up on the Faulhorn, at the foot of the summit; on the Heimwehfluh near Interlaken, etc.[27]

Thus the horn is known to have played a vital part in animal husbandry since records began: it was a piece of equipment without which certain farming routines could not take place. The long horn was used to call cattle, to soothe them during milking, to communicate with other people over long distances and to rally people together.

Musical potential

The music that can be played on a simple tube without lateral holes is limited by certain physical factors: its length, its shape and the method by which it is blown. It can only sound the notes from its harmonic series; additionally, the lowest few notes can be altered by a tone or two downwards. A number of factors, primarily relating to shape, dictate exactly which notes can be produced. A conical tube of about 8 feet long can produce around the first ten notes of its harmonic series; an experienced player can produce upwards of 16 harmonics from the longer alphorns in use today. (Throughout this book, the notes playable on the alphorn will be numbered from the lowest upwards. As they relate to each other according to the intervals found in the harmonic series, their place in the series, which uses the same numbering system, will be referred to when required to convey the relative positions of the notes to each other, as shown below. NB in the United States the terminology of 'partials' is often preferred to 'harmonics'. As partials are resonances found above a note, the numbering excludes the lowest note; thus the alphorn note / harmonic no. 2 is partial no. 1, etc.)

The typical modern Swiss alphorn is 11½ feet in length. This gives the harmonic series with *doh* as F sharp (or G flat) and the rich, haunting sonority of the pitches thus produced is sometimes retained by composers when music reminiscent of the sound of the Swiss alphorn is required in a concert work.

The harmonic series for a tube with *doh* as C is as follows. The tuning of the two harmonics no. 7 (flatter than written here) and harmonic no. 11 (halfway between the notes F and F sharp) are the most noticeably different from equal temperament; no. 13 is also slightly lower, and the notes above this are only approximations to those written here:

Fig. 1.15. The harmonic series.

The natural series of notes playable even on a well-proportioned tube are not exact, though, and the intermediate notes do not conform to equal temperament, just intonation or any other common Western tuning system. Modern alphorns, alongside Western brass instruments, are carefully profiled to adjust the majority of the notes to accord with the desired pitches.

Although the harmonic series quoted above forms the basis of early Western temperaments and key structure, two of the notes are avoided in classical music: harmonic no. 7, which is considered to be unpleasantly flat, and no. 11, which falls between two notes in standard use. In music composed for natural trumpets and French horns, these two harmonics are usually avoided. All of the harmonics from about no. 2 to no. 16, however, are used in alphorn music, including these two 'odd' notes: when playing to cows, or on a high mountain alone, or even with other alphorns, they cause no problem. To the musically educated, the presence of these unusual notes in alphorn music can create a haunting, evocative effect. Referring to the first harmonic, or fundamental, as *doh*, the note produced at the 11th harmonic falls above the normal note used in equal temperament for *fa* and in alphorn literature this note is referred to as the 'alphorn *fa*'.

Alphorn music, yodel and the *Kühreien*

The roots of alphorn music and yodel are much intertwined. Yodelling is often considered the vocal equivalent of alphorn music, with many traditional alphorn melodies imitated or suggested in yodelling. The *Ranz des Vaches* or *Kühreien* (cow procession melody) is always associated with the alphorn, yet it has words and is known as the song of the herdsmen. Not only does the music of yodel, in its exploitation of the jump in the voice between the chest register and the head register, resemble alphorn figurations and arpeggiations based on the harmonic series; even today, some Swiss yodel uses the tuning of the natural harmonics of the alphorn, including notes that are conspicuously 'out of tune' in comparison to any version of modern Western temperament. This tuning based on the natural harmonics has been retained because much Swiss yodel repertoire exists solely in the aural tradition and has not undergone the process of being adjusted to fit notation and subsequently been learned afresh from that. Although the *Kühreien* brings together the world of the alphorn and the yodel, alphorn music does not derive from vocal technique: its distinctive qualities derive primarily from its physical properties and secondarily from its function for the herdsman.

Because of the instrument's length in its longest form, its lowest notes are much lower than those of any other rustic instrument and are in the same octave as those of the modern orchestral tuba. In the alphorn's middle range, the notes available, restricted to open arpeggio notes of the harmonic series only, give the instrument a characteristic repertoire of phrases. As the bore becomes narrow towards the mouthpiece, it has almost a full scale at the top of its playing range, thus more 'normal' melodies are possible.

Alphorn music therefore derives specific melodic character from a combination of the above factors:

1. it uses only the notes of the harmonic series,
2. its length allows access to notes both lower and higher on the series than those accessible on shorter horns; it can make use of harmonic no. 11, known as the 'alphorn *fa*',
3. its use as a rustic calling horn, rather than a musical instrument in the usual sense, means that the 'out of tune' notes of the series are in common use and not avoided or adjusted as has normally been the case for example on an orchestral hand-horn.

The presence or absence of the 'alphorn *fa*' is disguised by constraints of notation in nineteenth-century printed alphorn music. However, two sources of evidence suggest it has been in common use for many centuries. Firstly, as intimated earlier, some Swiss yodel even today uses the scale that includes the exact tuning of the 'alphorn *fa*'. Secondly, an examination of the concert repertoire of the seventeenth and eighteenth centuries provides another possible clue. When the intention was to represent a rustic sound, various musical devices were utilised; for example, a drone effect to suggest bagpipes. Another common signifier was the presence of the raised fourth degree of the scale, sometimes referred to as the Lydian fourth, or the augmented fourth. It is possible that its presence is an imitation of the 11th harmonic in the series, which is introduced as 'too sharp' in its context: thus it might be a reference to the 'alphorn *fa*', familiar from actual folk repertoire.

The *Kühreien* or *Ranz des Vaches* (both terms appear with a variety of spellings: these are the most common), refers both to the journey with the cows up to the high mountain pastures and back, and to the music played along the way. As these journeys could last a few hours, a full *Kühreien* was of necessity extensive, with many different motifs following one another that would vary in metre, style and shape. These would be specific, repeated motifs, as the practice is still in use today whereby cows are taught to recognise their own calls: a cowherd would play phrases to call an animal as necessary on the journey or to attract its attention on the mountain. The music in each area was different, with each herdsman playing to the cattle in his care, using the motifs belonging to his own cattle, learned by ear from his associates or predecessors.

The use of the terms 'melody' or 'tune' applied to the *Kühreien* can therefore be misleading: music from any one herdsman was always improvised, with no extended melody, as such, ever specifically created or repeated. Once collectors began to write such music down, though, there are what are described as variants of a basic melody; however, this is not a true reflection of the genre. In some collections, many versions of the same melodic material are found alongside each other.

Defining features of a transcription of a *Kühreien*, therefore, are short repeating motifs, frequent changes of metre and style, phrase-lengths dictated by reasonable breathing with motifs that come to rest on a paused note and the inclusion of the 'alphorn *fa*'. Sometimes in the silence a natural echo might rebound off a distant mountainside, or another herdsman may play a response from a distance: this might be added in a transcription. An alphorn melody quoted by a composer is normally presented either unaccompanied or set against a quiet, peaceful background of long held chords. This reflects the stillness of a mountain landscape, and that traditionally a herdsman would play his alphorn alone.

A collection of transcriptions of *Kühreien* was printed in 1805 in Bern, *Acht Schweizer-Kühreihen, mit Musik und Text,* (Eight Swiss *Kühreihen,* with music and text), assembled by Sigismund von Wagner. Six are in fact *Kühreien,* while one is a *Lied* and the other a *Küherlied* (song, and cowherd's song). Wagner also considers it relevant to include three other melodies besides the eight, the *Ran des Vaches des Ormonts,* the music with text that begins '*Quand reverrai je*' and the *Ran de Vache du Dictionnaire de Rousseau.* The significance of these extra items will become apparent when this music is discussed in detail in Chapter 4.

All of these pieces were reproduced again in an extended volume printed in 1812 entitled *Sammlung von Schweizer Kühreihen und alten Volkliedern, nach ihren bekannten Melodien in Musik gesetzt* (Collection of Swiss *Kühreihen* and old folksongs, with their familiar melody settings), by Gottlieb Jakob Kuhn. He includes single melody lines for 26 tunes, mostly strophic songs, besides Wagner's six *Kühreien,* those from Oberhasli, Emmental (spelled in its caption Emmethal, a reflection of the local Swiss pronunciation), Entlebuch, two from Siebental and one from Appenzell.

Each of these *Kühreien* melodies is quite different from the next, and each has words too: although each uses just the notes available on an alphorn, it is by this date fully absorbed into the vocal repertoire. All of these *Kühreien* transcriptions, reproduced below, to a greater or lesser degree display the typical features of alphorn music, with just the open harmonics, repeating motifs, breath-length phrases ending with paused notes and the inclusion of the 'alphorn *fa*'. Each is quite different in structure from the flowing melodies with regular verse and chorus form of the items in the book that bear the title 'songs'.

The Preface to this 1812 volume quotes extensive passages from the writing of Johann Gottfried Ebel in his *Schilderung der Gebirgsvölker in der Schweitz* [*sic*] (Description of the Swiss Mountain People), Vol. 1, which had been published in Leipzig between 1798 and 1802. Although songs and *Kühreien* appear alongside each other, Ebel is at pains to describe the special manner in which a *Kühreien* should be sung, with full voice, in a natural, free manner:

> The *Kühreihen,* and in general the singing of our country people, absolutely must be heard in a certain environment that absorbs what the sounds give, with all the force of a full chest, an unsophisticated voice, almost coarse and hard. You cannot get the right idea of the effect produced by the *Kühreihen* unless you have heard them in the mountains themselves. When the cowherd calls his scattered herd on the hills, when he descends bright and carefree into the valley, his milk churns on his shoulders, he pours these feelings into his singing, and these completely natural feelings produce an impression that it is

impossible to express. The solemn silence of nature that surrounds it makes the heart receptive to all that is simple and natural; it proves to be a gentle and melancholy sensation and only heard like this is it possible to appreciate the full merit of the *Kühreihen.*

Sigismund von Wagner, in the introduction to his volume of 1805, comments that the texts occur in a variety of corrupt versions and that he has created lyrics that make more sense. Kuhn basically uses Wagner's lyrics, although he chooses at times to write them in a way that more reflects Swiss pronunciation. The melodies are in most respects the same as Wagner's, but Kuhn explains in his introduction that even with words, the tune is like a theme upon which each singer improvises *ad libitum* (although this is a slight misinterpretation of the genre) thus no two cowherds sing it in the same way and for this reason, it is very difficult to write something down. He explains that the phrases should be sung very slowly and smoothly, without artifice, and that the final notes of each phrase should be held as long as possible. Kuhn further describes the joyful spirit, reflected in the texts, of the cowherd as he returns to the village at the head of his fine herd, with the constant carillon of cowbells as he guides his procession through the mountains.

Fig. 1.16. *Sammlung* of 1812: *Kühreihen der Oberhasler.*[28]

Fig. 1.17. *Sammlung* of 1812: *Kühreihen der Entlebucher.*

Fig. 1.18. *Sammlung* of 1812: *Kühreihen der Emmethaler* [*sic*].

Fig. 1.19. *Sammlung* of 1812: one of the *Kühreihen der Siebenthaler*, with a different melody for the verse and the chorus.

The *Kühreien* music from Appenzell is a substantial source of material that assumed special significance in Switzerland: it forms the subject of Chapter 4.

Alphorn music and the classical composer

In any discussion in conjunction with orchestral or band instruments, the alphorn is classed as a brass instrument, because although it is normally made of wood, its sound is activated with a brass instrument method, by buzzing the lips at the end of a tube. There are at least five main categories of such 'brass' music found outside the concert hall: some of these relate to instruments made of wood, and others to a natural horn. These are the night-watchman's horn call, the rousing trumpet or bugle call, the call of the posthorn, the music of the hunt and the music of the alphorn. Each has unique musical qualities and stylistic characteristics, and composers reflect each of these worlds with distinctive representational music.

Music that represents the sound of the night-watchman's natural horn is typified by quiet single notes, as can be heard in Wagner's *Die Meistersinger von Nürnberg*, at the end of Act 2. Trumpet or bugle fanfares are designed to attract attention and therefore have bright, arresting rhythms based on a few notes: there is a complex repertoire of such calls used by the military, for example, to convey specific messages. Music for the posthorn has features of its own:

typically it combines an announcement fanfare with an elaborate flourish to finish. Many of these are quoted in Mahler's Symphony No. 3. Huntsmen may use a short horn of 8 to 12 inches in length to summon the hounds and send signals to each other; otherwise, they carry a long metal horn up to 14 feet in length that is coiled so that it can be worn when riding. A long horn has many notes available, and hunting horn signals can be sophisticated. Hunting groups often play together, as *cors de chasse* ensemble music is one of the peripheral pleasures of a hunting party: there is a substantial body of composed repertoire for groups of hunting horns, which often incorporates echo effects to reflect communication across field and forest. Composers evocatively re-create such scenes with music in the 'horse-riding' rhythm of 6/8, for example in the Trio of Beethoven's 'Eroica' Symphony.

Typical alphorn music has a number of features that distinguish it from these other styles. Alphorn-like melodies share with the trumpet and the long hunting horn the use of repeating motifs and echo effects, but in contrast to fanfares and hunting calls, the music of the alphorn is flowing and peaceful, as sudden sounds frighten cattle. Typically a *Kühreien* or *Ranz des Vaches* uses repeating short motifs with long held notes at the end of a breath, and there is little regularity of pulse and phrasing, as the motifs are improvised as required to call individual animals.

Many composers use the inclusion of an alphorn-like motif with these features to recreate the atmosphere of a peaceful mountain landscape in their compositions. The music explored in this book, therefore, is not only identified as reminiscent of an alphorn because of its restriction to the notes of the harmonic series. Both the context and the musical character of a motif will differentiate it from material indicative of other rustic brass instruments. In all the examples examined, it is the combination of a number of factors specific to alphorn music that indicate that it is into the world of this instrument that a composer is leading his audience.

The alphorn, then, is unusual as a musical instrument in that it has had a vital underlying extra-musical function in the rural community. Its musical potential is a factor in its use in communication with both animals and people. There are indications that its sound is not merely recognisable by both groups: it has long been realised that it should also be pleasing to both the bovine and the human ear. That composers should be moved by the evocative sound of the alphorn is the phenomenon that underlies the essence of this book.

Notes

[1] Brigitte Geiser, *Das Alphorn in der Schweiz* (Bern: Haupt, 1976), 10. Subsequent books published by this author appear with her married surname, Bachmann-Geiser.

[2] Conrad Gesner, *De Raris et Admirandis Herbis* (Zurich: Gesnarum, 1555), 52.

[3] Brigitte Bachmann-Geiser, *Das Alphorn vom Lock- zum Rockinstrument* (Bern: Haupt, 1999), 25.

[4] Michael Praetorius, *Syntagma Musicum* (Wittenberg: Wolfenbüttel, 1619), Vol. 2, 33.

[5] Moritz Capeler, *Pilati Montis Historia* (Basel: Rodolphi, 1767), 29. The spelling of the name of this author occurs in many different forms; the most commonly found today is given above.

[6] Capeler, *Pilati Montis*, 29: *Alp-horn, Cornu alpinum vulgo audit, est autem longa tuba tota ligno fabrefacta, variae longitudinis a 4 ad 12 quandoque pedum: curvatura lineam illam, quae Geometris Cissoides aemulatur: ab anteriori orificio 3 ad 5 digitorum amplo sensim gracitescit, ita ut quae ori applicatur apertura 1½ pollicis, interne ex tenuibus et longis assulis compaginatum est, quae extus per totam longitudinem lentis viminibus strictum colliguntur: et ut flatui nullae fissurae pateant, pice et cera undique inducta, solicite obturantur. Sonus Tubae gravis & penetrans, & licet in vicinia minus vehemens, tamen a longiore intervallo exauditur, addimus ejus figuram Tab. V. Fig. 2 etenim mihi non constat alibi reperiundam, & ne nihil omisisse videamur, addimus etiam praecipiuum pecuariorum melos, quod illis Vaccarum Chorea Kuh-Reyen dicitur, cui varias illi pastorales cantilenas accomodant.* ETH-Bibliothek Zürich. https://www.e-rara.ch/doi/10.3931/e-rara-22520. Public Domain Mark 1.0.

[7] The Hornbostel-Sachs system of musical instrument classification was devised by Erich Moritz von Hornbostel and Curt Sachs, first presented in *Zeitschrift für Ethnologie* Vol. 46 (1914), 553–90.

[8] Terminology is required in this book to differentiate between a number of different types of horn. The term 'French horn' is used throughout to define an instrument as the orchestral horn, both in the days of crooks and since the invention of pistons and valves. This terminology is consistent with the definition given in Percy Scholes, *Oxford Companion to Music* (Oxford: Oxford University Press, 1960), 490–1.

[9] Marcus Terentius Varro, *De Rerum Rusticum*, trans. W. D. Hooper (London: Loeb Classical Library, 1934), 2:364–5: *A partu decem diebus proximis non producunt ex haris matrem, praeterquam potum. Praeteritis decem diebus sinunt exire pastum in propincum locum villae, ut crebro reditu lacte alere possint porcos. Cum creverunt, patiuntur sequi matrem pastum domique secernunt a matribus ac seorsum pascunt, ut desiderium ferre possint parentis nutricis, quod decem diebus assecuntur. Subulcus debet consuefacere, omnia ut faciant ad bucinam. Primo cum incluserunt, cum bucinatum est, aperiunt, ut exire possint in eum locum, ubi hordeum fusum in longitudine. ... Ideo ad bucinam convenire dicuntur, ut silvestri loco dispersi ne dispereant.* Own translation.

[10] Polybius, *Histories*, trans. Evelyn Shuckburgh (London: Loeb Classical Library, 1927), 12:313–4.

[11] www.thelatinlibrary.com/vergil/aen7.shtml.: *At saeua e speculis tempus dea nacta nocendi / ardua tecta petit stabuli et de culmine summo / pastorale canit signum cornuque recuruo / Tartaream intendit uocem, qua protinus omne / contremuit nemus et siluae insonuere profundae; / audiit et Triuiae longe lacus, audiit amnis / sulpurea Nar albus aqua fontesque Velini, / et trepidae matres pressere ad pectora natos. / Tum uero ad uocem celeres, qua bucina signum / dira dedit, raptis concurrunt undique telis / indomiti agricolae, nec non et Troia pubes / Ascanio auxilium castris effundit apertis.*

[12] Reproduced with kind permission of the Fundation Pro Urba, Orbe-Boscéaz Roman Villa, Switzerland.

[13] The Miriam and Ira D. Wallach Division of Art, Prints and Photographs: Picture Collection, The New York Public Library. "Shepherd's horn, eighth century; Horn, or olifant, fourteenth century." New York Public Library Digital Collections. http://digitalcollections.nypl.org/items/510d47e3-3a1b-a3d9-e040-e00a18064a99. Public domain, unrestricted use.

[14] I have found more than 17 such illustrations. They can be examined, with their contexts, in my online Alphorn Artwork Archive, accessible through my website, www.AmazingAlphorn.com.

[15] British Library, London, manuscript Harley 5102 f. 77 v. https://www.bl.uk/catalogues/illuminatedmanuscripts/ILLUMIN.ASP?Size=mid&IllID=16605. Public domain, unrestricted use.

[16] *Chorbuch des Franziskaner Klosters*, Horb am Neckar. Reproduced with kind permission of the Stadtarchiv, Horb a. N.

[17] William Shakespeare, *King Lear* (London: Nathaniel Butter, 1608).

[18] Gesner, *De raris et admirandis herbis*, 52: *In suprema casa uaccaria, postquam delicatissimo pinguissimoque lacte refecti sumus, & lituū alpinum inflauimus (longum ferè ad pedes undecim* [sic.] *duobus lignis modicè incuruis & excauatis compactum, & uiminibus scitè obligatū) ...*

[19] François-René Chateaubriand, *Memoires d'Outre-tombe* (1849) Book 25, Chapter 11: *A six heures du matin un vieux berger, grand et maigre, parcourt le village; à différentes stations, il sonne d'une trompe droite, longue de six pieds qu'on prendrait de loin pour un porte-voix ou une houlette. Il en tire d'abord trois sons métalliques assez harmonieux, puis il fait entendre l'air précipité d'une espèce de galop ou de ranz des vaches, imitant des mugissements de boeufs et des rires de pourceaux. La fanfare finit par une note soutenue et montante en fausset. Soudain débouchent de toutes les portes des vaches, des génisses, des veaux, des taureaux; ils envahissent en beuglant la place du village; ils montent ou descendent de toutes les rues circonvoisines et s'étant formés en colonne, ils prennent le chemin accoutumé pour aller paître ... en un quart d'heure tout a disparu.*

[20] Zentralbibliothek Zürich, Varia, Alpwirtschaft I, 2. https://www.e-rara.ch/zuz/doi/10.3931/e-rara-36176. Public Domain Mark 1.0.

[21] Alexander Carmichael, *Carmina Gadelica, Hymns and Incantations collected in the Highlands of Scotland in the Last Century* (1899, reprinted Edinburgh: Floris, 1994), 335.

[22] Regiunalmuseum Surselva. https://commons.wikimedia.org/wiki/File:Tiba_1601.jpg. Creative Commons CC0 License. Heraldic stained glass window panels were common in aristocratic residences in Switzerland in the seventeenth and eighteenth centuries. Top panel vignettes often depict the domestic life of the family, and many show herdsmen with alphorns. See my online Alphorn Artwork Archive, accessible through my website, www.amazingalphorn.com.

[23] Bachmann-Geiser, *Das Alphorn*, 25: *Monseigneur, suyvant vostre commandement, j'ay mis poyne de trouver un cornet de Schwiss... vous luy pourrez faire dire chansons sur son cornet et autres petites carraces qu'il a accoustumé faire à ses vaches pour leur feire trouver leur desjuné bon...*

[24] Gottlieb Jakob Kuhn, ed., *Sammlung von Schweizer Kühreihen und alten Volkliedern* (Bern: Burgdorfer, 1818), copper engraving, title page. https://imslp.org/wiki/Sammlung_von_Schweizer-Kühreihen_und_Volksliedern_(Folk_Songs,_Swiss)

²⁵ Michael Praetorius, *Syntagma Musicum* (Wittenberg: Wolfenbüttel, 1619), Vol. 2, 33: *Auch findet man gar lange Trummetten von Past also fest und dichte zusammen ineinander gewunden darmit die Schaper aussm Voigt und Schweizerlande (die Wästerwälder genand) in den Städten herümbher lauffen und ihre Nahrung suchen.*

²⁶ Alois Lütolf, *Sagen, Bräuche und Legenden aus den fünf Orten Luzern, Schwyz, Unterwalden und Zug* (Luzern: Schiffmann, 1815), 413.

²⁷ Heinrich Szadrowsky, *Die Musik und die tonerzeugenden Instrumente der Alpenbewohner*, in *Jahrbuch des Schweizer Alpenclubs*, Vol. 4, 1867/8, 313: *In Berner Oberland befinden sich ungefähr 12 bis 14 Stationen für Alphornbläser: beim Staubbach; oberhalb Dorf Wengen, gegenüber Mettenberg; oben am Reichenbach; oben am Alpbigel, gegenüber dem Eiger, auf dem Wege nach Wengen-Scheidegg, von Grindelwald aus; an der Strasse nach Grindelwald, direct am Ufer der Lütschine; zwischen der Rosenlaui und Scheidegg; oben auf dem Faulhorn, am Fusse des Gipfels; auf der Heimwehfluh, bei Interlaken, u.s.w.*

²⁸ Gottlieb Jakob Kuhn, ed., *Sammlung von Schweizer Kühreihen und alten Volkliedern, nach ihren bekannten Melodien in Musik gesetzt* (Bern: Burgdorfer, 1812), and following three quotations. Universitätsbibliothek Basel. https://www.e-rara.ch/bau_1/doi/10.3931/e-rara-50794. Public Domain Mark 1.0.

Chapter 2

The Alphorn in Christmas Music, the *Pastorella*

This chapter outlines the special use of the alphorn in Christmas repertoire in the eighteenth and nineteenth centuries. The presence of herdsmen with their horns in the villages during the winter, and their participation in Christmastide activities in the representation of the shepherds in the Nativity story, offer us a unique set of examples of alphorn music from central Europe in this period.

Works that incorporate parts written for the alphorn, or herdsman's horn, feature prominently in archives in the eastern part of the Austro-Hungarian empire, primarily in the Czech-speaking provinces of Bohemia and Moravia. These works were composed for a village community to perform in church at Christmas, a dramatisation of the scenes from the gospel of St. Luke that included the shepherds, or *pastores* (Latin): the genre is thus identified with such titles as *pastorale*, *pastorala*, *pastorella*, Pastoral Mass or similar title, generally discussed now under the single term *pastorella*. It was normally part of midnight Mass, and was largely a rural phenomenon. A new *pastorella* was generally composed every year by the village schoolmaster, organist or cantor—often these posts were held by the same person.

Music was considered to be a valuable vehicle for the dissemination of the Christian message, so texts that would resonate with a rural population such as the scenes that involved the shepherds, both in the fields as they received the news of the birth of the Christ child and in Bethlehem when they visited the baby Jesus, were ideal subject matter for such special treatment. The words that related the shepherds' story in a *pastorella* were usually in a local dialect of Czech, and they vividly interpreted the gospel scenes in colloquial and chatty language, though occasionally they retained the gospel text in Latin when used in a monastic context. A *pastorella* could be a multi-movement work and was generally written for soloists or occasionally choir, with small orchestra; sometimes it was a purely instrumental composition.

This Christmas shepherds' music often reflected or included local songs or dance melodies and sometimes incorporated parts for rustic instruments: by far the most common folk instrument to be included in a *pastorella* is the herdsman's horn. As a necessary piece of equipment for the management of the animals in his care, this was the most obvious musical symbol of the shepherd. Over 100 examples of *pastorellas* that include a part for a herdsman's horn have been located, and the actual presence of this instrument brings a wholly appropriate sense of realism to Christmastide scenes with the shepherds both in the fields and beside the manger.

The *pastorella* developed in the Czech-speaking lands largely as a result of two circumstances: in this region, musical literacy was widespread by the end of the seventeenth century, and education was the remit of the Church. The revival of Habsburg support for Catholicism had led to a proliferation of monastic establishments; to these were delegated responsibility for education. By the second half of the eighteenth century, there were over 200 monasteries, convents and religious houses established by some 40 different religious orders in Bohemia, Moravia and Austrian Silesia. The main orders involved in education were the Jesuits for the older scholars and the Piarists and Franciscans for the younger children. While the Jesuits developed renowned choir-schools, for example in Prague, Brno and Olomouc, the Piarists and Franciscans, in collaboration with wealthy land-owners, had a church built in every village and a school alongside. Besides theological study, both literacy and music were considered a high priority, so that the Christian message could be better conveyed to the people.

Charles Burney (1726–1814), historian and musician, wrote a graphic description of musical education in Bohemia. He travelled throughout Europe in both 1770 and 1772 in order to gather information for his four volumes entitled *A General History of Music*, published between 1776 and 1789. His two extensive travel journals, however, were published first and offer fascinating insights into the social and musical life of that period. Burney visited a number of village schools in Bohemia in 1772 and was amazed to find that not only was every child literate, but each one played an instrument:

> I crossed the whole kingdom of Bohemia, from south to north; and being very assiduous in my enquiries, how the common people learned music, I found out at length, that, not only in every large town, but in all villages, where there is a reading and writing school, children of both sexes are taught music.
>
> At Teuchenbrod, Janich, Czaslau, Bömischbrod, and other places, I visited these schools; and at Czaslau, in particular, within the post of Colin, I caught them in the act.
>
> The organist and cantor, M. Johann Dulsick, and the first violin of the parish church, M. Martin Kruch, who are likewise the two school-masters, gave me all the satisfaction I required. I went into the school, which was full of little children of both sexes, from six to ten or eleven years old, who were reading, writing, playing on violins, hautbois, bassoons, and other instruments. The organist had in a small room of

his house four clavichords, with little boys practising on them all: his son of nine years old, was a very good performer.[1]

Burney relates that such schools were common throughout Bohemia, Moravia, Hungary and Eastern Austria. Villagers thus formed a musically literate congregation, from whom choirs and orchestras could be drawn to provide music for church services. Indeed the number of musicians from these rural regions who were appointed as performers and composers at most important European courts in the second half of the eighteenth century bears testimony to the remarkable ability fostered in these schools.

A further anecdote is recorded by the elderly Gluck (1714–1787), whose parents moved to Bohemia to work on the estates of Prince Lobkowitz when Gluck was a three-year-old. Speaking about his upbringing as a Bohemian, he told the painter Christian von Mannlich that everyone in Bohemia was a musician and that even in the smallest villages, the inhabitants sang and played different instruments at Mass:

> In my homeland everyone is musical; music is taught in the schools, and in the smallest villages the local people sing and play different instruments during High Mass in their churches.[2]

These quotations illustrate not only the significance of music in the lives of ordinary Czech people but also the participation of a congregation in music for worship. Within this context, the dramatisation of the Christmas Nativity scenes that involved the shepherds, which would resonate well with a rural congregation, developed and flourished.

There are large collections of unpublished manuscripts of *pastorellas* in the major monastic libraries of Central Europe, notably at Göttwieg near Vienna, Rajhrad in Bohemia, and Brno and Olomouc in Moravia. There is also an extensive body of manuscripts that come from the churches of various Czech villages and towns, now preserved in the České Muzeum Hudby (Czech Museum of Music) in Prague.

The Prague collection

The museum houses manuscripts of 393 *pastorellas*. Within this collection, 28 works specify a part for a herdsman's horn, of which 25 have an extant horn part, although in four of these works, the part includes notes that are not available in the harmonic series. They thus could not be played on a simple herdsman's horn: a different instrument would be needed for performance. Table 2.1 shows the composer, his dates of birth and death where known, the date and place of composition where known and the title of each of the remaining 21 works. The title *Offertorium* for many of these works reveals the time during midnight Mass for which these works were written: through the performance of a *pastorella*, the symbolism of the Offertory of the Mass is transferred to offerings that the shepherds could bring to the Christ child in the stable, which is often here the gift of music, or things to eat or to keep the baby warm. The works would be suitable for performance either as musical background to the offertory procession, or as music to be provided while members of the congregation placed actual gifts at the crib. One work is a part of the *Gloria* and relates this part of the Mass to the angel's words '*Gloria in excelsis Deo!*' declaimed to the shepherds in their fields. One of the *pastorellas* is a Gradual and two of the works celebrate other events in the Christmas period. The range of dates for this collection of works is around 1718–1856.

Table 2.1. Manuscripts in the České Muzeum Hudby, Prague that include a part for a herdsman's horn: dates, provenance and title.

Composer	Dates	Work	Provenance	Title
Dominico Czerni	1730–1766	1759	Prague	*Offertorium Pastorale*[3]
Ferdinand Daubrawský (3 works)[4]	1747–1829		Lomnice nad Popelkou	*Pastorella Czeska*[5]
František Dobravský			Hořice	*Pastorella*[6]
(?František) Duschek	?1731–1799		Pelhřimov	*Pastorella*[7]
Jan Augustin Fibiger	1760–1851		Bakov	*Pro Nativitate Domini*[8]
František Václav Habermann	1706–1783		Eger (now Cheb)	*Motetto pastoralni II*[9]
Holetschek				*Pastorella*[10]
František Václav Jech	b.1776		Rovensko	*Mottetto*[11]
Tomáš Norbert Kautník	1698–1755		Polička	*Offertorium Pastorale*[12]
Tomáš Kollovrátek (3 works)	1763–1831	1810	Choceň, Holice	*Offertorium Pastorale*[13], *Offertorium...*[14], *2do Pastorella*[15]
Jiří Ignác Linek (2 works)	1725–1791		Bakov nad Jizerou	*Pastorella*[16]
Matiegka		1833	Prague	*Pastorala*[17]
Josef Ondřej Nowotný	1778–1856		Želiv	*Offertorium Pastorale*[18]
Tadeáš Petipeský		1761	Přeštice	*Motteto de nativitate...*[19]
Jakub Jan Ryba	1765–1815		Rožmitál pod Třemšínem	*Pastoral Offertorium*[20]
Josepho Štietina	c.1700–1750		Ústí nad Orlicí	*Pastorella Nativitate...*[21]

The collection demonstrates how widespread the presence of herdsmen's horns was in the eighteenth and nineteenth century in this part of the Austro-Hungarian empire, now the Czech Republic, as shown on the following map:

Fig. 2.1. Present-day Czech Republic: known sources of works that include parts for herdsmen's horns in the manuscripts in the České Muzeum Hudby, Prague. Monasteries are shown with an additional ring.

Fig. 2.2. The village square, Ústí nad Orlicí, Czech Republic. Photo: Frances Jones.

The region is primarily not mountainous, and the villages where these works come from are typically small, many with no more than a hundred dwellings even today. There is generally a central square sometimes surrounded by grand buildings reminiscent of those in the centre of Prague or Vienna; beyond that, no buildings have an imposing appearance. In one corner of the square, there is normally a remarkably large Baroque church, with an adjacent school.

Most of these *pastorellas* include solo singers and organ; sometimes there is also a four-part choir. In addition, there is usually a string group, and in around half of the examples, there is some woodwind, occasionally percussion and sometimes other brass instruments besides a herdsman's horn. One work is unique in this collection, with no voices and no part for an organ: that of Fibiger from Bakov.

Table 2.2, below, shows the terminology and instrumentation of the compositions in this collection. Various names are found on these scores for the alphorn-like instrument used for herding in Bohemia and Moravia. Each is derived from the terms *pastores* and *tuba* or *tromba*, the words for herdsmen and pipe: *tuba pastoralis, pastorica,* or *pastoritia,* or *tromba* or *tramba pastore,* for example (Grove Dictionary of Music Online, 2012, uses the phrase '*tuba pastoralis* or alphorn' in discussion of the *pastorella*). Sometimes even within these works, a different version of the name is found on the cover from that on the part. For simplicity, though, I shall use the most commonly used term *tuba pastoralis* for the herdsman's horn throughout this chapter. The works in the following table are listed, as far as can be deduced, in chronological order: this shows an overall evolution of the instrumentation available. Voice parts here are Canto, Soprano, Alto, Tenor or Bass.

The sounding length (key) of the instrument is the same as the key of the work in every case. Table 2.3 on p. 36 compares details of the parts written for the *tuba pastoralis* in these works. It shows that the majority of parts in this collection use a specific set of four or five notes: with reference to the harmonic series shown earlier (p. 19), the tonic of a well-proportioned tube occurs at harmonics nos. 1, 2, 4 and 8; a major triad is created with harmonics nos. 4, 5 and 6, and harmonic no. 3 is a lower dominant. Most of these works use just the major triad of harmonics nos. 4, 5 and 6 plus the lower dominant of harmonic no. 3. This is the part of a tube's harmonic series where the intonation is least affected by the inconsistency of proportion between a tube's length and the rate of opening of its bore. Thus a piece of hollowed-out branch does not need to be very accurately proportioned to be able to produce acceptable intonation for these four notes; it may indeed have been the effect desired by the composer that the *tuba pastoralis* sounds more characterful if its intonation is not as 'perfect' as that of the other instruments around it. Occasionally, there is, in addition, the upper tonic at harmonic no. 8 or an upper mediant at harmonic no. 10.

Table 2.2. Prague works: name of horn and scoring.

Composer/work	Name of herdsman's horn	Voices and other instruments used
Kautník	*Tuba Pastoralis*	CATB, 2 clts, 2 hns, vn 1, vn 2, org
Štietina	*Tuba Pastoralis*	CATB, vn 1, vn 2, violone, org
Holetschek	*Tuba Pastoralis*	CAB, vn 1, vn 2, vne, org
Habermann	*Tuba pastoritia*	CATB, vn 1, vn 2, org
Linek (1)	*Tuba Pastorallis*	B, vn 1, vn 2, org
Linek (2)	*Tuba pastoralis*	AB, vn 1, vn 2, org
Czerni	*Tuba Pastorali / Pastoralis*	CATB, vn 1, vn 2, va, fundamento
Petipeský	*Tuba Pastoritia*	CATB, vn 1, vn 2, cemb, org
Duschek	*Tuba pastori / pastoricia*	CATB, chorus, fl, vn 1, vn 2, org
Daubrawský (1)	*Tromba / Tramba Pastoralis*	CAB, vn 1, vn 2, org
Daubrawský (2)	*Tromba Pastoralis*	CATB, 2 hns, vn 1, vn 2, org
Daubrawský (3)	*Tuba Pastorica / Pastoricia*	CATB, 2 hns, vn 1, vn 2, timp, org
Fibiger	*Tuba Pastoricia / Pastoralis*	clarino 1, clarino 2, princ, march, timp [i.e. 2 high trumpets, principal trumpet, marching drums, timp]
Kollovrátek (1)	*Tuba Pastoritia*	CATB, 2 clts, 2 hns, clarino 1, clarino 2, timp, org
Kollovrátek (2)	*Tuba Pastoralis*	CATB, 2 clts, 2 hns, vn 1, vn 2, vne, org
Kolovrátek (sic) (3)	*Tuba Pastorellis / Principal*	CA, 2 clts, 2 hns, vn 1, vn 2, timp, org
Ryba	*Tuba Pastoralis*	CATB, 2 clts, 2 hns, vn 1, vn 2, org
Jech	*Tuba Pastoris / Pastorica*	CATB, 2 clts, 2 hns, clarino 1, clarino 2, vn 1, vn 2, va, vne, timp, org
Nowotný	*Tromba Pastorale*	CATB, 2 clts, 2 hns, flugelhorn, vn 1, vn 2, va, vne, org
Dobravský	*Tuba Pastorallis / Pastoralis*	SCATB, fl, 2 clts, 2 hns, tbne, bass flugelhorn, vne, org
Matiegka	*Tuba Pastoralis /* Posthorn	CA, 2 hns, vn 1, vn 2, org

The fourth column of Table 2.3, below, shows that *tuba pastoralis* parts reflect the music of individual players rather than a consistent recognised compositional style. Since the composers of *pastorellas* were members of their local community, it seems not unlikely that the parts were written for a friend or a neighbour: each part appears to have been written for an individual herdsman whose playing was known to the man who was writing the work in question. It is interesting to note that the majority of the works are for an instrument in C or D. It appears likely that this may be because an instrument providing these notes, of around 3½ to 4ft in length, would have been easy to carry; it also affords the possibility that these performances could have made use of trumpets of the day, which were not uncommonly constructed in C or D.

Table 2.3. Prague works: key, harmonics used and description.

Composer/work	Key	Harmonics used	*Tuba pastoralis* part description
Kautník	C	3, 4, 5, 6	bugle-like calls, sometimes solo, sometimes among the other instruments
Štietina	D	4, 5, 6	bugle-like solos, also a representation of the midnight bell
Holetschek	C	3, 4, 5, 6, 8	sounds the tolling bell of midnight, twice. Additional bugle-like solo passages
Habermann	D	3, 4, 5, 6, 8	virtuosic solo part
Linek (1)	C	4, 5, 6 plus 8-12	florid solo phrases interspersed with harmony notes within the instrumental texture
Linek (2)	D	3, 4, 5, 6, 8	bugle-like florid fanfare passages, replicated in the other instrumental parts
Czerni	D	3, 4, 5, 6, 8	bugle-like calls, with much florid additional passagework added in pencil
Petipeský	G	3, 4, 5, 6	virtuosic arpeggio writing, replicated in the other instrumental parts
Duschek	D	3, 4, 5, 6	some short bugle-like calls within the texture, then a brief florid solo passage
Daubrawský (1)	D	3, 4, 5, 6	bugle-like part, used among the other instrumental parts
Daubrawský (2)	D	3, 4, 5, 6	bugle-like calls, alternating with horns
Daubrawský (3)	D	3, 4, 5, 6	bugle-like solos, alternating with horns
Fibiger	C	3, 4, 5, 6, 8	*tuba pastoralis* the primary and most complex part, with bugle-like calls
Kollovrátek (1)	C	3, 4, 5, 6	bugle-like solos
Kollovrátek (2)	C	3, 4, 5, 6, 8	bugle-like solos
Kolovrátek (3)	C	3, 4, 5, 6, 8, 10	plays bass or basic horn line, and a few bugle call sections marked 'solo'
Ryba	F	3, 4, 5, 6	substantial virtuosic bugle-like solos
Jech	D	3, 4, 5, 6	mostly silent. Two passages of florid solo writing
Nowotný	G	3, 4, 5, 6	elaborate melodic solos, some within the texture. Alternative part written for flugelhorn
Dobravský	D	3, 4, 5, 6	simple bugle-like calls. It doubles, or may be an alternative to, the bass flugelhorn part. At times doubled by horn 1
Matiegka	G	3, 4, 5, 6	bugle-like solos

Fig. 2.3. *Pastýřská trouba*, Czech, nineteenth century, approximately 3ft long. České Muzeum Hudby, Prague. Photo: Frances Jones.

The geographical setting for each work, its composer, its content and the use of the herdsman's horn all reveal fascinating information, as does the use by each composer of the *tuba pastoralis* in the context of other instruments, voices and text. We may also gain a broader window onto the music played by herdsmen in the region. It would be reasonable to suppose that the idiosyncratic notes and rhythms written here reflect the motifs in current use by the individual herdsman for whom each part was written, not only because the players and their playing were likely to have been known to the composer, but also because the function of these works was the realistic representation of the herdsmen in the Nativity story. These parts may thus be actual transcriptions of eighteenth- and nineteenth-century herdsmen's horn calls. There follows a detailed examination of each of the works.[22]

P[adre] Dominico Czerni Minoritta, *Offertorium Pastorale*

Czerni (1730—1776) was born in Nimburg in Bohemia. He became a Franciscan Minorite priest in Prague and was renowned in his day as a composer and choral director at St. Jakob's Church in Prague. This work was composed in 1759 and is scored for Canto, Alto, Tenore and Basso, with the accompaniment of 2 violins, viola, *fundamento* (continuo) and *tuba pastoralis obligato* [*sic*].

There are a number of dates on the manuscript, which is a full score. The source is acknowledged at the end with '*Partitura jost sestavena se hlarů, Ex rebus Chori Pontensis Ordinis S. P. Francisci Minorum Convent: 1759*' in handwriting that matches that in the rest of the material. The typography appears modern, as does the pre-printed manuscript paper. At the end, in pencil, '*28.V.24, Deo gratias!*' is written, which suggests that this copy was made in 1924. On the first page, 390/1950 is to be found: 390 might be a catalogue number, while 1950 might be the date on which the material was obtained and catalogued by the museum.

This is a lively one-movement work of 224 bars in the key of D major. The work remains for the most part in D with brief statements of the melodic material in the dominant and subdominant. There is much use of tonic pedals and the rustic signifier, the scale with a raised fourth. The word *fundamento* is written as an identifier for a pair of bracketed staves in the lowest place in the score, although throughout, the stave apparently allocated to the right hand of a keyboard is left blank. The bass line is not figured.

There are two types of vocal writing. The text is delivered in simple strophes, syllabic, direct and homophonic, while the strings are given similar material to the voice parts, although with some decoration and ritornello passages in addition. The text, in Latin, is repeated many times by solo voices in turn, interspersed with the same text for *tutti* voices. In contrast, there are two vocal passages, of 21 bars and 14 bars respectively, where no text is given: here the voices and strings have long overlapping notes that create a calm chordal backdrop to the elaborate music of the *tuba pastoralis*. There is, in addition, an unusual feature that is also found in a few other *pastorella* settings (including the work of Habermann, p. 54): the repeating of the final syllable of one of the words, for example in the third *tutti* line of the transcription below, *Jerusalem, -lem, -lem* or later, *Betlehem, -hem, -hem*. This may be intended to convey the impression of an echo or represent the stammering of frightened shepherds, the bleating of sheep, or the repeating call notes of the *tuba pastoralis*.[23]

The narrative is distributed between the voices as follows:[24]

Alto	*Io Sion consolare,*	O Sion [i.e. Christians] be comforted!
	applaude Jerusalem, lem,	applaud, Jerusalem
	jube Deo resonare,	resound to God
	qui natus in Betlehem,	who is born in Bethlehem
	Jerusalem,	Jerusalem
Tutti	*Gaude Jerusalem,*	Rejoice, Jerusalem!
	exsulta Betlehem,	Praise, Bethlehem!
	Jerusalem, Jerusalem, lem, lem,	Jerusalem
	Io Sion consolare,	(etc.)
	applaude Jerusalem,	
	Jube Deo resonare,	
	qui natus est in Betlehem, hem,	
	Io consolare,	
	jube resonare, Jerusalem,	
	(21 bars of vocal parts without text)	
	Plaude Jerusalem,	
	exulta Betlehem,	
	io consolare, Jerusalem	
Canto	*Io Sion consolare,*	
	applaude Jerusalem, lem,	
	jube Deo resonare,	
	qui natus in Betlehem, hem, hem,	
	Jerusalem, lem, lem,	
Tutti	*Gaude Jerusalem,*	
	exsulta Betlehem,	
	Jerusalem, Jerusalem, Jerusalem,	
Basso	*Io Sion consolare*	
	applaude Jerusalem, lem,	
Tenore	*jube Deo resonare,*	
	qui natus in Betlehem, hem.	
Tutti	*Io Sion consolare,*	

applaude Jerusalem, lem,
Gaude Jerusalem,
exsulta Betlehem,
io consolare, Jerusalem
io consolare,
jube resonare Jerusalem,
io Sion consolare,
applaude Jerusalem,

(14 bars of vocal parts without text)

Gaude Jerusalem,
exsulta Betlehem,
io consolare,
jube resonare Jerusalem.

Although the *tuba pastoralis* is used in the work, there is no specific reference to shepherds in the text. However as the birth of the Christ child is the subject matter, there would be some relevance to Czerni's use of the instrument, since the shepherds were among the visitors to the stable described in St. Luke's gospel. There is no tempo indication, although the style of the string and vocal writing implies a feel of *Allegretto* or *Allegro*. The *tuba pastoralis* part displays considerable virtuosity, using the five notes of harmonics nos. 3, 4, 5, 6 and 8. The *tuba pastoralis* notes are written in C, as is the custom for natural horn parts; thus the *tuba pastoralis* must be an instrument in D, with notes that sound a tone above those written, although this is not specified.

The music for *tuba pastoralis* is marked *oblig.*, which could be interpreted as either 'optional' or 'obligatory'. Whereas the *tuba pastoralis* part is independent of, and much of the time supplementary to, the vocal and other instrumental parts, there are four passages of three or four bars where the strings are given repeated crotchets on a tonic chord, which form a background for bugle-like calls for the *tuba pastoralis*. This would imply that the reading of 'obligatory' is more likely.

While most of the transcription is in black ink, there are a number of additional flourishes added to the *tuba pastoralis* line of the score, in pencil. These additional notes are shown on the part transcribed as Fig. 2.4 in square brackets. It is possible that these extra notes were present on an alternative original part; they might have been added to enhance a performance for which this manuscript was produced (although the date in pencil at the end records the month of May); they might represent possible suggestions of improvisation-like material for the player, or they may merely imply that such improvisation was expected. As the source of this work is a monastery in the centre of Prague, rather than a village, there may have been some uncertainty as to the availability of a *tuba pastoralis* player for a performance of this work. The part could therefore have been made suitable for performance on a different instrument.

Tuba pastoralis

Offertorium Pastorale

Dominico Czerni
Transcription Frances Jones

Fig. 2.4. Czerni, *Offertorium Pastorale*, transcription of the *tuba pastoralis* part. Notes added in pencil are shown in square brackets.

Ferdinand Daubrawský, *Pastorella Czeska* (1)

Daubrawský (otherwise Doubravský), 1747–1829, was cantor at Lomnice nad Popelkou, a typical little Czech village. The church of St. Nicholas was built in 1782 and the road that surrounds it is named Doubravského. None of the three *pastorellas* examined herein by this composer provide any evidence of a date of composition.

This *pastorella* is scored for Canto, Alto, Tenore and Basso, 2 violins, 2 horns in D, timpani in D and A, organ and *tuba pastoricia* (*tuba pastorica* on the cover). The violin 1 part is missing. It is in the key of D. It is 237 bars in length, in one continuous section, marked *Allegro non molto*. The harmonies are simple and the vocal writing homophonic.

The narrative describes the Nativity as a contemporary event from the point of view of the shepherds: they must go to worship the baby Jesus and sing and play the violin to him. It is a typical example of the way in which the Christmas story was brought to life by the composer, to make the story relevant for the congregation. The different voice passages are interspersed with instrumental sections: the position of these is indicated by a blank line below. The text is as follows: [25]

Basso	*Vzhůru pastuškové,*	Arise, shepherds,
	do Betléma půjdeme,	we shall go to Bethlehem,
	co nového pasiruje	this new event
	ať také vidíme.	let us see.
	Narodil se tam Spasitel,	The Saviour has been born,
	v hospodě v chlivečku,	in a small stable,
	nemá, kde by pohodlně	he has nowhere to comfortably
	položil svou hlavičku.	lay his little head.
	Leží mezi hovádkami,	He lies between the beasts,
	vola a oslička.	the ox and the ass.
	Jozef starý jej kolébá	Joseph rocks the cradle
	a jeho matička.	and his mother too.
	Muzikanti, nemeškejte	Musicians, hurry
	zahráti Ježíšku,	to play to baby Jesus,
	hodně hřmotně a vesele,	very loudly and cheerfully,
	nějakou novou písničku.	a new song.
Alto	*Přestaňte, muzikanti, na housle hráti,*	Stop, musicians, playing the violin,
	nechejte nás Ježíškovi také zaspívati.	let us also sing to baby Jesus.
Canto and Alto	*Gloria in excelsis Deo,*	Glory to God on high.
	Gloria in excelsis Deo.	
Tenore	*Co pak to má znamenati,*	What will it all mean?
	slyším hráti a spívati,	We hear music and singing:
	Sláva buď na Výsostech Bohu	Glory be to God on high
	a na zemi pokoj lidu.	and on earth peace among people.
Basso	*Nediv se, bratře milý,*	Do not be surprised, dear brothers,
	nemeškej tuto chvíli	come, hurry,
	malého Ježíška přivítati,	welcome little Jesus,
	jemu čest a chválu, též díky, vzdávati.	give him honour, praise and thanks.

Tutti	*Zdráv buď, Mesiášku,*	Hail, Messiah,
(although	*zdávna vinšovaný,*	long-awaited,
Tenore is	*s přečisté panenky*	from the Virgin most pure,
silent	*nám narozený.*	born to us.
where		
marked)	*Vítáme tě společně,*	We welcome you together,
	náš Spasiteli,	our Saviour,
	neb se nám skrze tebe	for us all
	stalo všem spasení.	you will be our salvation.
	Z nebe si na svět stoupil, (not Tenore)	From heaven you came into the world,
	to pro naše spasení,	for our salvation,
	bys nás, hříšné, vykoupil, (not Tenore)	in order to redeem us sinners,
	Ježíšku přemilý.	most beloved baby Jesus.
	(twice)	
	Vzhůru tedy, pastuškové,	Therefore arise, shepherds,
	půjdeme k Betlému,	go to Bethlehem,
	zahrajeme Ježíškovi,	let us play to the baby Jesus,
	dítěti malému.	the little child.

Fig. 2.5. Daubrawský, *Pastorella Czeska* (1), *tuba pastoricia* part. [26]

The *tuba pastoricia* has a sounding length of D and is given four notes, harmonics nos. 3, 4, 5 and 6. It has an integral role in the work. It announces the first shepherd (Basso) with 12 bars of flourishes over held tonic chords, then is given an 8-bar passage to introduce the second shepherd (Alto). Thereafter it adds background rhythms on the tonic while the *tutti* voices sing, with further flourishes forming punctuation between phrases. It is the primary voice in the closing instrumental section. Its function is therefore to introduce the shepherds, to support them and to provide a concluding symbolic representation of the joy of music-making to celebrate the birth of the Christ child.

Ferdinand Daubrawský, *Pastorella Czeska* (2)

This work is also in the key of D, although the scoring is different from the previous work examined: it has three solo voices, Canto, Alto and Basso, a chorus, 2 violins, organ and *tramba* [*sic*] *pastoralis* (*tromba pastoralis* on the cover). The work is shorter, at 146 bars in length, and is in two sections. First is an introductory *Andante* in 3/4 time, in which the three voices present their messages in turn, with instrumental interludes. The *tromba pastoralis* does not appear in this section. The second section is marked *Tutti Chorus, Allegro*, and is in common time. Four bars of ornate violin melody are followed by the first appearance of the *tromba pastoralis*, which introduces the choral section of the composition. The final 16 bars of the organ part are missing. The harmonic palette is more varied than that of the previous work, and Daubrawský makes use of the scale with the raised fourth. The string writing doubles the voice parts and is more lyrical and elaborate when the voices are not being used. The vocal writing is again simple and homophonic.

The text is similar in sentiment to the previous work: the shepherds receive the news of the birth of the Christ child. They sing of their intention to go and give the gift of music to the baby Jesus.

Canto	*Radostnou novinu zvěstuji vám,*	Good news to proclaim to you,
	že jest se narodil Spasitel nám.	that our Saviour is born.
	Z čisté Panny narozený,	Born of the pure Virgin,
	nám zajisté k potěšení	we truly rejoice that he
	a našim duším k spasení.	brings salvation to our souls.
Basso	*Hej, hej. Poslyšte noviny*	Hey, hey! Listen to the news
	pastuškové milí,	dear shepherds,
	což anjel zvěstoval,	this angel has proclaimed
	radostně prospíval,	in cheerful song
	že se nám narodil náš Spasitel,	that our Saviour is born,
	všeho světa Vykupitel.	Redeemer of the world.
Alto	*Já, ačkoliv již snad poslední,*	And finally me,
	slyším přeradostné noviny, anjelské spívání,	I hear the good news in the angel's song,
	bohu čest vzdávání.	giving honour to God.
	Anjelské spívání, chválu, čest vzdávání.	Angels sing praise and honour.
	Poďmež i my spolu a klekněme,	Let us go together and kneel,
	Ježíškovi libě zahrajeme.	and play sweet music to baby Jesus.
Tutti	*Tebe Boha chválíme,*	God be praised,
Chorus	*vděčně díky činíme.*	gratefully we offer our thanks.
	Rač nás uslyšeti, Milostivý Králi náš,	Please hear us, our gracious King,

kterýž všechno v rukouch máš,   who hold all in your hands,
buď nám milostivý.   be gracious to us.
Popřej tvé božské milosti,   Give us your grace,
budeme mít na tom dosti.   that is all we ask.
Dej se k tobě dostati,   May our praise reach you,
tebe věčně chváliti.   praise you forever.

As with the previous work, Daubrawský uses a *tromba pastoralis* in D and gives it harmonics nos. 3, 4, 5 and 6. It is again used to add realism to the shepherds' story. In this work it is used to announce the *tutti* voices, it provides an *obbligato* line at the same time as the singing, and it features in the final instrumental section. Overall, though, it has a less substantial part than in the previous *Pastorella*.

Fig. 2.6. Daubrawský, *Pastorella Czeska* (2), *tramba pastoralis* part.

Ferdinand Daubrawský, *Pastorella Czeska* (3)

The third *pastorella* by Daubrawský to be investigated is divided into two parts, a *Moderato* in 2/4 in the key of D followed by an *Andante* in 3/4 in A. It is scored for Canto, Alto, Tenore and Basso, 2 horns in D, 2 violins, organ and *tromba pastoralis* in D. It is the longest of the three works examined, with 244 bars.

The musical content is again cheerful, with a predominance of simple tonic and dominant harmony, with use of the scale with a raised fourth. An instrumental opening leads to extended flourishes (24 bars) on the *tromba pastoralis* over unobtrusive background chords; these announce the first entry of the Alto voice. The Basso, then Tenore, then finally Canto singers take up the melody in turn. An instrumental interlude without *tromba pastoralis* then leads to homophonic passages for *tutti* voices and the section concludes with a further solo section for the *tromba pastoralis*. The *Andante* forms the central 40 bars of the work and comprises instrumental passages that alternate with sections for the *tutti* voices. Neither the orchestral horns nor the *tromba pastoralis* are used in this section. The instruction *da capo* signals a return of the opening *Moderato*.

The text is the most personal and detailed of the three Daubrawský *pastorellas* with parts for *tromba pastoralis* in this collection. The Canto, Alto, Tenore and Basso singers take the parts of four herdsmen, each encouraging the others to come to Bethlehem to see the baby Jesus. The Alto will take two lambs to keep the baby's feet warm and to protect his hands from being scratched by the straw, and the Canto will cook him some porridge to warm him. They sing praises all together to welcome the holy birth and prepare to play for the infant. The subsequent *Andante* section, without the loud instruments, is an invitation to the Christ child to sleep while they play for him. The *tromba pastoralis* does not appear in this section: it has already played its part. It has announced the herdsmen and accompanied them in the fields before their journey to Bethlehem. The *da capo* intimates that the discussion ensues once again.

The text reads as follows:

Alto	*Do Betléma půjdeme,*	Go to Bethlehem,
	dary sebou vezmeme,	take your gifts,
	Ježíškovi miláčkovi	sweet baby Jesus
	je darujeme.	is there.
	Tuhle máš, můj Ježíšku,	Here for you, my baby Jesus,
	dvě ovčičky,	two little lambs,
	zahřej s níma tvé malé	with which you can warm
	outlé nožičky	your tiny feet
	by ti zima nebylo,	to keep you warm,
	a seno nepíchalo	and so that the hay
	rozmilé ručičky.	does not scratch your pretty hands.
Basso	*Já též půjdu k Betlému,*	I too will go to Bethlehem,
	v nově narozeného,	to the new-born child,
	k Ježíškovi, miláčkovi	to see the baby Jesus,
	se podívati.	to see the sweet child.
	Nemeškejte pastýři	Hurry, shepherds,
	stáda svého přivítat	leave your flock to greet
	Spasitele lidu všeho.	the Saviour of all people.
	Který jest narozený,	He is born,
	a to s přečisté Panny	and with the Virgin most pure
	nám k potěšení.	let us all rejoice.
Tenore	*Já taky, já taky,*	Me too, me too,
	půjdu s vámi pastuši	I'll go with you shepherds,
	na Ježíška se divati,	to see Jesus,
	jej přivítati,	welcome him,
	vítáme tě, Ježíšku,	we welcome you, baby Jesus,
	náš přemilý miláčku,	our sweet dear one,
	neb si se pro nás vtělil,	bring us freedom,
	abys nás vysvobodil.	you will free us.

Canto		
	Co pak já dám,	What then shall I give,
	když nic nemám,	for I have nothing
	malému Ježíšku?	for the baby Jesus?
	Kdybych věděl,	If I knew
	že by jedl,	what he would like to eat,
	uvařil bych kašičku,	I would cook porridge,
	nakrmil bych outlé dítě	to feed to the little child,
	tak sprostným dárečkem,	a simple gift,
	abych po smrti byl učiněn	so that when it is prepared
	jeho miláčkem,	for the beloved child,
	nes bych jej do Betléma	I would carry it to Bethlehem
	k Ježíšku malému,	to give to baby Jesus,
	abych spatřil a vyzdvěděl	to see whether
	zdaž zima jemu.	he is cold.

Tutti		
	Narodil se Spasitel,	The Saviour is born,
	radujme se,	let us rejoice,
	všeho světa Vykupitel,	Redeemer of the world,
	radujme se.	let us rejoice.
	Spívejme mu vesele	Let us sing
	s ochotností.	with cheerfulness.
	Slušnou chválu vzdávejme,	We gladly praise you
	vší radostí.	with all joy.
	Zdráv buď, náš Spasiteli	Hail, our Saviour,
	který si narozený	he is born
	z přečisté Panny.	of the Virgin most pure.
	Vzhůru pastuškové	Arise, shepherds,
	k Betlému,	to go to Bethlehem,
	zahrejte Ježíšku	to play to baby Jesus,
	malému.	the infant.

Tutti (though occasionally Tenore and Basso are silent)		
	Usni, usni, náš Ježíšku,	Sleep, sleep, our baby Jesus,
	polož tvou malou	rest your little head
	všechnu rozmilou	most holy one,
	a přesvatou hlavičku.	sleep well.
	Usni libě, náš poklade,	Sleep well, our treasure,
	Ježíšku nejkrásnější.	beautiful baby Jesus.
	Matička tě kolébá,	Your mother rocks you,
	tobě líbezně spívá,	singing sweetly,
(no T, B)	*usni libě, můj poklade,*	Sleep well, our treasure,
	synáčku nejmilejší.	most beloved son.
	Přijmi od nás letošní čas,	Accept from us now
(no T, B)	*od nás všech konanou musicu,*	this music we play together,
	tu tobě darujem	we give to you
	i lásky obětujem,	in love and sacrifice,
	nejmilejší, nejkrásnější,	sweetest, most beautiful,
	narozený Ježíšku.	new-born baby Jesus.

The *tromba pastoralis* is again in D, and the harmonics used are nos. 3, 4, 5 and 6. The instrument plays two solo interludes while the strings and organ provide a simple harmonic support. The first of these acts as an introduction to the entry of the first singer, while the second brings the introductory section to a close before the scene changes to the stable in Bethlehem.

Fig. 2.7. Daubrawský, *Pastorella Czeska* (3), *tromba pastoralis* part.

The role of the herdsman's horn in these three works is to enhance the realism of the scene where the herdsmen in the fields discuss the news of the birth of the Christ child; it plays no further part in the narrative once the scene changes and they arrive at the crib. Doubrawský uses individual singers to represent individual herdsmen: there is the possibility, of course, that they may be the actual village herdsmen. The style of writing for the *tromba pastoralis* across the three works is similar, the instrument is of the same length, the same four notes are used and the technical expectations and figurations used are similar. It is reasonable to suppose that the player for whom these parts were written was the same for all three works.

František Dobravský, *Pastorella*

This work has little in common with the previous three compositions apart from its title, its use of the *tuba pastoralis* and the similarity of the given and family names. With the variety of spellings of names found in the Czech lands, it is feasible that this composer could have been from the same lineage as the composer of the previous works; however, the following examination of the material suggests that this musician may be from a later generation. There is no date of composition given.

This work comes from the village of Hořice, which is around 20 miles from Lomnice nad Popelkou. Again this is a small village that has a large Baroque church at its centre and a central square lined with splendid buildings. The church was built in the 1740s and is dedicated to the Birth of the Virgin Mary.

This *pastorella* is scored for Soprano, Canto, Alto, Tenore and Basso, flute, 2 clarinets in A, 2 horns in D, trombone, violone, organ and *tuba pastoralis* (*tuba pastorallis* on the cover) in D. It is unclear whether the five voice parts sing together in the sections marked *tutti*, or whether a separate chorus is intended.

The work is in the key of D and is marked *Andante*. It takes the form of 16 opening instrumental bars followed by five verses in which the same melody is sung an octave apart by the Soprano and the Tenore. There follows a refrain for all to sing in simple harmony. There is prominent use of the rustic signifier, the raised fourth degree of the scale. The text reads:

Soprano and Tenore (five verses, each followed by the refrain)	1. *Radostnou novinu, křesťane milí, zvěstujem vesele v tu chvíli.*	Joyful news, dear Christians, we bring merry tidings in this time.
	2. *Jasná noc pastýře k pastvě zbudila, zpěv, hudba v povětří jest byla.*	On a clear night shepherds in the pastures awoke with music and singing in the skies.
	3. *Dvanáctou hodinu dnes v noci právě, zpívali andelé přeslavně.*	At the stroke of midnight the angels sang wonderfully.
	4. *Všechno se k Betlemu hrne sú prkem, staří mladí plesaj' svým zvukem,*	Everyone is hurrying to Bethlehem, old and young dance to the music,
	5. *Protož i my také vesele pějem, příští Mesiáše zvěstujem.*	And thus we also sing with joy announcing that the new Messiah has come.
Soprano, Canto, Alto and Tenore	Refrain: *Že se narodil Spasitel, všeho světa Vykupitel,*	Know that the Saviour is born, Redeemer of the whole world,
plus Basso	*v Betlemě městě, vězte, to jistě, vězte to jistě.*	in the town of Bethlehem, believe the truth, believe!

The *tuba pastoralis* in D uses harmonics nos. 3, 4, 5 and 6. It plays in bars 8 to 16, a part that is entirely doubled by horn 1, then is silent during the narrative. It joins in the final seven *tutti* bars, where it has an independent bugle-like part. The same music is also written out for bassflugelhorn in C: this may be an alternative in the circumstance that one or the other was not available. It appears that the presence of the *tuba pastoralis* for the performance of this work would have been to enhance the impact of the depiction of Nativity, as the part of the story that involves the shepherds is described.

Fig. 2.8. Dobravský, *Pastorella, tuba pastoralis* part.

Duschek, *Pastorella*

Although no first name appears on this manuscript, perhaps the German name Franz Xaver and the Czech name František belong to the composer of this work: this is a composer born in 1731 and died in 1799, who studied music in Prague where he became an influential teacher, pianist and the most prominent Bohemian composer of his day. Mozart stayed with him during his time in Prague. He was primarily known for his secular compositions. However, most sacred works thought to be by this composer are of doubtful attribution: they may be by another F. Dušek, by B. Dušek, F. B. Dussek or J. L. Dussek.

The cover of this manuscript records that this is a copy of material from Pelhřimov, a large town and regional centre, and that it was transcribed on 26 December 1903 by Ondřej Horník. This *pastorella* is scored for Canto, Alto, Tenore, Basso and chorus, 2 flutes, 2 violins, organ and *tuba pastoricia* (*tuba pastori* on the cover). It is a multi-sectioned work of 144 bars. The opening 32 bars form an introduction of accompanied recitative, initially in the key of G, then the key signature is changed to D. The first main section of the work is marked *Coro, Andante* and is in A major in 6/8 tempo. A further recitative, in the key of D, leads to an *Aria*, in G, marked *Largo*, for the Canto voice. There follows the text '*Gloria in excelsis Deo*' set as a duet for Canto and Alto; further recitative leads to another chorus, in 3/8, and seven instrumental bars bring the work to a close.

The text describes the shepherds' reaction to the events of the Nativity story in an informal manner, and the words and the setting are lively and graphic.

The Tenore and Basso represent the voices of shepherds: they express the urgency, maybe even panic, of the shepherds as they wake each other upon the appearance of great light and fire in the sky: perhaps it is the Day of Judgement. Duschek particularly brings the story to life by use of the shepherds' names and repeated exhortations to wake up. Not only that, he also uses informal versions of the names: *Matouši, Janeku, Mikši, Vavrouši* and *Bárto* are Matthew, John, Michael, Laurence and Bartholomew, but in versions that would correspond in English to something like Matt, Jack, Micky, Larry and Bart.

The shepherds are reassured by the angel, as the Canto is designated, who sings in an aria of the glad tidings of the birth of the Christ child, with text that is taken from the story in the gospel of St. Luke. Canto and Alto together sing the words of the angels, '*Gloria in excelsis Deo*', and the scenario ends with the shepherds' arrival in Bethlehem and their greetings to the baby Jesus. The text reads:

Tenore (recitative, with chords and short instrumental punctuation between some phrases)	*Zhůru chaso, zhůru chaso, zhůru vstávejte, dvanáctá hodina byla, stáda shánějte. Zhůru chaso, zhůru vstávejte. Stáda dohromady shánějte. divné věci se dnes dějou. Kterak obstojíme, strachy a hrůzou, nebe celé se otvírá, velkým bleskem zem přikrývá město Betlehem celé v ohni plápolá a snad bez soudu spáleno je docela.*	Arise, arise young men, wake up, the midnight hour is passing. Arise, get up. Gather your flocks together, amazing things are happening today. As we stand, in fear and trembling, the heavens open, great lightning strikes the earth and the town of Bethlehem is ablaze with the fire and without Divine authority may be burning to the ground.
Basso (recitative)	*Ach, co je to za věci nové, snad se přiblížili již poslední dnové.*	Oh, what new and strange things, perhaps the Day of Judgement has come.
Tenore (recitative)	*To jsou věci nevídaný, ba nikdy neslýchaný.*	These are unprecedented things, never seen before.
Basso (recitative)	*Vstaň Matouši, vstaň ty, Janeku, vstávej brzy Mikši, nelenuj, Vavrouši, ty, Bárto ospalej, vzhůru taky vstávej.*	Arise Matt, you too, Jack, get up quickly Micky, don't be lazy, Larry, you, sleepy Barty, wake up too.
Tutti (coro)	*Vespolek všickni vstávejme, k Betlému rychle chvátejme, Vespolek všicky vstávejme, k Betlému rychle chvátejme. Vespolek všicky vstávejme, a dále rychle chvátejme.*	Let's all get up, hurry to Bethlehem, Let's all get up, hurry to Bethlehem, Let's all get up, Let's go there quickly.

Canto (recitative, with punctuating chords)	*Nebojte se pastýřové,* *zvěstuji vám věci nové,* *zvěstuji vám radost* *zdávna vinšovanou,* *a nikdy neslýchanou.*	Fear not, shepherds, I bring glad tidings, I bring news of great joy, long-awaited, of new things, unheard of.
Canto (Aria)	*Narodil se vám Spasitel,* *všeho světa Vykupitel,* *narodil se v Betlémě,* *leží v chlívě na slámě,* *narodil se z Panny čisté,* *leží v chlévě, špatném místě,* *anjelové jej chválejí,* *jemu vesele spívají:*	Born for you, a Saviour, Redeemer of all the world, born in Bethlehem, lying in a stable in the hay, born of the pure Virgin, lies in a poor stable, there the angels sing to him with praise:
Canto and Alto	*Gloria, gloria, gloria,* *gloria in excelsis Deo.*	Glory to God on high.
Tenore (recitative)	*Ach, jak krásně, jak líbezně,* *anjelové jemu spívají,* *jak radostně jak míle* *jemu posluhují.*	Oh, how beautiful, how lovely, the angels sing to him, how joyfully, how well they serve him.
Basso (recitative)	*Nuž i my také začněme* *toho velkého mocnáře* *skroušeným srdcem pozdravme.*	So let us too greet this great King with a humble heart.
Tutti	*Budiž od nás pozdravený,* *ó děťátko spanilé,* *milionkrát zvelebený,* *ó poupátko rozmilé.*	Let us greet you, oh Child full of grace, a million praises, oh pretty rosebud.
Tutti, repeated	*Tebe pozdravujem s vroucností,* *tobě se klaníme s vděčností.*	We greet you with devotion we worship you with gratitude.

Fig. 2.9. Duschek, *Pastorella, tuba pastoricia* part.

The *tuba pastoricia* is in D and uses harmonics nos. 3, 4, 5 and 6. It appears only in the final chorus, where the text begins '*Budiž od nás pozdravený*' (Let us greet you). Here it has a few bright fanfares, followed by a substantial celebratory flourish to bring the work to a conclusion. In this instance Duschek does not use the instrument at the time when the shepherds are in the fields and visited by the angels, rather it is brought in at the end of the narrative as a device to celebrate the birth of the Christ child. The motifs do not resemble those of Daubrawský's parts: these are more virtuosic and call for more technical skill.

Jan Augustin Fibiger, *Pro Nativitate Domini*

Fibiger (1760–1851) is a composer about whom little information has been identified other than first names and dates. This work comes from the village of Bakov, where Linek (see p. 70) was cantor from the 1750s.

As mentioned earlier, this work is unique in this collection in that there are no vocal parts, and there is no part for organ. It has a total of 24 bars: two sections, each of which is repeated. It is in the key of C major and is scored for 2 *clarini*, *principale*, timpani, march and *tuba pastoralis*, or in modern terminology, two high trumpets, one standard trumpet, timpani, a pair of drums and a herdsman's horn. It was a style of music that was played on Christmas night. The instrumentation suggests that it was suitable for use out of doors; thus, it may have been intended for performance outside the church either before or after midnight Mass.

The *tuba pastoralis* is in C and uses five notes, harmonics nos. 3, 4, 5, 6 and 8. It is the most prominent instrument, and its music alternates with that of the two *clarini* in bright fanfare-like phrases.

Fig. 2.10. Fibiger, *Pro Nativitate Domini, tuba pastoricia / pastoralis* part.

František Václav Habermann, *Motetto pastoralni II*

Habermann (1706–1783) was born in Eger (now Cheb). After holding musical appointments in Spain, France and Italy, he settled in Prague, where he was choirmaster for two monastic churches. He was commissioned to write music to celebrate the coronation of Empress Maria Theresa as Queen of Bohemia in 1743. He was also a renowned teacher; students included F. X. Duschek (see earlier) and Mysliveček. At the age of 67, he returned to take up the post of cantor at Cheb, where he remained for the rest of his life.

The date of this work is not known. This manuscript is in full score, in the hand of Ondřej Horník. The copy was made on 20 December 1905, and its provenance is given as Ústí nad Orlicí. On the cover the composer's name is spelt Habermañ, inside it reads Habermann (the first is a shorthand version of the second); the cover gives the work as *Moteto pastoral* and inside it is *Motetto pastoralni II*. The scoring is for Canto, Alto, Tenore and Basso, 2 violins, organ and *tuba pastoritia*. It is in the key of D, in a single section marked *Allegro* of 60 bars in length. The violin parts are lively and energetic and weave elaborate figurations around the predominantly tonic harmony.

The text is in Latin. The vocal writing is largely *tutti* and homophonic, with syllabic word underlay. It is a simple prayer to the Christ child. A fascinating feature of the work is seen on line 6 in the text below, which was also found in the *Offertorium Pastorale* of Czerni: the repetition of the end of the word *optime*, with *-me, -me, -me*, an idea that recurs here a number of times. It is noted that both of these composers had connections with the monastic traditions in Prague, where one composer may have come into contact with such word painting from the other, or from a common source.

Tutti	*Vive ergo nostuere,* *vive ergo nostuere,* *bone pastor domine,*	Living One, look on us Good Shepherd, Lord,
	nostri semper curam gere *vive puer optime,* *vive puer optime -me -me -me*	always carry our cares, O greatest living Child. etc.
	nostri semper curam gere, *vive puer optime,* *vive puer optime -me -me -me*	
	vive puer optime, *vive puer nostuere,* *bone Pastor Domine,*	
	nostri semper curam gere *vive puer optime, -me -me -me*	
	vive puer optime, *vive puer optime -me -me -me* *vive puer optime, optime!*	

The *tuba pastoralis* is in D and uses the five harmonics of nos. 3, 4, 5, 6 and 8. The part is virtuosic, as energetic as the violin parts, with much semiquaver figuration particularly when the voices are given long held notes. The part begins after the initial statement of the text. The reference to the name of the Good Shepherd is the only textual connection with a *tuba pastoralis*.

Fig. 2.11. Habermann, *Motetto pastoralni II*, transcription of the *tuba pastoritia* part.

Holetschek, *Pastorella*

No information about this composer has been found, nor has the place of composition been identified, but the date 28 December 1839 appears at the end of the organ part. The work is scored for Canto, Alto, Basso, 2 violins, violone, organ and *tuba pastoralis*. It is 109 bars long, in the key of C and is in a number of short sections.

Its text is in both Latin and Czech. The first section is a setting of the opening of the *Gloria* of the Mass, the angel's words from the gospel of St. Luke, Chapter 2. It is sung by the Canto and Alto in simple harmony, the lines supported by the violins. The next section, marked *Andante*, is a setting of a gentle folk-like melody played on the violin and organ over a tonic drone, while the *tuba pastoralis* plays twelve slow notes on the tonic (harmonic no. 4) with the instruction '*Hodiny s'e bjgi neb traubigj*' (the clock strikes the hour).[27] After four further bars of solemn *tuba pastoralis* figuration, the key changes to G major and the *tuba pastoralis* plays another twelve slow notes, this time on G (harmonic no. 3). This may represent a different church clock striking the hour of midnight. Replication of the sounding of midnight by the *tuba pastoralis* is also found in this collection in the *pastorella* of Štietina (p. 86).

The key now changes again, to E flat, and the Czech narrative begins. The Basso takes the role of a shepherd, who tells his friends to listen: that at the moment of midnight, the Christ child is born. The music reverts to C major when the angels (Canto and Alto) sing '*Gloria*' again, and the shepherds encourage each other to go to Bethlehem. The Czech text leads back into the Latin with an invitation to sing the words of praise from the *Gloria* of the Mass, '*laudamus te*', etc. It would therefore appear that this work may have been written to take place not at the Offertory of the Mass, but as an interlude during the *Gloria*.

Canto and Alto	*Gloria gloria in excelsis Deo*	Glory to God on high
	Gloria gloria in excelsis Deo	
	et in terra pax hominibus	and on earth, peace to all men
	bonae voluntatis.	of good will.
	Gloria gloria in excelsis Deo	
	(the clocks strike)	
Basso	*Vy milý pastýřové,*	Listen, dear shepherds,
	odbila dvanáctá hodina.	the twelfth hour has struck.
	V té době jest Syn Boží	At this moment the Son of God
	narozený z jedné prosté panny,	is born of a simple virgin,
	a to v Betlémě v chlévě.	in Bethlehem in a stable.
Canto and Alto	*Gloria gloria in excelsis Deo*	

Alto	*Slyš, slyš, slyš,*	Hear, hear, hear,
	jak anjelé spívají	hear the angels sing
	a pastýřům zvěstují,	proclaiming to the shepherds,
	jak oni spívají,	as they sing,
	čest Bohu jak vzdávají,	giving praise to God,
	do Betléma pospíchají	go quickly to Bethlehem
	k nově narozenému.	to the newborn.
Tutti	*Vy milý pastýřové pospěšte,*	You, dear shepherds,
	v této době	hurry at this time
	to malé děťátko přivítat,	to welcome this little baby,
	jemu dary obětovat,	to bring him gifts,
	čest a chválu vzdávat,	give honour and praise,
	pobožně jemu spívat	sing to him with the holy words
	laudamus te,	we praise you,
	benedicimus te,	we bless you,
	adoramus te,	we adore you,
	glorificamus te,	we glorify you,
	tobě, Ježíšku.	to you, baby Jesus.

Fig. 2.12. Holetschek, *Pastorella*, *tuba pastoralis* part.

The *tuba pastoralis* in C uses harmonics nos. 3, 4, 5 and 6. In this work it is put to imaginative use in the representation of the striking of midnight on what appear to be two different clocks. It also plays slow bugle-like calls in between, which might represent the peaceful watch of the shepherds overnight. Once the narrative begins, the *tuba pastoralis* is played alongside the voices until the end of the work, adding cheerful arpeggio figurations to the texture.

František Václav Jech, *Mottetto in D, Ofertorium [sic] Pastorale*

Jech was born in Jilemnice in 1776; this work comes from Rovensko, which is about 20 miles away. The title page reads *Mottetto in D*; on each part is written *Ofertorium Pastorale* or an abbreviation or variant spelling, sometimes in addition, sometimes instead. The work is 87 bars in length with a *da capo* and is scored for Canto, Alto, Tenore and Basso, 2 clarinets in C, 2 clarini in D, 2 horns in D, 2 violins, viola, violone, organ, timpani in D and A and *tuba pastorica* (*tuba pastoris* on the cover).

The orchestration is rich. The instruments are sometimes used all together and at other times in a variety of reduced combinations to provide a number of different sonorities. There is a 19-bar instrumental introduction which is used as a *ritornello* that reappears as interludes in the narrative; it is also used as a *da capo* section that brings the work to a close. Its thematic material is also given to the voices. The opening statements are followed by seven bars for the *tuba pastorica*, accompanied by static chords on the tonic played by the strings and organ. This heralds the arrival of the voices. The *tuba pastorica* is not used again until after the narrative is finished, when similar motifs over held chords return.

The vocal writing is entirely homophonic, and *tutti* except for the central section when Canto and Alto alternate with Tenore and Basso. Much of the material is sung in unison or at the octave and is doubled by the strings and wind instruments where possible as well. The Czech text tells in an informal manner of the desire to greet and honour the arrival of baby Jesus. In this instance, shepherds are not mentioned, but individual musicians are told of the need to wake up and celebrate the arrival of the newborn child: they will play horns and the loud cheerful bass. The use of the familiar name Franto (a pet name for František) gives a personal touch to the story. As the voices primarily sing all together, they do not in this instance take the role of different characters in the story, neither does the orchestration highlight the specific instruments when they are named. However, some dramatic enhancement is created with the interplay between the high and the low voices.

Tutti	*Ježíšku, náš rozmilý Spasiteli,*	Jesus, our beloved Saviour,
	k tobě my přicházíme v tuto chvíli,	we come to you at this time,
	chceme čest, chválu vzdávati,	we want to give you praise,
	z příští tvého radost míti,	and rejoice in your coming;
	přijmi od nás dary malé,	accept our small gifts,
	které v musice konáme,	that we give you in music,

	tak tebe, dítě spanilé,	to you, baby full of grace,
	srdcem i ústy chválíme.	may our hearts and mouths give praise.
	Vzhůru, vy muzikanti, hodně hrejte,	Arise, musicians, make music,
	na všecky inštrumenty chválu vzdejte.	give praise on all the instruments.
Canto and Alto	*Franto, ty hodně hřmotně a vesele drbej basu,*	Franto, on the loud and cheerful bass,
Tenore and Basso	*Valdhorny, hlas vydejte a vzbuďte ospalou chasu.*	Horns, start playing, and wake up the sleepy lot!
Canto and Alto	*Tak půjdeme Ježíškovi čest, chválu prospěvovat.*	They will give honour to the baby Jesus.
Tenore and Basso	*Srdce naše, též i duši budeme obětovat*	Our hearts and souls we will also offer.
Tutti	*Přijmi od nás, Ježíšku, letošní čas, až víc umět budeme, přijdeme zas. Buď tisíckrát pozdravený, že ses ráčil z čisté panny pro nás, hříšné, naroditi, bys mohl všechny spasiti.*	Accept now from us, baby Jesus, our humble but sincere offerings. Be greeted a thousand times, that you have deigned to be born of a pure virgin, for us sinners, for our salvation.

A contemporary illustration from 1717 of musicians playing at the scene of the Nativity is found in the painted ceiling above the nave of the magnificent church of the former Benedictine monastery at Michelfeld in Bavaria, 50 miles from the Czech border:

Fig. 2.13. Shepherds play instruments at the crib, ceiling painting by Cosmas and Egid Asam, in the monastery church at Michelfeld. Photo: Frances Jones.

Jech gives the *tuba pastorica* in D four notes in this work, harmonics nos. 3, 4, 5 and 6. It is played just twice; on each occasion it is given a phrase of seven bars with an up-beat. The part appears to be a collection of calls that a herdsman would play, with phrases quite different from the parts Jech writes for the orchestral horns. Although shepherds are not mentioned in the text, the narrative is presented using informal language in a familiar setting in order to enhance the realism of the Nativity story, and the *tuba pastorica* adds an extra touch of local colour to the scene.

Fig. 2.14. Jech, *Mottetto Ofertorium Pastorale, tuba pastorica* part.

Tomáš Norbert Kautník, *Offertorium Pastorale*

Kautník, or Koutník, (1698-1775) was born in Choceň. He studied music in the Piarist schools in Litomyšl and later Kroměříž, then returned to take up the post of organist and schoolmaster at Choceň in 1729, where he remained until his death, which apparently occurred while he was playing the organ. There are at least 52 surviving religious compositions by Kautník.

Choceň is a small town; the large Baroque church at one end of the central cobbled square, dedicated to St. Francis of Assisi, was completed in 1703. It is typical of the scale and magnificence of the provincial churches for which these rural *pastorellas* were written.

Fig. 2.15. Church of St. Francis of Assisi, Choceň, where Kautník was organist for 46 years. Photo: Frances Jones.

Two works composed by Kautník that include a part for a *tuba pastoralis* survive in České Muzeum Hudby in Prague, although one uses notes that could not be played on a natural horn. The second work, *Offertorium Pastorale*, exists in the form of a hand-written full score made on 21 April 1944, signed Diblík. It quotes Kautník as the composer and the source as Choceň. It is 139 bars long, in C major, and scored for Canto, Alto, Tenore and Basso, 2 clarinets in C, 2 horns in C, 2 violins, organ and *tuba pastoralis*.

An instrumental introduction of 19 bars that includes flourishes on the *tuba pastoralis* leads to the entry of the voices in a homophonic unaccompanied rendition of the text '*Gloria in excelsis Deo*'. After a further instrumental passage, the narrative in Czech begins. This is divided into four sections with instrumental interludes in between, shown with a line space in the transcription of the text below. Kautník makes substantial use of the scale with the raised fourth degree.

All the singing is *tutti*. The *Gloria* is in four-part harmony, thereafter all the text is sung in unison, high voices an octave above the low voices, except for the final chord that divides into four parts. The vocal sections are accompanied only by the organ, apart from the *Gloria,* which is *a capella,* and the final 6 bars, when the full orchestra plays with the voices. One simple melody is used for each of the sections in Czech; it is used twice in the key of C and twice in the key of G, then the final text concludes with different music. The shepherds' story is told in their own words as they encourage each other to go to Bethlehem. They decide to take whistles and bagpipes to play for the baby Jesus.

Tutti	*Gloria, Gloria*	Glory
	in excelsis Deo,	to God on high.
	in excelsis Deo.	
	Nuž tedy pastýřové, všichni poběhněme,	Well then, shepherds, let's run, all of us,
	uhlídáme, kde co máme, hodně již	collect our things and hurry;
	hybejme;	
	uhlídáme, kde co máme, hodně již	collect our things and hurry;
	hybejme;	
	Uvidíme děťátko, prosté pacholátko,	We will find the little child, our Lord,
	což to bude vemte hude našemu Paňátko.	we must take our instruments,
	což to bude vemte hude našemu Paňátko.	we must take our instruments.
	Všichni honem najednou dary sebou	Hurry all, we must take our gifts
	nesme	collect our things and hurry,
	uhlídáme, kde co máme, hodně již	collect our things and hurry.
	hybejme,	
	uhlídáme, kde co máme, hodně již	
	hybejme.	
	Vemte sebou píšťaly, všelijake dudy	Let's take our whistles and various
	najednou začneme tomu novému králi.	bagpipes
	Tobě všichni z ochotnosti	we must go now to see the new King.
	dáváme dary a příjmi nás všechny	All of us want to give gifts to you;
	do nebeského království.	accept us all
	Amen.	into the heavenly kingdom.
		Amen.

The *tuba pastoralis* in C uses harmonics nos. 3, 4, 5 and 6 and the part consists of different bugle-like flourishes, sometimes in declamatory style and sometimes in a melodic fashion. Most of the time, when the *tuba pastoralis* is used, it is accompanied only by strings and organ which hold a tonic chord in support, in the manner of a bagpipe's drone. The *tuba pastoralis* introduces each of the vocal entries apart from the first one and joins in the climax at the end of the work.

Offertorium Pastorale

Tuba pastoralis

Tomas Norbert Kautník
transcribed Frances Jones

Fig. 2.16. Kautník, *Offertorium Pastorale*, transcription of the *tuba pastoralis* part.

Tomáš Kollovrátek, *Offertorium Pastorale*

Tomáš Kollovrátek was born in 1763 and died in 1831. Of the six *pastorellas* in the Prague collection written by Kollovrátek, five come from Choceň, and one is from Holice, around twelve miles away. It is therefore possible that Kollovrátek may have been cantor at Choceň after the death of Kautník.

Three of the six works of Kollovrátek in this collection in the style of a *pastorella* include the *tuba pastoralis*. This *Offertorium Pastorale* has the date 1810, which has been changed to 1820, on the cover. It is written for Canto, Alto, Tenore and Basso, 2 clarinets in B flat, *clarino*, 2 horns in C, 2 violins, timpani in C and G, organ and *tuba pastoritia*. It is in the key of C and is 153 bars in length.

A lively instrumental opening of 22 bars leads to eight bars of *tuba pastoralis* solo over held tonic chords played by the rest of the instruments. This heralds the vocal music which is entirely *tutti* and homophonic, although the Tenore and Basso are omitted where the text requires a hushed sound. Much of the instrumental accompaniment doubles the voice parts, although there is more florid writing for the strings at times. There is one instrumental interlude of eight bars; otherwise, the singers tell their story continuously. The orchestra brings the work to a close. The piece rarely strays from tonic and dominant tonality.

The text is taken from a collection of Latin vocal music published in 1582 known as *Piae Cantiones* (Pious Songs): it is part of the Gradual used in the Mass for the Epiphany (Twelfth Night). Kollovrátek has not used the entire text from *Piae Cantiones*, but made a selection for his setting from the fourteen verses of the original to suit his needs; he has also added the text '*in hoc novo Anno*' (in this new year) a number of times into the work. It is probable therefore that it was intended not for midnight Mass on Christmas night, but for use in the celebration of Mass on the Feast of the Epiphany, which commemorates the visit of the three kings. It is unusual for a work that includes the *tuba pastoralis* to concentrate not on the story of the shepherds in the fields when they are told of the birth, but on the arrival of the magi at the stable.

A notable moment occurs at the description of the crib: here the music takes on a special reverence. The instruments fall silent, the voices join together in unison or at the octave and the melody they sing is a fifteenth-century Czech Christmas carol that is quoted in other *pastorellas*: *Narodil se Kristus Pán* (Christ the Lord is born). The melody is used for the text '*Hic jacet in presepio qui regnat sine termino*' (Here lies in the manger he who reigns without end). The melody uses the minor 3rd of the scale as well as the raised fourth degree, a feature commonly used in compositions that imitate folk repertoire. There is no hint of this material in the music that precedes it; however, the orchestral writing thereafter takes on some of the features of this melody and the tune returns in the voice parts for a second time towards the end of the work, with the words '*Laudetur sancta Trinitas*' (Praised be the Holy Trinity).

Immediate repetitions of words are omitted below:

Tutti; Tenore and Basso are omitted in quiet bars	*Puer natus in Betlehem unde gaudet Jerusalem.*	A child is born in Bethlehem Jerusalem rejoices.
	Laetamini in Domino in hoc novo Anno.	Be glad in the Lord in this new year.
	Hic jacet in presepio qui regnat sine termino	Here lies in the manger he who reigns without end.
	Laetamini in Domino in hoc novo Anno.	Be glad …
	Cognovit bos et asinus quod puer erat Dominus.	The ox and the ass knew that this child was the Lord.
	Reges de Saba veniunt, aurum thus mirham offerunt. Alleluja.	Kings come from Sheba, offering gold, frankincense and myrrh. Alleluia.
	In hoc natali (not T, B) *natali gaudio.*	On this joyful birthday praise to the birth.
	Laetamini in Domino, in hoc novo Anno.	Be glad …
	Laudetur Sancta Trinitas benedicamus Domino.	Praised be the Holy Trinity let us bless the Lord.
	Laetamini in Domino in hoc novo Anno.	Be glad …

The *tuba pastoritia* is in C and uses four notes, harmonics nos. 3, 4, 5 and 6. The inclusion of a part for *tuba pastoritia* is not easy to explain in this work, for a few reasons. There is no reference to shepherds in the text, and it would appear to be a work written for a service other than Christmas midnight Mass. The fact that the text is in Latin and a setting of a regular part of the words of the Mass also make it an unexpected composition in which to find this instrument: this might not be a dramatic interlude designed to bring the Christmas story to life, but part of a normal sung Mass. The text is formal: it does not introduce the names of individuals or instruments, or make other personal references. The title *Offertorium Pastorale* is the only oblique reference to the rustic. The instrument is used sparingly: it heralds the first vocal entry with a bugle-like call, it has four bars of music while the voices hold the word '*Anno*' and it appears again in the final eight-bar instrumental close.

Fig. 2.17. Kollovrátek, *Offertorium Pastorale, tuba pastoritia* part.

Tomáš Kollovrátek, *Offertorium pro Festis Natalitijs*

This work is scored for Canto, Alto, Tenore and Basso, 2 clarinets in C, 2 horns in C, 2 violins, violone, organ and *tuba pastoralis*. It is 276 bars long and is in one section in C major, marked *Allegro*.

50 bars of instrumental introduction include two short flourishes for the *tuba pastoralis*. The vocal writing is entirely homophonic, with some antiphonal writing between the high and low voices in simulation of conversation. Almost all of the text is set syllabically, apart from the word '*Gloria*' which attracts flowing semiquaver runs, initially just in the Canto voice with held notes in the other parts and subsequently in all the voice parts in unison or at the octave.

This typical *pastorella* text includes conversations of the shepherds and uses a personal name in familiar form, *Mikšíčku* (or Micky). It is possible that this is the actual name of the person playing this part in the Christmas story: this would enhance the realism of the scene. The shepherds rejoice at the birth of the Christ child with exhortations to sing '*Gloria*' and hurry to Bethlehem to see the baby. They describe the gifts they will bring: a lamb, a fat calf and a kid; they will take a violin and sing and play to the Christ child. Kollovrátek again uses a variant of the melody of *Narodil se Kristus Pán* in this work, for the text '*pospěšme my k Betlému, pospěžme Panáčkovi malému hojné dary dejme mu*' (Let us hurry to Bethlehem, to the wondrous baby boy, let us give him gifts). Repeated lines of text have been omitted below:

Canto and Alto	*Nuž, my všichni pospolu,*	Well, let us all together,
	Panáčkovi malému,	to the little Lord,
	chválu vzdejme a plesejme, Pánu našemu.	give thanks and rejoice to our Lord.
	Gloria in excelsis Deo, Gloria.	Glory to God on high, sing Gloria.
Tutti	*Plesejme.*	Rejoice.
	Plesej nebe, plesej země, všecko plémě,	Heaven rejoice, all the earth, all creatures,
	a raduj se, všecko lidské plémě,	and rejoice, all humanity,
	že se narodil nám Spasitel,	that our Saviour is born,
	všeho světa Vykupitel,	Redeemer of all the world,
	Gloria, gloria.	Gloria, gloria.
Canto and Alto	*Nuž, my všichni pospolu,*	Well, let us all together
	pospěšme my k Betlému,	hurry to Bethlehem,
	panáčkovi malému hojné	to the wondrous baby boy
Tutti	*dary dejme mu,*	let us give him gifts,
	nuž, my všickni pospolu,	well, all together,
	pospěšme my k Betlému, pospěžme	let us hurry to Bethlehem,
	Panáčkovi malému hojné	to the wondrous baby boy
	dary dejme mu.	let us give him gifts.
	Já jemu, já jemu	I shall give him, I shall give him
	daruji to malé jehňátko	I shall give a little lamb,
	i také to tlusté, tlusté telátko,	and also a fat, fat calf,
	to kůzlátko.	and a kid.
	Mikšíčku, vem sebou	Micky, take with you
	tvoje nové malé housličky,	your new little violin,
	zahráme Ježíškovi	we will play to baby Jesus
	před těma jesličky,	around the crib,
	budem hráti a spívati,	we will play and sing,
	před těma jesličky.	around the crib.
Canto and Alto	*Tedy pospěšme tam, pastýři,*	So hurry there, shepherds,
	stáda našeho vartýři.	guardians of our flocks.
	Panáčka přivítejme,	Welcome baby Jesus,
	chválu jemu vzdávejme.	give praise to him;
	zdráv buď, milý a spanilý,	hail, dear one full of grace,
	Ježíšku malý.	little baby Jesus.
Tutti	*Začneme, začneme*	We'll start, we'll start
	všichni pospolu	all together
	Gloria, ať se jen všudy rozlíhá, rozlíhá.	with Gloria, let it resound everywhere.
	Začneme Gloria, ať se všudy jen rozlíhá	We'll start with Gloria,
	sláva jeho nestihlá, nestihlá.	which has not been heard before.
Canto and Alto	*Spívejme mu Gloria, ať se všudy rozlihá,*	Let Gloria resound for ever,
	rozlíhá, há rozlíhá	resound, resound.
Tenore and Basso	*sláva jeho nestihlá, ať se*	praise his glory,
Tutti	*všudy rozlíhá.*	let it resound everywhere.
	Gloria, gloria, gloria,	Gloria, gloria, gloria,
	Amen, amen.	Amen, amen.

The *tuba pastoralis* in C uses five notes, harmonics no. 3, 4, 5, 6 and 8. It is given two short flourishes in the introduction, over held chords in the other instruments; it then joins the final cadence of the introduction before the voices enter. A brief call before the final text '*Začneme, začneme*' invites the participants to sing '*Gloria*' to the baby Jesus. The *tuba pastoralis* is the main voice in the final twelve bars of the work while the other instruments again hold tonic chords in imitation of a calm drone.

Fig. 2.18. Kollovrátek, *Offertorium pro Festis Natalitijs, tuba pastoralis* part.

Kolovrátek, 2do Pastorella

The spelling of the composer's name is here at variance with the spelling on the other two works in this investigation, and no first name is given. Although the source of the manuscript is a Holice, approximately twelve miles from Choceň, these three works may be by the same composer, as stylistically the *tuba pastoralis* parts show some similarity, and all are pitched in the key of C.

Within the folio entitled *2do Pastorella* is a pair of *pastorellas*, scored for Canto and Alto, 2 clarinets in C, 2 horns in C, 2 violins, timpani in C and G, organ and *tuba pastorellis* (*tuba principal* on the part). The first is marked *Andante*, of 87 bars in length; the second is marked *Allegro moderato* and is 62 bars long. Both are in 3/8, and each consists of an opening introduction followed by two verses of text, the voices singing syllabically in simple harmony. The melody of the first *pastorella* is different from the melody of the second.

The text of each verse is divided into parts by instrumental interludes, shown by line spaces below. Repeated lines have been omitted in this transcript:

Pastorella 1

2 verses,
Canto and Alto

1. *Radostná novina,*
přešťastná hodina,
Panenka Maria
porodila syna.

   Glad tidings,
   most joyous hour.
   The Virgin Mary
   has borne a son.

   Plesejme radostí,
   nastal den milosti.
   Dnes Panenka čistá
   porodila Krista.

   Sing with joy,
   the day of grace has come.
   Today the pure Virgin
   has borne Christ for us.

2. *Nebeští anjelé*
zpívají vesele.
Radost nám zvěstují,
Boha zvelebují.

   Angel from heaven
   sing merrily.
   We proclaim the joy,
   magnify God.

   S nimi se radujme,
   takto prozpěvujme:
   Sláva na výsosti
   božské velebnosti.
   Bůh jest narozený.

   Let us rejoice with them,
   singing as follows:
   Glory on high
   to the divine Majesty.
   Christ is born.

Pastorella 2

2 verses,
Canto and Alto

1. *Sem, sem pastýři,*
sem, sem vesele,
pospěšte vy všichni
k Betlému směle,
narozenému
děťátku malému.
Chválu děťátku,
chválu vzdejte.

   Come, come shepherds
   come with joy,
   hurry, let us go bravely
   to Bethlehem,
   born there
   is a little baby.
   Give praise to the baby,
   let us give thanks.

   Sem, sem pastýři,
   sem vesele,
   pospěšte vy všichni
   jen směle,
   děťátku malému
   chválu vzdejte.

   Come, come shepherds
   come with joy,
   hurry all
   be brave,
   to the little baby
   let us give thanks.

2. *Ó přešťastná jest*
tato novina,
Maria splodila
krásného syna.
Právě teď, půlnoční
půlnoční hodinu,
anjelé zvěstují
všemu lidu,

   Oh, rejoice
   at this news,
   Mary bore
   a beautiful son.
   Now, at midnight
   the midnight hour,
   angels proclaim
   to all the people,

   že se narodil Spasitel
   všeho světa,
   světa Vykupitel.
   Radost nám
   zvěstují andělé,
   že se narodil
   v Betlémě.

   that the Saviour is born,
   for the whole world,
   to redeem the world.
   Let us proclaim
   with the angels
   that he was born
   in Bethlehem.

The *tuba pastorellis* in C is given harmonics nos. 3, 4, 5, 6, 8 and 10 (an upper mediant). In both of these *pastorellas* there is a mix of single notes in the instrumental texture alongside the orchestral horns and independent short herdsmen's motifs under which the accompanying instruments hold static chords. The *tuba pastorellis* is the dominant voice at the close of this pair of *pastorellas*.

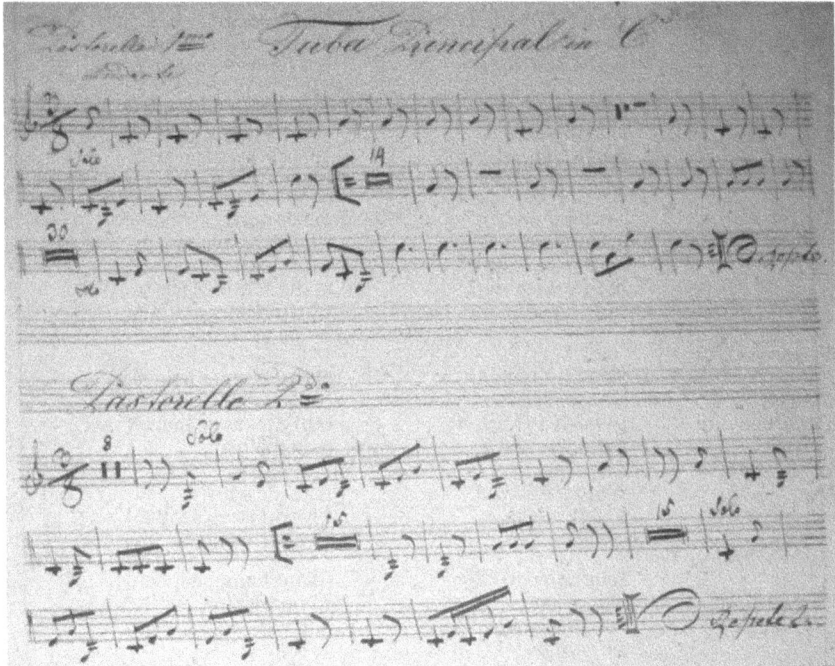

Fig. 2.19. Kolovrátek, *2do Pastorella, tuba principal* part.

Jiří Ignác Linek, *Pastorella* (1)

Jiří (Georgy on the cover of this work, Georgio on the next work) Linek (or Linka, or Lynka), 1725–1791, was born and died in the small village of Bakov, where he also spent his working life as schoolmaster and cantor. The large Gothic church, with its adjacent school, is dedicated to St. Bartholomew and dates from the 1560s. There is a monument to Linek in the churchyard. 44 sacred compositions by Linek are known.

Fig. 2.20. Monument to Linek in front of the church in Bakov. Photo: Frances Jones.

This *pastorella* is scored for Basso solo, 2 violins, organ and *tuba pastorallis*. It is in the key of C, in 3/4 *Allegro moderato* tempo and is 58 bars in length. The work opens with 12 bars of an instrumental introduction, followed by a second section of 46 bars that is repeated to accommodate four verses of text. The instrumental introduction returns at the end in the form of a *da capo*. The word setting is syllabic, and the music for the voices is the same as that of the introduction. Much of the time the line of the Basso is duplicated by the strings or the organ; the voice also mimics the calls of the *tuba pastoralis* at times. Pedal points are used to represent the bagpipes that are mentioned in the narrative.

The text is light-hearted and personal. The shepherd tells his friends to get up quickly and go with him to Bethlehem, with gifts of a ram and a lamb to keep baby Jesus warm. They will take bagpipes and play and sing to the Christ child.

Familiar versions of personal names enhance the realistic feel of the text. Each verse is in two sections separated by an instrumental interlude that is indicated below with a blank line; repeated lines of text are also omitted:

4 verses   1. *Zhůru bratři, Bárto, Mikši,*   Arise, brothers, Barty, Micky,
Basso   *rychle vstávejte,*   get up quickly,
                   se mnou pospíchejte do Betléma.   hurry with me to Bethlehem.

                   Vemte kejdy a gaduchy,   Take your bagpipes,
                   budeme spívati,   we'll sing
                   musicírovati u Betléma.   and play in Bethlehem.

              2.. *Bárto starý, vezmi dary,*   Old Barty, take gifts,
                   jehňátko bílý,   take a white lamb,
                   by bylo jmilý Ježíškovi.   baby Jesus would like that.

                   K tomu plíšek, neb kožíšek,   Its fleece will keep him warm
                   by se moch zahříti,   and protect him
                   před zimou ukrýti, náš Ježíšek.   from the cold, our Jesus.

              3. *Mikši hloupý, neseš kroupy,*   Stupid Micky, you are carrying barley
                   berany zapíráš,   instead of a sheep
                   zubkyně taky máš, jsi hodný lhář.   That is wrong, you must take a sheep.

                   Vem berana na ramena,   Take a ram on your shoulders,
                   Pánu jej obětuj,   offer it to the Lord,
                   krup se sám napěchuj notně doma,   and eat the barley yourself.

              4. *Obětujte a darujte,*   Sacrifice and give,
                   každý dle možnosti   each whatever you have
                   panáčku v hojnosti udělujte.   give in abundance to the child.

                   Já jsem chudý, jdu jen z dudy,   I am poor, I just have my bagpipes,
                   pěkně mu zapískám, milost u něj   I will blow a tune
                   zejskám, pak zavejskám.   as a joyful present for him.

The *tuba pastoralis* in C is played throughout the piece. It uses harmonics nos. 4, 5, 6, 8, 10 and 12; in addition, five fast notes of a scale are written in ascent up to harmonic 12. This is likely to be an instruction to 'whoop' up to the note, as these pitches themselves cannot be played accurately (see similar figures on pp. 152, 153). The instrument is given many figurations while the bass sings and there is antiphonal interplay between the horn and the singer.

Fig. 2.21. Linek, *Pastorella* (1), *tuba pastorallis* part.

Jiří Ignác Linek, *Pastorella* (2)

This second *pastorella* by Linek with a part for a herdsman's horn in the collection in Prague is scored for Alto and Basso, 2 violins, organ and *tuba pastoralis*.

This work is in the key of D and is 109 bars long. It begins with eight bars of recitative, unaccompanied apart from held notes on the organ. This is followed by an *Andante* in 6/8, although the voice parts retain quasi-improvisatory recitative throughout. At times the strings share lively semiquaver figurations, sometimes they imitate the arpeggiating notes of the *tuba pastoralis*, and at other times they play the same as the voices, but overall the string writing forms a cohesive structural framework upon which the narrative is superimposed.

The text is an informal conversation between two shepherds, using familiar names, and is chatty and amusing. While the news of the events of Christmas night is relayed by the Alto, the Basso queries each comment with 'what?', 'who?' and 'where?' in a surprised and uncomprehending manner. There is no record of how these works were performed, but this style of writing might suggest that this was acted as a little music-drama, rather than merely sung in the style of a concert performance. The Basso is not portrayed in this instance as someone who has just woken up, rather as someone who is not particularly intelligent, as he explains that although he heard loud singing of the angel close by, he did not know the meaning of the message 'Gloria in excelsis Deo' as he does not understand Latin! There follows detailed conversation concerning what gifts to take: they decide on a lamb and a goat. They then discuss what instruments they and each of their fellows should play for the infant: bagpipes, whistle, fiddle and bass. The story ends with 'good night' sung to the baby Jesus, followed by an instrumental close.

The text reads:

Basso, recit.	*Hej, hej, Jene, co se to děje v Betlémě se svíti, co co pak to, co co pak to, co pak to má býti? Běž, běž, nemeškej, bež, běž, běž, nemeškej, oznam a pověz co se tam děje, co nového.*	Hey, hey, Johnny, what is happening in Bethlehem a light is shining, what, what then, what then, what is it, what then is there? Go, go, hurry, go, go, go, hurry, go and say what is happening there, what is the good news.
Alto	*Hleď, Kubo, divná věc jest,*	Behold, Jake, this wondrous thing,
Basso	*Co pak,*	What?
Alto	*Bůh se nám narodil jest,*	God is born for us.
Basso	*Kdo pak,*	Who?
Alto	*Teď v Betlémském chlévu, při anjelském spěvu.*	Now in a stable in Bethlehem, the seraphim are singing.
Basso	*Kde pak,*	Where?
Alto	*Jak sme jen vyhnali, světlo sme spatřili v Betlémě.*	We'd only just driven the flocks out when we saw the light in Bethlehem.
Basso	*Divná věc,*	Where is the wondrous thing?
Alto	*Co pak jsi neslyšel anjele spívati překrásně?*	Didn't you hear angels singing so beautifully?
Basso	*Já slyšel spívati, hlasitě volati Gloria in excelsis Deo. Neumím latinsky, nevím co to.*	I heard singing, loud singing Gloria in excelsis Deo. I don't understand Latin, I don't know what it means.
Alto	*I co pak druhých nezavoláš?*	Won't you call the others?
Basso	*I ano.*	But yes, you're right.
Alto	*Musíme mu nésti dary od nás.*	We need to take our gifts to him.

Basso	*Máš právo.*	You're right.
Alto	*A co pak to?*	And what else?
Basso	*Já nevím co.*	I don't know.
Alto	*Já ti povím.*	I'll tell you.
Basso	*a já již vím,*	I know now,
Alto	*Co pak to chceš jemu darovat?*	What are you going to give to him?
Basso	*Já jemu daruji jehňátko.*	I will give him a lamb.
	Čím pak to chceš jeho obdarovat?	So what do you want to give him?
Alto	*Já jemu daruji kuzlátko.*	I will give him a young goat.
Alto and Basso	*Já daruji jemu,* *robátku malému,*	I will give him a little kid.
Alto	*Cokoliv mám,*	That's what I can do.
Basso	*Všecko mu dám,*	That's all I have,
Alto and Basso	*věř, bratře, že sobě nic* *nenechám.*	Believe me, brother, I won't keep anything back.
Alto	*Co pak ostatní mu mají dáti?*	What should the others give him?
Basso	*Oni mu musejí zahráti.*	They must play to him.
Alto	*Ty, Vašku, ty na dudy hrej,*	You, Wally, play on the bagpipes,
Basso	*a ty, Macku, kejdy drbej,*	and you, Macky, play your whistle,
Alto and Basso	*ty Macku, Kubači,* *Frantochu, Ferdači*	you Macky, Jake, Frank, Ferdi
Alto	*hodně řezej,*	play the fiddle,
Basso	*basu řezej*	play the bass
Alto and Basso	*Ježíškoj malému, jen hodně* *hrej.*	to baby Jesus, play out.
Alto	*Vinšuj Ježíšku dobrou noc,*	Wish the baby Jesus good night,
Basso	*Měj se dobře, dítě,* *Bona nox,*	Farewell, child, Good night,
Alto and Basso	*Dobrou noc.*	Good night.

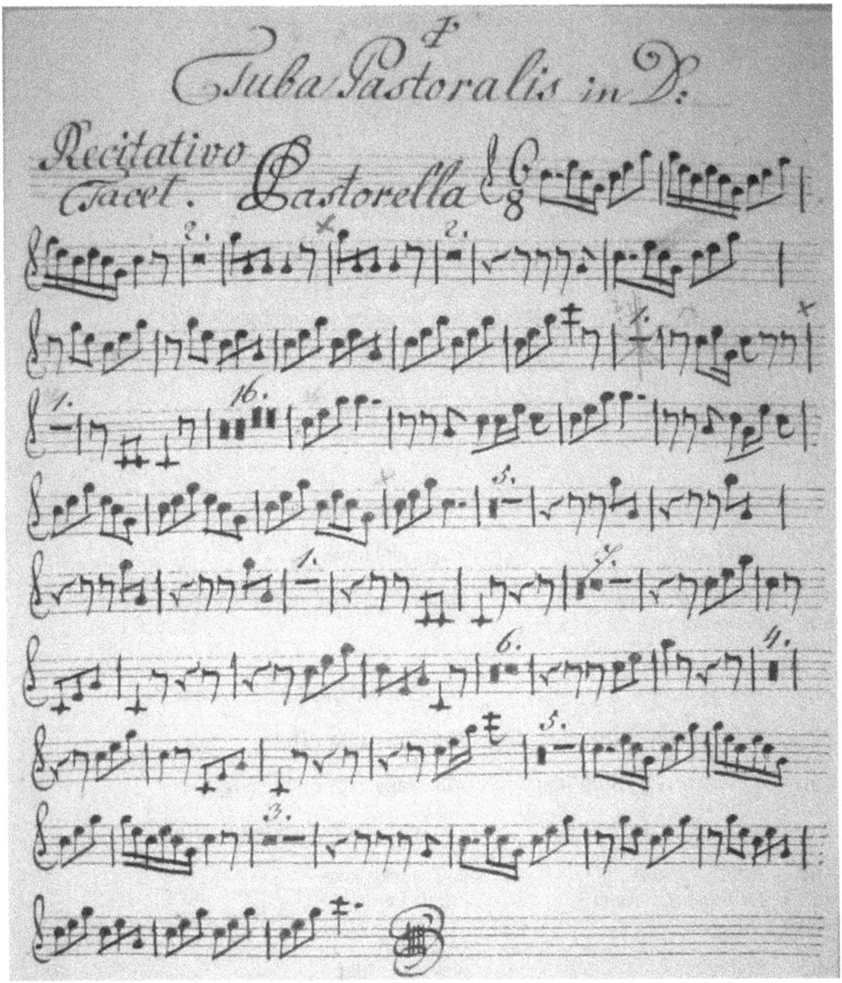

Fig. 2.22. Linek, *Pastorella* (2), *tuba pastoralis* part.

The *tuba pastoralis* in D uses harmonics nos. 3, 4, 5, 6 and 8. This is one extra note, a perfect fourth higher, than in the other *pastorella* by Linek examined here. If that note had been available for the other work, there is little reason for it not to have been used; it is therefore possible that this more florid part is written for a more skilled player. This player also has a different instrument: this *tuba pastoralis* has a sounding length of D whereas the other *pastorella* of Linek uses an instrument in C.

The *tuba pastoralis* is the primary instrument in the opening and closing instrumental sections of the *Andante*; it also participates throughout the unfolding story. Often its typical bugle-like figurations are also given to the violins; sometimes its calls are imitated by the voices. The *tuba pastoralis* is also given interjections that are not horn calls, but rather a few notes to add colour, in the style of music for an orchestral horn.

Matiegka, *Pastorala*

There are four musicians in the Czech historical record named Matiegka (with a variety of spellings). One lived from 1728 to 1809 and a second, identified as his son, lived from 1767 to 1793. Both were famous horn players from Prague, and the father was renowned as the teacher of Jan Václav Štich, who under the assumed name of Giovanni Punto became a horn player legendary throughout Europe. Joseph Erasmus Matiegka, composer of *pastorellas* from Ústí nad Orlicí, may be related to these, although the source for this manuscript is not given. The text on the cover of this work reads A. Matiegka, with an omission mark after the 'A'. Searches have not revealed any composer of similar family name with a given name that begins with A, and it is possible, in comparison with other manuscripts, that this letter may be an abbreviation for the word '*Authore*'. The date 7 January 1833 appears on the cover in pencil, in a hand that does not resemble any other writing on the manuscript.

The work, labelled *Pastorala* on the cover, and variously *Pastorale*, *Pastorela*, *Pastorala* and *Pastorella* on the eight parts, is in the key of G. It is 94 bars long and is a graceful *Andante*. It is scored for Canto and Alto, 2 horns in G, 2 violins, organ and *tuba pastoralis*. However, the part for herdsman's horn is labelled *Posthorn* on the part. The violins at times double the voice parts but at times are independent. The orchestral horn parts are simple: they add a little weight to the harmony.

This is the only text in this collection that is a direct setting of verses from the gospel (Luke 2.21). It describes the events commemorated on the Feast of the Circumcision, celebrated on the eighth day of Christmas: this indicates that it was likely to have been composed for Mass on that day rather than for Christmas midnight Mass. Repeated lines of text have been omitted below:

Canto and Alto	*A když se jest bylo dní osm splnilo,*	And when he was eight days old,
	dítě, obřezáno bylo.	the child was circumcised.
	Nazváno jest jméno jeho Ježíš,	He was given the name Jesus,
	kterýmž bylo nazváno od anjela	the name he was given by an angel
	prv než se v životě počalo.	before he was conceived in the womb.

The *tuba pastoralis* in G is given four different notes, harmonics nos. 3, 4, 5 and 6. The part is integral to the musical structure of the piece. It joins in the opening, without being a soloist, but sixteen bars before the entry of the voices it has an extended passage of calls over a background of held tonic chords from the other instruments, in simulation of a bagpipe drone. The *tuba pastoralis* is not played while the voices are singing. The closing instrumental section follows a similar form to the introduction: its second half is another extended passage of horn calls over unchanging tonic chords, which brings the work to a close.

The reason for the presence of a *tuba pastoralis* in this work is not clear, as shepherds form no part of the narrative and the text does not describe the events of Christmas night. The designation on the player's part, *posthorn*, despite the words *tuba pastoralis* on the cover, is even more intriguing. The part is notated at 'low' pitch, i.e. an octave below the other *tuba pastoralis* parts in the collection. Notation and its connection with actual sounding pitch will be part of a later general discussion about the instruments in this collection of works.

Fig. 2.23. Matiegka, *Pastorala, tuba pastoralis* / posthorn part.

Josef Ondřej Nowotný, *Offertorium Pastorale*

Of the eleven different musicians with this surname in the historical record, the composer of this work, who lived from 1778 to 1856, is the only one noted as a composer of *pastorellas*. The source of this composition is the Premonstratensian monastery at Želiv. The magnificent church there is dedicated to the Nativity of Our Lady.

This work is 104 bars in length, in one section and strays little from the key of G major. It is scored for Canto, Alto, Tenore and Basso, flute, 2 clarinets in C, 2 horns in G, 2 violins, viola, violone, organ and *tromba pastorale* (*tramba pastorale* on the cover). There is also a part for a flugelhorn in G. This is given all the material of the *tromba pastorale* and much additional music which at times is a decorated version of the *tromba pastorale* part, and at times the line of the uppermost voice or violin part. Thus it would appear to be an alternative part to that of the *tromba pastorale* that includes additional material possible on a flugelhorn that cannot be played on a herdsman's horn.

Fig. 2.24. The monastery church at Želiv, for which Nowotný's *Offertorium Pastorale* was written. Photo: Frances Jones.

The description *Moteto* is written at the beginning, and the tempo is an *Allegretto* in 6/8. A richly scored orchestral introduction alternates elaborate string figuration with calls on the *tromba pastorale* (or flugelhorn): these are played over held drone-like chords for the strings and orchestral horns. After 24 bars the Canto enters, with a simple 16-bar melody. Four bars of *tromba* solo then lead to a repeat of the music and text; this time the Alto sings the melody heard before, while the Canto is given a harmonising upper part and the strings a more elaborate accompaniment. A further four-bar *tromba* interlude leads to the same material again; this time the Tenore has the melody, the Alto the upper harmony part and the Canto an elaborate additional decorative line with semiquavers and demi-semiquavers. After a third *tromba* passage, all four voices sing the opening melody once more, to a new text, in simple four-part harmony, while the strings are given complex figures in accompaniment. Thus the sense of increasing excitement builds gradually throughout the work. In the final four bars, though, when the voices have fallen silent, the calls of the *tromba*, over a drone backdrop, bring the work to a *pianissimo* close. Nowotný incorporates the scale with the raised fourth degree in this work.

The text describes the birth of Christ. It is appropriate for use in a monastery: it is in Latin, in the form of a metrical, rhyming hymn or motet and uses theological, prayer-like language.

Canto	*Ave Jesu novo nate*	Hail Jesus newborn
	fili unijenite	the only Son [of the Father]
The same text is used	*qui in mundum hunc venisti*	who has come into this world
three times: the second	*ad salvandos homines,*	to save mankind,
time the Alto is added;	*fac ut benedicat nos*	grant that he may bless us
the third time, the	*pater tuus omnipotens,*	heavenly Father
Tenore as well.	*et ut per te salvatorem*	and through you the Saviour
	Salva sit humana gens.	may the human race be saved.
Tutti	*Alleluja de cantate*	*Alleluia*
	Alleluja canite	sing *Alleluia*
	Jesu Salvatori nostri.	to Jesus our Saviour.
	Devote obvenite	Come with devotion
	ut per illum	that through him
	dignissimum	[we may be] most worthy
	intrare celestia	to enter into heaven
	ubi infinite	where for ever
	canunt angeli Alleluja.	angels sing *Alleluia.*

The *tromba pastorale* in G uses harmonics nos. 3, 4, 5 and 6. It is involved only as a solo voice. In the repeating section with the text '*Ave Jesu*', before the *tutti* voices are used, it is given four-bar or eight-bar interludes; at each of these, orchestral detail is suspended in order to create a bagpipe-like drone effect. In the *Alleluia* section, the *tromba* calls are superimposed upon the *tutti* texture. The presence of the *tromba* in this work could be seen as formal and symbolic, rather as Bach might use a trumpet fanfare, unlike its use in the *pastorellas* in the vernacular where it appears in association with the shepherds in the Nativity story, to heighten the sense of realism.

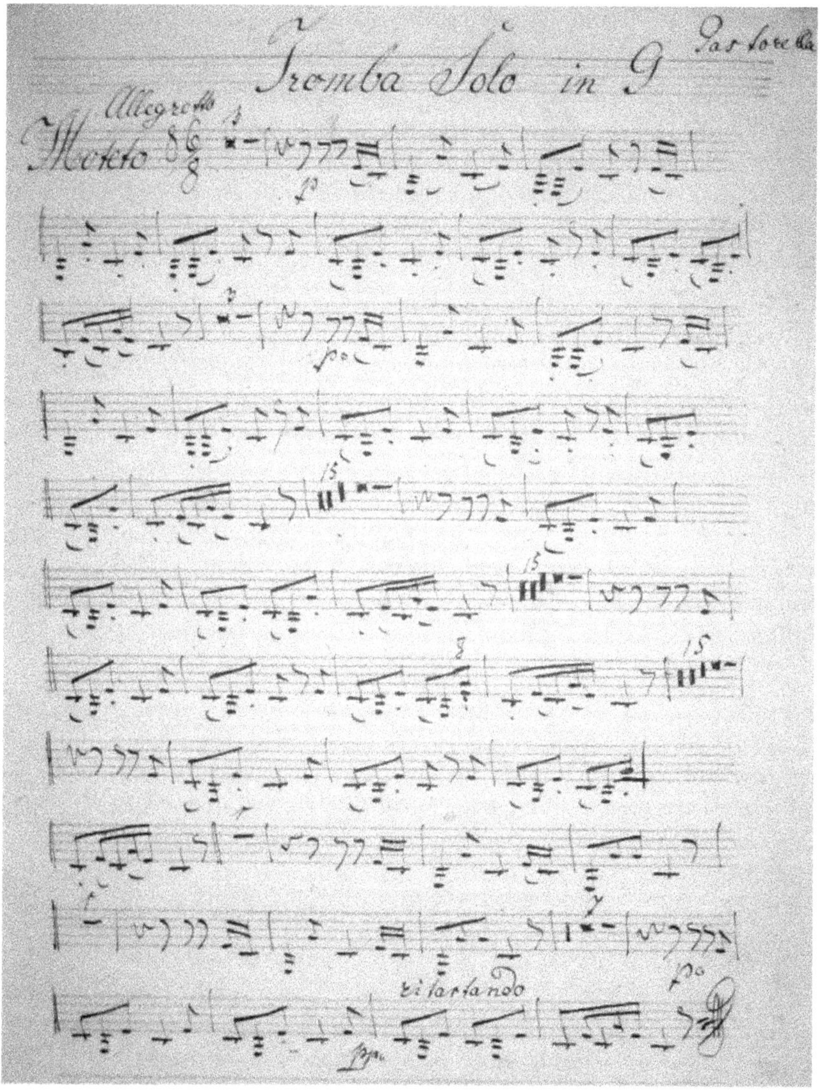

Fig. 2.25. Nowotný, *Offertorium Pastorale, tramba / tromba pastorale* part.

Tadeáš Petipeský, *Motteto de Nativitate pro Sacro die Certatio pastoralis*

There are nine surviving works composed by Petipeský, of which three, including this work, were written in Přeštice. The dates of composition of these works range from 1758 to 1771; this Motetto was written on 16 December 1761. The imposing Baroque church in Přeštice for which it was composed is dedicated to the Assumption of the Virgin Mary and stands on rising ground above the central square of this otherwise typical small Czech town.

This work has two covers. The outer one, which has more modern handwriting, gives the title *Motetto*; the inner one, the original, has the organ part on the reverse, with the spelling *Motteto*. The work comprises 132 bars and is in the key of G, in a gentle 3/8 with the tempo indication *Affetuose*. The scoring is for Canto, Alto, Tenore and Basso, 2 violins, *cembalo*, organ and *tuba pastoritia*. The *cembalo* only plays the voice parts during the sections for *tutti* voices.

A 26-bar instrumental introduction is based entirely on horn-call motifs shared between the *tuba pastoritia* and violin 1, over a bagpipe-like drone. Thereafter the work is organised into a refrain '*Ach usni, děťátko, paňátko*' (Oh sleep, little baby), sung to a horn-call phrase by the Tenore, answered by the rest of the voices with a simple verse setting. The Basso repeats '*Ach usni, děťátko, paňátko*' before the second verse. This refrain does not precede the third verse: instead, the strings provide a brief interlude based on the horn motif before the final stanza. The *tuba pastoritia* returns for the final instrumental coda, with music similar to that of the introduction, where held chords provide a backdrop to elaborate horn figurations that are echoed by violin 1. The verses are each set to the same melody, the first and the third in the tonic and the second in the dominant key.

The text uses a repeating refrain as if to hush the baby Jesus to sleep. The verses recount that the singers (there is no specific mention of shepherds) must hurry to the manger to give praise to the Christ child. The singers enumerate various instruments that they will play to give cheer to the infant: cimbalom, zither, flute and organ, although the music does not reflect these sounds. There is also an invitation to nightingales to sing to the holy child.

Tenore	*Ach usni, děťátko, paňátko.*	Oh sleep, little baby.
Canto, Alto, Basso	1. *Nynej, rozkošné,* *nynej rozmilé pacholátko,* *nynej, nynej,* *polož nožičky,* *vztáhni ručičky,* *budem ti hráti na cimbálky,*	Sleep, lovely one, sleep, pretty babe, sleep, sleep, rest your feet, stretch out your hands, we will play the cimbalom,
Basso	*Ach usni, děťátko, paňátko.*	Oh sleep, little baby.
Alto, Tenore, Basso	2. *K jeslem pospěšme,* *dítě vítejme,* *čest a chválu* *jemu vzdávejme;* *Ježíšku malý,* *kvítku spanilý,* *ó Pane nad pány, Ježíšku.*	Let us hurry to the manger, let us greet the child, honour and praise let us give to him, little baby Jesus O graceful flower, O Lord of lords, little Jesus.

Canto, Alto, Basso	3. *Nástroje vzhůru,* *cythary vzhůru ať jsou,* *ať zní flétny, varhany,* *spívejte ptáčkové,* *libí slavíčkové,* *Ježíška vesele vítejte.*	Raise your instruments, make the zither ready, sound the flutes and the organ, sing, birds, sing, sweet nightingales, to give a cheerful welcome to Jesus.

The part for the *tuba pastoritia* in G uses harmonics nos. 3, 4, 5 and 6 and is, unusually, written in concert pitch. It is virtuosic and repetitive. The two motifs given to the instrument are both taken up by the violins, thus they are an integral part of the thematic structure of the composition. The *tuba pastoritia* plays only in the instrumental introduction and the closing coda. The final bar is unusual: as the work comes to a peaceful close, the cadence complete, a final high 'flicked' note is given to the *tuba pastoritia* on the last beat of the bar, a phenomenon seen occasionally elsewhere (see pp. 120, 147). It would appear both from the individual style of the material used and from this end note characteristic of herdsman's horn playing, that Petipeský has notated material actually played by the herdsman for which the part is written.

Fig. 2.26. Petipeský, *Motteto de Nativitate, tuba pastoritia* part.

Jakob Jan Ryba, *Pastoral Offertorium*

Ryba (1765–1815) is the best-known exponent of the *pastorella*. He was born in Přeštice, the source of a number of Petipeský's *pastorella* manuscripts. Ryba's father held positions as schoolmaster and organist at several small towns in the area. The young Ryba initially learned singing, violin and keyboard skills from his father, before furthering his musical studies in Prague. He then, in turn, took up a career as a schoolmaster, choirmaster, organist and composer in various towns and settled from 1788 in Rožmitál pod Třemšínem where he remained for the rest of his life. Ryba's best-known work is *Missa Pastoralis, Hej, mistře*, written in 1796. There are manuscripts of 33 *pastorellas* by Ryba in the České Muzeum Hudby in Prague, of which only this one has a part for a herdsman's horn.

The work comes from Polička, one of many sources where Ryba's *pastorellas* are found. The manuscript in the Prague collection that bears the catalogue number MXIVG79 includes two of Ryba's *pastorellas*. *Pastorella 1* is scored for Canto, Alto, Tenore and Basso, flute, 2 horns in G, 2 violins, organ and posthorn in G. This work is in the key of G. The instrumentation is different for *Pastorella 2:* the horn parts are for instruments set up in the key of F, and there is neither flute nor posthorn; instead, there are parts for two clarinets in C and a *tuba pastoralis* in F: the work is therefore written in the key of F. *Pastorella 2*, with the part for a *tuba pastoralis*, is the work to be examined here.

The composition is 82 bars in length. It is unsophisticated and has a restricted harmonic framework, rarely straying from the tonic key. It opens in declamatory style, with the *tuba pastoralis* given prominent and sometimes florid interjections. The strings then introduce the opening strains of the popular Czech Christmas carol *Narodil Kristus Pán* which was also incorporated into two of Kollovrátek's *pastorellas* examined earlier. In common with many other quotations of this melody in the *pastorella* genre, it is presented in unison and an octave apart. Harmony returns after the two-bar motif has been stated. The Basso is the first voice to enter, with new material. Through the first sung section, it appears solo, answered by the other three voices together in harmony. In the next vocal section, the Tenore is the voice that sings alone, answered by the other parts. The voices return to the *Narodil* melody towards the end of the piece, with the words '*Laudetur sancta Trinitas*', which was also the case in one of Kollovrátek's settings. The melody is highlighted because only here do the voices once again sing in unison and at the octave. Ryba's *Pastoral Offertorium* makes prominent use of the scale with the raised fourth degree, which is a feature of the *Narodil* melody.

The Latin text, which describes the events surrounding the birth of Christ, is derived from the text in *Piae Cantiones* that was also used in a *pastorella* by Kollovrátek, one in which the *Narodil* melody was similarly incorporated. The original text has 14 verses, each comprising a rhyming couplet followed by the word *Alleluia*; Ryba has selected five for this work. With repeated lines or words omitted here , it reads as follows:

Puer natus in Betlehem	A child is born in Bethlehem
unde gaudet Jerusalem	therefore Jerusalem rejoices
Alleluja	Alleluia
Hic jacet in praesaepio	Here lies in the manger
qui regnat sine termino	he that reigns without end
Alleluja	Alleluia
Reges de Saba veniunt	Kings come from Saba
aurum thus myrham offerunt	offering gold, frankincense and myrrh
in hoc natali gaudio	In this joyful day
benedicamus Domino.	let us bless the Lord.
Alleluja	Alleluia
Laudetur Sancta Trinitas	May the Holy Trinity be praised
Deo dicamus gratias	let us give thanks to God
Alleluja.	Alleluia.

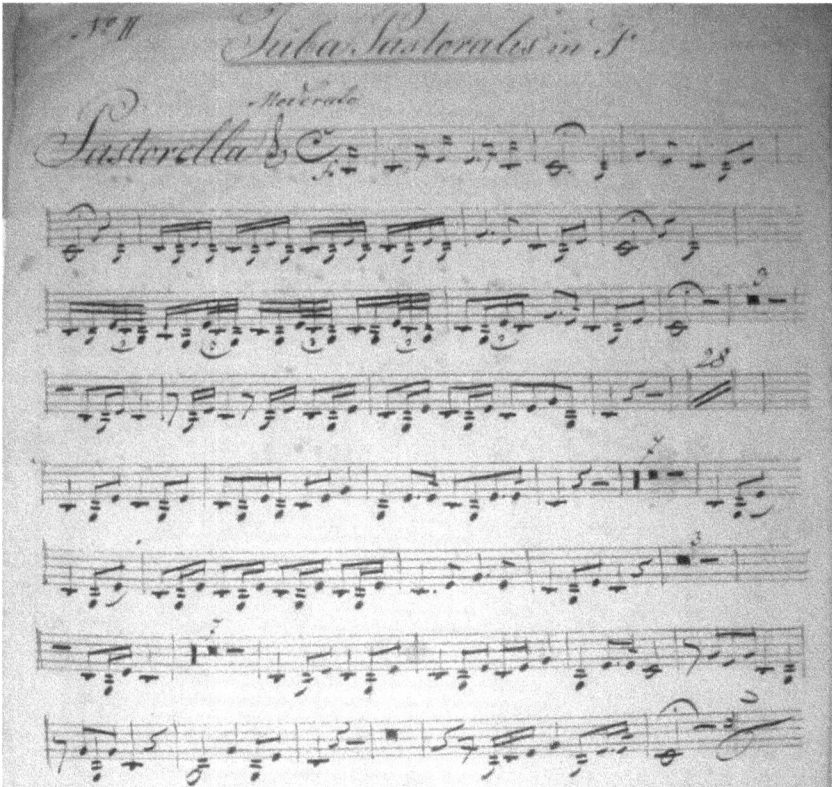

Fig. 2.27. Ryba, *Pastoral Offertorium, tuba pastoralis* part.

The *tuba pastoralis* is in F and uses harmonics nos. 3, 4, 5 and 6. The instrument is used several times throughout the work, although not while the voices are singing. At each appearance of the *tuba pastoralis*, the other instrumental parts mark the pulse on tonic harmony in replication of the rhythmic drone accompaniment of a hurdy-gurdy. The *tuba pastoralis* is given bugle-like flourishes, some stately, others quite athletic. In general, the figurations are not imitated by any other part, except on one occasion when the clarinet is given similar motifs where Ryba has modulated into a key in which neither the *tuba pastoralis* nor the horns can be played.

Josepho Štietina, *Pastorella Nativitate D[omini] N[ostri] J[esu] Christi*

Štietina was the schoolmaster at Ústí nad Orlicí from about 1741 to 1754. This is the village where Matějka worked and also was the provenance of the work by Habermann.

The beautiful late Baroque Church of the Assumption in the village of Ústí nad Orlicí was completed in 1776. It is not known where the musicians would have sat or stood to perform a *pastorella*, but the organ loft of this church reveals a space large enough for at least 15 or 20 musicians to perform music there as part of the celebration of Mass. The sound of a *tuba pastoralis*, out of sight from the congregation, in a church of this size, would have been magnificent.

Fig. 2.28. The organ loft, Church of the Assumption, Ústí nad Orlicí. Photo: Frances Jones.

This work is written for Canto, Alto, Tenore and Basso, 2 violins, violone, organ, *tuba nocturna* and *tuba pastoralis*. It is 97 bars long and in the key of D major. The work falls into two sections. After four introductory bars at *moderato* tempo for the strings with organ, the *tuba nocturna* intones twelve slow crotchets on the same note to mark the moment of midnight, a device seen earlier in the *pastorella* of Holetschek. This is followed by the Canto (marked 'Angel') who wakens the shepherds with the words '*Gloria in excelsis Deo*'. The *tuba nocturna* then sounds the twelve notes again.

The narrative is thereafter shared between the voices, with instrumental interjections. Appropriate tempo changes are used as the text is handed from one character to the next. Once the discussions with the angel are finished, the music settles into a new section with the heading *pastorella*, which features the entry of the *tuba pastoralis*. 17 bars of horn calls with lively string accompaniment lead into this second part of the work, in which the shepherds decide upon their plans.

The text is a graphic conversation both between the shepherds and the angel, and among the shepherds themselves. It relates the Christmas story in a lively manner. The shepherds decide to play some music for the Christ child, and they discuss what food they will take for him: porridge and cream. They will also take presents of a lamb to keep him warm with a tinkling bell to amuse him, and their own blankets stripped off the bed.

Canto (Angel)	*Gloria in excelsis Deo.* *Velkou radost zvěstuji* *této půlnoční hodiny,* *pastýři, vzhůru povstaňte,* *šťastné noviny poslyšte.*	Glory be to God on high. I proclaim great joy to you at this hour of midnight, shepherds, arise, listen to happy news.
Alto	*Kdo pak nás to volá a spáti nám nedá?* *Kdo pak to zde hraje a nás probuzuje?*	Who calls us that we cannot sleep? Who plays and wakens us?
Canto	*Vzhůru, vzhůru!* *Pastýři ospalý.*	Awake, awake! You sleepy shepherd.
Alto	*Kdo pak mi to praví?*	Who is that talking to me?
Canto	*Otevři tvé oči,* *vidíš divné věci.*	Open your eyes, you can see wonderful things.
Alto	*Ó poslíčku nebeský,* *oznam mi hned věci ty,* *ať já mý bratří zbudím* *a jim to vše oznámím.*	Oh heavenly messenger, tell me these things, so I can waken my brothers at once and tell them everything.
Canto	*Narodilo se děťátko,* *vinšované pacholátko,* *ó pastýři, déle nelež,* *vstaň a nelež,* *vstaň a do Betléma* *hned běž, běž, běž.*	A baby is born, longed for little child, O shepherd, do not sleep any more, get up and sleep no more, get up and go to Bethlehem off you go, now, go, go, go.
Alto	*Vstaň, vstaň, milej bratře, vstaň,*	Get up, get up, dear brother, stand up,

	nětco povědít mám,	I have things to tell you,
	vstaň bez meškání, vstaň,	be quick, get up, get up,
	narodil se v Betlémě Spasitel,	Our Saviour is born in Bethlehem,
	a to v chlévě, poď se mnou,	in a stable, come with me,
	poď tam, poď tam.	come there, come there.

Basso   *Co, co pak a kdo pak tobě to pověděl,*   What, what and who has told you this?
         dyť bych snad já také něco podobného věděl.   Why, perhaps I might hear about it too.

Alto   *Anjel v krásném blesku*   The angel in splendour
        mně se jest ukázal,   has shown himself to me,
        bych vám to všechno   and has told me
        vyjevil přísně jest rozkázal.   to reveal everything to you.

Tenore   *Jestli tomu tak jest,*   If this is so,
        šťastný jsi, ach šťastný,   and you are very lucky,
        zanechám já mé stádo,   I will leave my flock,
        půjdu s tebou taky.   and go with you too.

Alto   *Poď, poď, poď,*   Come, come, come,
        nechtěj meškat dlouho,   do hurry up,
        nechme pásti stádo,   the flock can feed itself,
        nezdržuj se, dlouho,   no time to lose,
        dokud mně mysl hněte vidět   I want to see the holy child
        to svaté dítě   I have a strong desire
        mám kuráže z toho.   to do just that.

Tenore   *Půjdeme my hnedky s tebou teď*   We will go at once
and   *do Betléma,*   to Bethlehem
Basso   *podíváme se na něho,*   to see him,
        co pak tam dělá,   and what he is doing,
        máli pak co jísti,   we must take him some food,
        musíme mu nýsti.   in case he needs some.
        Nejprv však zahrajem,   But first we will play to him,
        pak dary odvedem.   then give our gifts.

Tenore   *Již jsme odbyli muziku,*   Now that we have played some music,
        vyndejme dary,   let's get out the presents,
        poď přijímat a odbývat,   put them somewhere safe,
        Jozefe starý.   old Joseph,
        Já mu dám krupičku,   I have some nice food,
        pěknou na kašičku,   porridge for him,
        též smetánku mu naleju   also some cream
        hned do hrníčku.   that I'll pour into his cup.

Alto   *Já mám jehňátko běloučký,*   I have a pretty white lamb,
        pěkný k pohledu,   to give him,
        má zvoneček velmi libý, to mu povedu,   it has a sweet tinkling bell,
        vždycky kudy chodí, ustavičně zvoní   it rings all the time, a pretty tinkling.
        klink, klink, klink, klink, klink, klink,   ting-a-ling, ting-a-ling, ting-a-ling,
        obveselím ho s ním,   he can have fun with it,
        klink, klink, klink, klink, klink, klink,   ting-a-ling, ting-a-ling, ting-a-ling,
        obveselím ho s ním.   he can have fun with it.
Basso   *Co pak já dám neb*   What can I give him,

ostávám již naposledy.
Něco vidím, to já sklidím
tam na posteli,
pěkný dvě peřinky,
by zahřál nožičky,
neb se hněte, zimou třese,
dítě maličký.

as the last person?
I see something,
I will strip the bed,
two nice blankets
to warm his feet,
for the baby is feeling the cold,
is shivering.

Tutti *Přijmi od nás odevzdaný tobě, Ježíši,*
po smrti pak duše
naše uveď v tvou říši,
kdež by tě chválily,
věčně velebily,
a na tvou přejasnou
tvář na věky patřily.

Accept these gifts we bring you, Jesus,
after our death
bring our souls into your realm,
where they will praise you
and glorify you for ever
and behold you
in your everlasting glory.

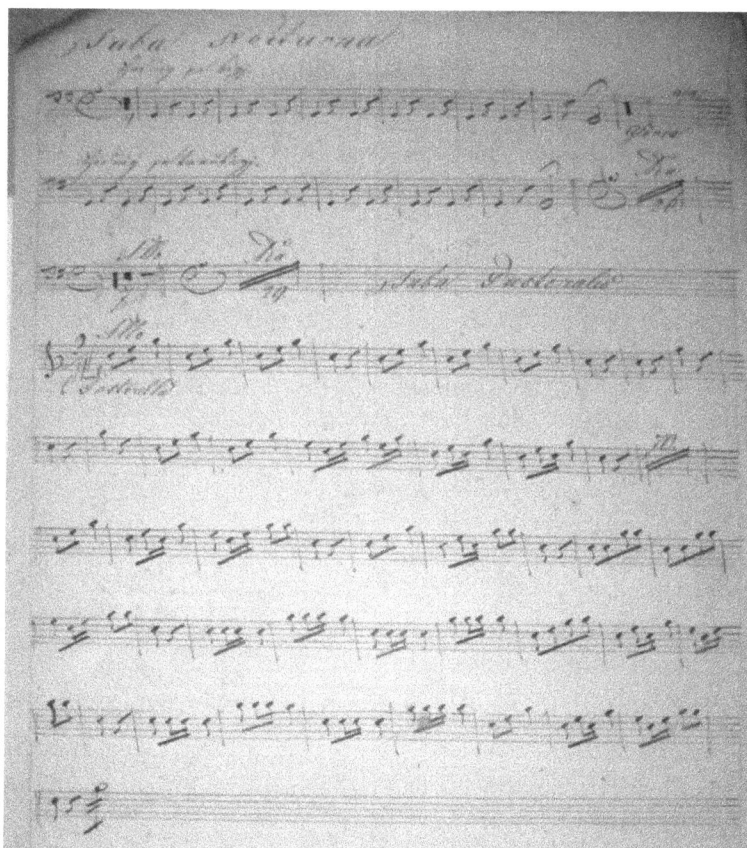

Fig. 2.29. Štietina, *Pastorella Nativitate, tuba nocturna* and *tuba pastoralis* part.

The *tuba nocturna* plays just one low note, a written G, twelve times; then after the angel has sung, it has the same again. There is no mention of the key of the instrument or whether the intended pitch is a sounding G. Thereafter there are 62 bars rest before the *tuba pastoralis* is used. The music for both instruments appears on one sheet of paper with the bars enumerated in between, which suggests that the intention was that one player would play the *tuba nocturna* first and then take up the *tuba pastoralis*. This might imply that Štietina wrote the music with a specific player in mind, who was maybe a herdsman who also held the post of night watchman in the village. This could be supported by the fact that the *tuba pastoralis* part uses just three notes, harmonics nos. 4, 5 and 6. These figurations were possibly those used by the player, transcribed by Štietina for inclusion in this composition. The *tuba pastoralis* music is for an instrument in D although this is not marked on the part.

The instruments

All the *tuba pastoralis* parts in these 21 works in the collection in Prague are written for an instrument where harmonic no. 4 is the tonic of the key of the work, because only then do harmonics nos. 3, 5, 6 and 8 give the intervals written. Table 2.4 shows the tonic of each of the instruments used in this collection. The approximate length of the instrument can be deduced because the length to a large extent determines the pitches of the harmonics for any tube: column 3 gives the approximate length of a tube that would produce each series. It is not known in which octave the *tuba pastoralis* parts were expected to sound, so possible alternative lengths are shown: this is because the parts are not written at their sounding pitch, but to be transposed from C, as was the custom for natural horn parts. For horns in C, the notes are normally expected to sound an octave below what is written.

Table 2.4. Prague works: key and length of herdsman's horn.

Tonic	Composer/work	Approximate length
F	Ryba	12ft or 6ft
G	Matiegka, Nowotný, Petipeský	10ft or 5ft
C	Fibiger, Holetschek, Kautník, Kollovrátek (all 3 works), Linek 1	8ft or 4ft
D	Czerni, Daubrawský (all 3 works), Dobravský, Duschek, Habermann, Jech, Linek 2, Štietina	7ft or 3½ft

There are many reasons why it is only possible to gauge an approximate length for a *tuba pastoralis*:

1. as 'concert pitch' was not standardised in the eighteenth and nineteenth century, the sounds produced by a *tuba pastoralis* specified as in a certain key could actually be around a tone above or below modern concert pitch,

2. the pitch of a tube is slightly altered if there is a flare at the end; thus the tonic of a *tuba pastoralis* depends not only on the length of the piece of wood from which it has been made but also on how much and how suddenly it opens out at the end,

3. temperature affects pitch: we cannot know how cold it was at midnight in December in a church in central Europe in the eighteenth or nineteenth century and to what extent this was taken into account.

The sounding pitches of the instruments used in these works are shown below: the notes for the F instrument at approximately 12ft, the G instrument at 10ft, the C instrument at 8ft and the D instrument at 7ft. Instruments of half these lengths produce notes one octave higher.

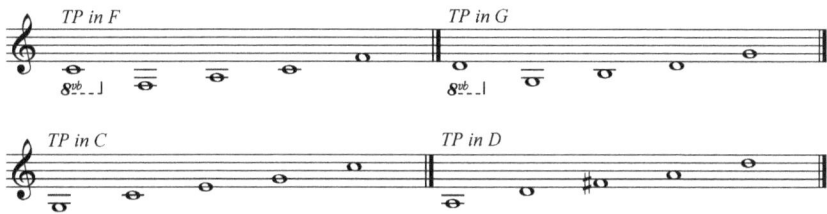

Fig. 2.30. Sounding pitch of harmonics nos. 3, 4, 5, 6 and 8 for the *tuba pastoralis* in F at around 12ft, in G at 10ft, in C at 8ft and in D at 7ft in length.

The use of the instrument in the *pastorella*

The herdsman's horn adds an element of realism to a *pastorella*, an enhancement of the scenes of the Nativity narrative that involve the shepherds. It accompanies their wonder at receiving news from the angel, their discussions in the fields, their desire to go to Bethlehem to worship the baby Jesus and their arrival at the crib. At times the role of the horn in the narrative is specific; at times, it is general. It is used to introduce the shepherds, to summon them to go to Bethlehem, to represent the tolling of the midnight bell and to provide music for joyful celebration. Sometimes the horn appears merely as a cheerful sound in the musical texture, present because the herdsman who plays it is there and the story is that of the herdsmen from the gospel.

Occasionally the text does not refer to the shepherds: the music alone alludes to their presence at the crib; there are also times when the horn motifs are given to the vocal or other instrumental parts, and the horn itself is present but silent. Sometimes its calls are given a background of quiet held chords that might represent the landscape at night, or a gentle bagpipe drone; sometimes the horn calls have a rhythmically pulsed drone accompaniment in the manner of a hurdy-gurdy.

The social context

The relationship between the herdsman and his animals, his village and his landscape is fundamental to the use of the *tuba pastoralis* in the *pastorella*. It is possible to extract some information about village life from this examination of the music that includes parts for the *tuba pastoralis*. For example, it is unlikely that parts would have been written for such an unusual instrument but for the fact that herdsmen who used rustic horns were present in each location. That around 100 *pastorellas* that include a part for a *tuba pastoralis* are known, suggests that a herdsman was a normal figure in village life in this region and that playing on his pastoral horn was part of his regular routine. The Deutsches Hirtenmuseum at Hersbruck, mentioned earlier, is but 70 miles from the Czech border: here the routine in which the village herdsman collected the animals daily to take them to pasture is described, whereby he called them from their stalls in the mornings by blowing his horn in the various corners of the village square and also signalled his return of the animals to their owners at the end the day in the same way. It appears that this daily routine was normal in the Czech lands too: a nineteenth-century painting by Adrian Ludwig Richter illustrates the scene.

Fig. 2.31. Herdsman blows a horn (detail). Adrian Ludwig Richter *Der Schreckstein bei Aussig* (now Ústi nad Labem, Czech Republic), 1835.[28]

The boundary between the participants in the *pastorella* and the characters portrayed from the Christmas story is deliberately blurred to enhance the relevance of the Nativity story for the congregation. It is not possible to say whether the people who assumed the roles of the shepherds in the *pastorella* were also the village herdsmen. However, in that the underlying intent with these works was to make the Christmas story relevant to the lives of the worshippers using realistic and familiar references, it would seem appropriate. A number of personal names occur in these texts, and most of these are in the familiar form. Some of the comments are so personal that they could be specific references to known characters in the village: 'Hey, hey, Johnny, what is happening?' or 'Stupid Micky, you are carrying barley instead of a sheep'. In that the singers were from the local community and the work was written specifically for them by one of their number, it would be particularly realistic if these were the actual names of the participants; thus the effect upon the rest of the congregation would be most heightened. Instances where the herdsman's written part also includes music of the night watchman and the posthorn may indicate a dual role for the player within the village community.

The musical significance

With regard to the motifs that the herdsmen played to the animals in their care, it can be seen that most of the *tuba pastoralis* material written here is unlike music written for orchestral horns. Many parts involve just one or two specific and individual motifs, repeated a number of times: these sound like the motifs that a known herdsman might repeat as he wanders around the village square to gather the animals together. If a part for a herdsman's horn is incorporated into a Christmas work, this implies that the herdsman is the person asked to play it; if a specific herdsman plays on his horn in the church at midnight Mass, it would be wholly appropriate that it should be his own personal motifs that he would be expected to play. It is thus reasonable to suppose that the notes and rhythms written reflect the motifs in current use by the individual herdsman for whom each part was written—not only because the players and their playing would have been known to the composer, but also because the function of these works was the realistic representation of the herdsmen in the Nativity story.

The key of the composition would have to have been selected to accommodate the key of the particular herdsman's instrument. There are a number of features transcribed that are particular characteristics of playing on a herdsman's horn: a 'whoop' up to an initial high start note, or a high note flicked up at the end of a piece: these suggest accurate transcriptions of music played by a herdsman. Thus these works may provide a unique window on the music played by herdsmen in this region at this time.

It is important to note that these works are written by country people for and about their own kind. Any amusement in the narrative is laughing with, not laughing at, the rustic scenario. This is in contrast to music composed for the enjoyment of the nobility at court in the eighteenth century, in which 'rustic' often implied uncouth, something to be looked down upon and ridiculed, where peasants were depicted as beggars and drunkards.

These samples of herdsmen's horn music display a style of call different from a Swiss *Kühreien*. There is no narrative of a journey to the pastures, no litany of individual calls to individual animals, no pleasing constructed melodic design. These calls, a repeating motif for rounding up the animals, have elements of a fanfare, though not a strident military one; there is often a cheerful, lively feel. Alongside that, these settings have a recurring backdrop of stillness, or a bagpipe or hurdy-gurdy drone. The setting of a quiet landscape is conveyed, but there is also an implication that interaction with other rustic musicians was normal too.

As an example of the cultural and historical importance of the herdsman's horn in regions of Europe outside the Alps, these works not only give samples of the sort of motifs played by herdsmen in this period, their function and location, and a unique niche for the use of such music in the composed repertoire. They may also provide a clue to the effectiveness of alphorn motifs when quoted by composers in mainstream nineteenth-century music, which will be the subject of Chapter 5. It is possible that when a composer chose to use an alphorn motif in a composition as a representation of an Alpine landscape, he was in part, consciously or unconsciously, calling upon the memory in his audience of a backdrop of local herding routines that stretched back many centuries in many parts of the continent. By the nineteenth century, high art music was no longer composed and published for the nobility: it reached a wide public. With the rapid growth of urban industrial centres, the new audiences included those who had moved into the cities from the villages. A reference to a herdsman in the Alps would thus be seen not as the representation of a vagabond, of a despised lower class. For both the composers and for their audiences, there may have been the subconscious feeling that a herdsman was one of them, someone to whose music they would respond with the warmth of filial familiarity. In addition to the magnificence of mountain scenery, the music of the alphorn could be heard even by lowland dwellers as a symbol of the freedom of a lost idyllic and idealised rural past.

Notes

[1] Charles Burney, *The present State of Music in France and Italy* (London: Becket, 1771) and *The Present State of Music in Germany, the Netherlands and the United Provinces* (London: Becket, 1773), 4–5.

[2] Joseph Christian von Mannlich, 'Gluck à Paris en 1774: Memoires sur la musique à Paris à fin du règne de Louis XV', *La Revue musicale,* Vol. 15 (1934), 260: *Dans mon pays tout le monde est musicien; on enseigne la musique dans les écoles et dans les moindres villages les paysans chantent et jouent des différents instrumens pendant la grand'messe dans leurs églises.*

[3] České Muzeum Hudby, Prague catalogue number MXXVIIIF242.

[4] These will be referred to as Daubrawský 1, 2 and 3; similar references will be used for the works of Kollovrátek and Linek.

[5] ČMHP MVIIID111, 130 and 110.

[6] ČMHP MVIIID187.

[7] ČMHP MVIIIF23.

[8] ČMHP MXXIXD249.

[9] ČMHP MXIF8.

[10] ČMHP MXXB282.

[11] ČMHP MXF198.

[12] ČMHP MXXIXB187.

[13] ČMHP MXID54.

[14] ČMHP MXID94.

[15] ČMHP MXID42.

[16] ČMHP MVIB155 and MVIB342.

[17] ČMHP MXIIE151.

[18] ČMHP MXLA157.

[19] ČMHP MIIIA146.

[20] ČMHP MXIVG79.

[21] ČMHP MXVA202.

[22] A transcription of each work, and detailed document of discrepancies between parts, alterations required to create a performing edition, etc, have been made as part of the PhD research project from which this book draws much of its content. There is also documentation of experimentation relating to the acoustic properties of conical and cylindrical tubes to ascertain how accurately a *tuba pastoralis* would need to have been made to produce the harmonics used in these works. Information is available from frances@AmazingAlphorn.com

[23] These last three suggestions are made by Jiří Berkovec in *České Pastorely* (Prague: Supraphon, 1987), 50.

[24] All translations from the Latin have been made with the kind assistance of Elizabeth Rees.

[25] All the Czech manuscript texts for this study have been generously deciphered and transcribed for me by Tomáš Havelka in Prague. For the English translations I have been assisted by Pavel Blazek, James Naughton, David Cairns and Josepha Collins. Punctuation and capitalisation have been rationalised.

[26] All reproductions of parts in this chapter are photographs taken by me on 14/15 April 2010 and are reproduced here with kind permission of the České Muzeum Hudby, Prague.

[27] The Old Testament Book of Wisdom (ch.18 vv. 14,15) implies that Christ will be born at midnight. Tradition thus places importance on the role of the night watchman to sound the strokes of midnight to announce the moment of the holy birth. The equivalent to midnight Mass in the Methodist and Presbyterian Churches is known as the Watch Night service.

[28] The Yorck Project. https://commons.wikimedia.org/wiki/File:Adrian_Ludwig_Richter_008.jpg. Creative Commons CC0 License.

Chapter 3

Leopold Mozart's *Sinfonia Pastorella* for Alphorn and Strings

Leopold Mozart's iconic work in the repertoire for alphorn, his *Sinfonia Pastorella* in G for alphorn or *corno pastoricio* and strings, has much in common with the eastern European *pastorella* explored in the previous chapter. It also incorporates motifs associated with the Italian *pastorella*, the *pastorale* and music for *Kindelwiegen* (the practice of crib-rocking), and has many thematic connections with other works by well-known composers.

Fig. 3.1. Leopold Mozart, c.1765. Attributed to Pietro Antonio Lorenzoni.[1]

Leopold Mozart (1719–1787) grew up in Augsburg in Bavaria. Although he studied philosophy and law at the Benedictine university in Salzburg, his employment throughout his life was in the field of music, as a violinist, violin teacher and composer. His primary legacy, though, was the role of musical mentor for his son, Wolfgang, born in January 1756: throughout this chapter, I have chosen to refer to the composer of this *Sinfonia Pastorella* by his first name, Leopold, as the use of the surname alone normally carries the implication of Wolfgang.

Leopold wrote a number of works that included parts for unusual instruments in the autumn of 1755. In October he sent a *Musikalische Schlittenfahrt* (Musical Sleigh Ride) to his Augsburg publisher, Johann Jakob Lotter, which included parts for five sleigh-bells and a whip. He followed this in November with *Die Bauernhochzeit* (Peasant Wedding) which included parts for bagpipes, hurdy-gurdy and *hackbrett* (cimbalom). Then in December of the same year, a month before Wolfgang's birth, Leopold wrote a Christmas *pastorella* scored for alphorn, two flutes and strings. He wrote to Lotter to complain that it was difficult to find enough time to respond to a request for a few new pastoral symphonies, although he did have one ready, that pleased him:

> Monsieur Gignox wants a couple of new *Pastorell Synfonien*? He seems to think that it's as easy to produce them as it is to put bread on the table, but there's no way I have time to compose them. He does know this because he accused me of not even having enough time to read a letter he sent me. But, you know, I have a brand new *Pastorell Synfonie*, but I'm telling you I don't want to give it to him. I'd intended to send it to Wallerstein along with some other works. It's a really good piece. It is for obbligato herdsman's horn and two flutes. Shall I send this then? Alright, I will send it in the next post, but above all, please don't tell anyone, or Wagner will get to hear about it and will certainly gossip about it to [Hans von] Rehling. You know my circumstances.[2]

Unfortunately, no work with this instrumentation has been found. Leopold's letter mentions a request for 'a few new *Pastorell Synfonien*', and although there are references to three such works in his letters to Lotter written in 1755, it is not specified whether all of these works included a part for an alphorn.

However, one *Sinfonia Pastorella* by Leopold for alphorn and strings has survived. There are at least six extant manuscript copies of this composition. No contemporary printed copy has been located, despite the letter to Lotter quoted above and the fact that this publisher produced several Leopold's works (notably his *Violinschule* which first appeared in 1756). It is possible that the work did not reach print format in Leopold's day because the expectation of its widespread use was substantially less than would have been the case for works with more conventional instrumentation.

None of the six manuscripts found for this investigation is in Leopold's own handwriting, and there are many discrepancies between the copies. Each version differs from the others with regard to paper, layout and handwriting. Each set is consistent within itself in these aspects, apart from the set from Öttingen where the violin parts are in a different hand from the rest of the set. There is a variety of title, name of the solo instrument and even instrumentation (see Tables 3.1 and 3.2).

All specify the composer as Leopold Mozart, although the manuscript in Vienna has the forename Wolfgang crossed out and replaced with Leopold. The manuscript from Öttingen shows the surname as Mozhart; the 'h' has been subsequently crossed through. Table 3.1 shows basic details of the six manuscript versions and the various descriptions used:

Table 3.1. Leopold Mozart, *Sinfonia Pastorella*, manuscript versions.

Location	Format	Title	Instrumentation
Chor-Stift Lambach, now at the Stadtbibliothek, Augsburg. ms.MGII42.	ms set of parts	*Sinfonia Pastorella*	*2 Violini, Viola obligato e Basso, con un Corno Pastoritio ma non obligato benché d'effetto assai buono*
Fürst zu Hohenlohe-Bartensteinisches Archiv, Schloss Neuenstein, now at the Staatsarchiv, Ludwigsburg. ms.Ba 120 Bü 161.	ms set of parts	*Sinfonia Pastorale (Sinphonia Pastorale* on the Violin 1 part)	*Violino Primo e Secondo, Viola Obligato, Fundamento con Corno Pastoricio*
Fürstlich Öttingen-Wallersteinischen Bibliothek, now at the University of Augsburg. ms.D-HR/III41/24/o.	ms set of parts	*Sinfonia Pastorale ex G* (cover), *Sinfonia / Sinfonia Pastorella* (parts)	*Violino Primo, Violino Secondo, Corno Primo, Corno Secondo, Alto Viola, Basso Corno di Pastore/ Kühe Horn (Corno Pastoricio* on part*)*
Preußischer Kulturbesitz, Staatsbibliothek, Berlin. Mus.ms15328.	ms score	*Divertimento Sinfonia Pastorale*	*Violino I, Violino II, Viola, Basso, Corno pastoricio in G*
Archiv der Gesellschaft der Musikfreunde, Wien. ms.XI29298(H26029).	ms score	*Pastorale für Streichquartett und Corno Pastoriccio*	*Violino Primo, Violino Secondo, Viola, Basso, Corno pastoricio* (spelling different on part from cover)
Bayerische Staatsbibliothek, München. Mus.ms.6218D-R,540.	ms score	*Sinfonia Pastorale ex G*	*Violino Primo, Violino Secondo, Corno Primo, Corno Secondo, Alto Viola, Basso Corno di Pastore/ Küh-Horn*

Detailed examination of all of these manuscripts reveals which are copies of others, because of the presence of many clear inaccuracies, for example, bars with an incorrect number of beats, notes that are foreign to an otherwise clear harmony, inconsistencies of articulation, etc., that have been faithfully repeated. In some cases, new errors are introduced, while others are corrected. The likely correlations of the manuscripts are thus deduced: the earliest manuscript is either that of Lambach or Bartenstein. One is a copy of the other, as most of the same inaccuracies occur in both. The Öttingen set is derived from the Lambach manuscript, with the addition of two orchestral horn parts. Of the three scores, the one in Berlin is copied from Bartenstein, the Vienna copy is taken from the score in Berlin, and the Munich score, which includes the horn parts, is copied from the Öttingen set.[3]

Table 3.2 gives details of four modern editions which were published in 1978, 1979, 2001 and 2016:

Table 3.2. Leopold Mozart, *Sinfonia Pastorella*, published versions.

Publication	Format	Title	Instrumentation
ed. Marvin McCoy (self-published, Minneapolis, 1978)	score, parts and piano reduction	*Sinfonia Concerto* for Alphorn and Strings	Alphorn, Violins 1 and 2, Viola, Cello/Bass
ed. Kurt Janetzky (Zürich: Kunzelmann, 1979)	score	*Sinfonia Pastorale G Dur*	*Corno pastoriccio (Alp- oder Hirtenhorn, Jagdhorn, Wald- oder Ventilhorn) und Streicher*
ed. Christian Broy (Augsburg: Wißner, 2001)	score	*Sinfonia Pastorale G-Dur*	*Corno pastoriccio, Corno I* and *II in G, Violino I* and *II, Viola, Basso*
ed. Frances Jones (Oxford: Edition HH, 2016)	score, parts and piano reduction	*Sinfonia Pastorella*	*Corno pastoricio, Violino I* and *II, Viola, Basso*

Of the modern editions, the publication by McCoy includes much more material for the solo alphorn than is present in any of the manuscript versions: this additional material is discussed later (see p. 119). McCoy issued three sets of orchestral parts, to provide string accompaniment for alphorn in F, alphorn in F sharp or alphorn in G. The publication of Janetzky is based on the Lambach score, and Broy's version is taken from the Öttingen set. Both are issued in score format, thus they are not available for performance. The new, historically-informed performing edition prepared by the author, quoted above, is based on a critical analysis of the six manuscript copies described here.

The locations of the manuscripts of Leopold's *Sinfonia Pastorella* show a wide distribution. Two copies are from the private collections of residences of the nobility in south-central Germany, that of the Prince of Hohenlohe-Bartenstein and that of Prince Öttingen-Wallerstein. The Lambach manuscript is from the

Benedictine monastery there, around 50 miles north-east of Salzburg. The copies in the municipal archives of Berlin, Munich and Vienna do not record their original source.

None of the surviving manuscripts bears a date, although there are some indications from the details available. Firstly, it might be one of the *pastorellas* referred to in Leopold's letters of December 1755. Secondly, the watermark on the paper of the copy from Öttingen dates from 1751: this copy could thus not have been made before that date; there is, however, no indication as to how long the paper might have been stored before it was used. Thirdly, the version in Vienna originally showed Wolfgang's name on the cover, so this copy must date from a time after Wolfgang had become the more famous composer with this surname.

With regard to the time of year when it was written, a link between this *Sinfonia Pastorella* and Christmastide is confirmed not only by its title, but also by the musical content of the work: the majority of its themes are derived from Christmas carols. The letters to Lotter mention that three *pastorellas* were written just before Christmas in 1755, and the presence of Alpine herdsmen in the streets of towns and cities during the winter months, who played their horns for entertainment, is noted by a number of seventeenth- and eighteenth-century writers. The herdsmen would not be in the fields with the cattle during the winter; thus they would be available to play 'shepherds' music' during Christmas festivities.

Instrumentation

The scoring for this *Sinfonia Pastorella* is in most of the sources herdsman's horn in G, two violins, viola and bass. The copies from Lambach and Bartenstein state that the viola is optional; the Bartenstein manuscript uses the term *fundamento* instead of basso, which could imply a keyboard continuo part although there are no figures. The Berlin catalogue reference gives the accompaniment as *Streichquartett*; the other versions do not specify whether the string parts were intended for single players or for orchestra. The Lambach manuscript shows the comment: '*Corno Pastoritio ma non obligato benché d'effetto assai buono*' (the herdsman's horn is not essential but adds greatly to the effect), which may reflect that there was some doubt as to the availability of a herdsman's horn or player there.

The most prominent discrepancy of scoring, however, is that the version from the library of Prince Öttingen-Wallerstein includes two additional orchestral horn parts: the parts are marked Horn in G in the outer movements and Horn in D in the central movement. This instrumentation is also found in the score from Munich which is a copy of this version and is replicated in the modern Broy publication which is also taken from the Öttingen parts. The horn parts in the Öttingen-Wallerstein set are in the same handwriting and on the same paper as the rest of the work; thus they do not appear to be a later addition to a pre-existing set of parts. Equally, there is no evidence that horn parts were formerly present in the Bartenstein and Lambach sets and have subsequently been lost: the title pages, which are consistent in paper type and handwriting with the parts therein, provide instrumentation lists that do not mention orchestral horns. There are no sections in the versions without orchestral horns where essential musical content is obviously missing: the work is complete without the horn parts. It therefore appears that Leopold wrote the work without orchestral horns and he or someone else also had a version made with additional horn parts for use at Öttingen.

In every manuscript the solo horn specified is the rustic instrument: Leopold uses the term *Hirten Horn* (herdsmen's horn) in his discussions with Lotter and in each of the six manuscripts the solo instrument is referred to by some variant of the Italian version *corno pastoricio*, with the alternative of *Kühe Horn* (horn for cows) in the Öttingen manuscript and its copy in Munich. The part could be played on a normal orchestral horn in G; there is no contemporary comment, however, to suggest that this was expected as an alternative.

The musical content

The alphorn music written by Leopold in this work is more varied than that found in many of the parts for herdsmen's horns in the Czech village *pastorellas*. Whereas those parts were often restricted to just one or two different repeating calls that a herdsman might use in the village square to gather the cattle together each morning in order to lead them to pasture, Leopold's music here has similarities with the more sophisticated *tuba pastoralis* parts written for the urban *pastorellas* of Habermann, Czerni and Nowotný, where functional herding calls have been developed into art music. The proximity of Salzburg to the mountains is such that Alpine herdsmen are likely to have been regular street entertainers around the city during the winter months: an alphorn player busking in a town for a human audience would need to play more than just a single call that his cattle would recognise. He would have to play a variety of music in order to entertain and earn a few coins; indeed as has been seen already, there is scope for considerable virtuosity on an alphorn despite the constraint of the natural harmonics. The variety of motifs included in Leopold's work might thus be a reflection of the range of alphorn music heard on the streets of Salzburg; alternatively, Leopold may have composed his own alphorn-like motifs to use in this work. The first alphorn theme of Leopold's third movement in this work is a pre-existing Christmas carol.

There is no record as to whether Leopold's *Sinfonia Pastorella* was written for a specific player, or whether the alphorn part is a transcription of one player's music. The work could have been intended either for the player who used these different calls, or for someone who could learn them by ear or from Leopold's score. This work provides evidence not only that composers such as Leopold were familiar with a range of music that alphorn players could play, but also that there was the expectation that an alphorn player was available, prepared and able to perform on his instrument with other musicians.

Leopold demonstrated his familiarity with the complications that could arise when a rustic player is included in a performance with experienced musicians when he wrote in his directions for a different work that a player who may have difficulty playing from written music should stand alongside an experienced musician for assistance: 'It would be good if they also had a little hackbrett or cimbalom so that it could be played from the violin part, and it could be good if the violin and the bass sat together …'[4] The part for the alphorn in Leopold's *Sinfonia Pastorella* is mostly doubled by another voice: this could help an alphorn player who might be less familiar with the skills required to keep with an accompaniment. It also allows for there to be no alphorn player at all: indeed the manuscript from Lambach notes that the work can be performed without the solo horn part.

There is an indication that the parts from Öttingen were used, as there are pencil annotations in the parts for the orchestral horn 1 and horn 2. The score from Munich also includes pencil annotations. There are no players' markings in the parts from Lambach or Bartenstein. The copies from Berlin and Vienna are full scores and thus archive material or conductors' scores, rather than parts from which a performance could be given.

The work is written for an alphorn in G; thus, in order for a performance of this work to have taken place with a herdsman's horn, there would need to have been a horn of the correct length available in that location. A tube that sounds the harmonic series of G produces the four notes used in this work, in ascending order G, C, E and G: these are harmonics nos. 3, 4, 5 and 6 of a tube of approximately 5ft in length. Alternatively, these pitches can be played on a tube of approximately 10ft, using harmonics nos. 6, 8, 10 and 12, although if a horn of this length had been intended, there would have been no reason not to use the intermediate harmonics, most of which are reasonably 'in tune'. A third option is that the notes intended are harmonics nos. 3, 4, 5 and 6 on a 10ft horn, in which case they would sound an octave below those of a 5ft horn. It is customary for natural horn in G parts to be written in C with the notes intended to sound a perfect fourth lower: Fig. 3.2 shows the four written notes of the alphorn part and the sounding pitch of these harmonics for a 5ft horn.

Written pitches   Sounding pitches

Fig. 3.2. Written pitches and sounding pitches of the alphorn part in Leopold Mozart's *Sinfonia Pastorella* for an alphorn in G of approximately 5ft in length.

Fig. 3.3. Contemporary depiction of a herdsman with a horn of around 5ft in length. Detail, map of Switzerland, 1712.[5]

With regard to the relationship of this work to the genre of the Czech *pastorella*, this composition is one of just a handful of *pastorella*-type works that include a part for a herdsman's horn that have been found outside the Czech-speaking, eastern part of the Austro-Hungarian empire. The title *Sinfonia Pastorella* (or the other equivalents found in Table 3.1) is the primary link with the genre of *pastorella* so prevalent in Czech culture in the mid-eighteenth century; in addition, Leopold's core thematic material is melodies that are used in *pastorella* repertoire.

There are two significant differences between this work and the majority of the Czech *pastorellas* examined in the previous chapter. Firstly there is no text: its Christmas message is transmitted by means of purely musical allusions. The title *Sinfonia* provides the information that is is an instrumental work: there are other examples of orchestral works that use *pastorella* material with the title

Sinfonia Pastorella, or Pastoral Symphony, some of which will be considered later in this chapter. Secondly, there are a number of extant manuscript copies of the work, none of which are in Salzburg where Leopold lived. Most of the Czech *pastorellas* discussed in Chapter 2 were written for local village use, by the resident cantor, with idiosyncratic and personal texts in a local dialect. There is just one copy. Examination of the musical material in Leopold's work shows that it was inspired not so much by these (there is no record that he ever visited a Czech village) but by the type of Christmas *pastorella* that was used in monasteries, houses of the nobility and city cathedrals. These were more formal, and if there was a text, it was in Latin (for example those of Habermann and Nowotný). A *pastorella* for general distribution among musically sophisticated audiences, with a Latin text, or indeed none, conveys its narrative by means of a specific collection of recognised Christmas melodies and motifs.

There are three carols that occur many times in these pan-European Christmas *pastorellas.* They are identified by their opening texts as 1) *Nězábudka pri potôčku* (in Slovak) or *Parvule pupule* (Latin), 2) *Hajej můj synačko* (Czech) or *Resonet in laudibus* (Latin), a crib-rocking melody, and 3) *Es hat sich halt eröffnet* (German) or *Joseph adstabit* (Latin). These carols and their melodic motifs occur as references to Christmas in the instrumental works of many mainstream Baroque composers including Johann Sebastian Bach, Heinrich Biber, Arcangelo Corelli, Gottfried Finger, Johann Fux, George Frideric Handel and Antonio Vivaldi; elements of these melodies are found in the works of later composers too, such as Josef Haydn, Wolfgang Amadeus Mozart and Ludwig van Beethoven. These three Christmas carols form the principal thematic material for each of the movements in Leopold's composition.

In form, Leopold's *Sinfonia Pastorella* has three independent movements, which immediately sets it apart from the rural Czech *pastorella*s examined earlier. There is no implication here that it was written to be an integral part of the celebration of midnight Mass on Christmas eve: a three-movement instrumental composition has more in common with a work for non-liturgical performance. Each movement, nevertheless, forms part of a whole that can be seen to represent three principal scenes of the Christmas narrative. The first movement appears to be a reflection of the shepherds in the fields, the second movement a lullaby for the baby Jesus in the crib and the third movement the visit of the shepherds to the Holy Family in the stable.

First Movement

The first movement opens with a theme commonly used to begin a European *pastorella*. The melody is a carol from Bohemia and Poland, *Nězábudka pri potôčku* (Sleep, baby Jesus). Fig. 3.4 shows a comparison between the opening of the carol and the opening motifs of four other Christmas *pastorellas*; there follows Leopold's version of the motif.

Fig. 3.4. (a) is the carol *Nězábudka pri potôčku* that was frequently used as the opening motif in a *pastorella*; (b) to (e) are the opening bars of four such works;[6] (f) is the opening of Leopold Mozart's *Sinfonia Pastorella*.

This motif was popular in Italy. There was a potential for word-play between the Italian term *la pastorella* (the shepherdess), and the word *pastorella* that had come to mean the music associated with the shepherds in the Christmas story. The frolics of Arcadian shepherds and shepherdesses were a common subject in Italian literature and music; nevertheless from the seventeenth century, when the word 'shepherdess' appeared in the title of an Italian composition, the music would sometimes feature this Christmas *pastorella* motif, despite an otherwise secular context. As an example, Antonio Vivaldi (1675–1741) wrote a Concerto in D for flute, oboe, violin, bassoon and continuo entitled *La Pastorella*: the presence of the definite article in the title gives it the translation of 'The Shepherdess'. However, its first movement uses a version of the Christmas *pastorella* theme given above. Italian composers often prefixed the motif with an up-beat, to accommodate the definite article in the title *La Pastorella*.

Fig. 3.5. Vivaldi, Concerto in D *La Pastorella*: first movement, flute part, bars 7–8.[7]

A further potential for play on words, alongside the double meaning for the word *pastorella*, appears in compositions inspired by Battista Guarini's *Il Pastor Fido* (The Faithful Shepherd).[8] Although Guarini's text is a typical story of love between shepherds and nymphs, the title *Il Pastor Fido* may also be used for the 'faith-filled', or 'devotional' shepherd who is always, even today, an essential figure in a Christmas crib on mainland Europe. Vivaldi's catalogue includes a set of six sonatas, Op. 13, which bear the title *Il Pastor Fido*; they are scored for flute, oboe, violin, musette, vielle and continuo. However, the set is now generally attributed to the French composer and musette player, Nicholas Chédeville (1705–1782). The Christmas *pastorella* opening motif quoted above is used to open three of the movements in these sonatas:

Fig. 3.6. Vivaldi / Chédeville, *Il Pastor Fido*. The opening bars of the flute parts of (a) Sonata No. 1, second movement, (b) Sonata No. 1, fourth movement, and (c) Sonata No. 5, third movement.[9]

In Leopold's work, initial statements of the *Nězábudka pri potôčku* theme in the strings are followed by lively arpeggiations for the alphorn, typical horn calls that could be intended to symbolise the herdsmen calling to one another to go to Bethlehem. The calls are accompanied by static tonic chords from the strings, in the styles of both the bagpipe (long held notes) and the hurdy-gurdy (rhythmically pulsed). A second theme from the strings is followed by scurrying triplet figures and harmony in the dominant key; the strings then echo the alphorn's arpeggiation figures. A brief development of the material follows before the return of the initial music.

Second Movement

The second movement of Leopold's *Sinfonia Pastorella* appears to depict Mary's gentle lullaby as she rocks her newborn child in the manger. It is scored for strings alone, and the absence of the loud alphorn in this central movement highlights the tranquillity and wonder of the scene. It is as if this is the most important picture at the centre of a triptych: the alphorn player frames the scenario by appearing only in the side panels, remaining at a reverential distance from the sacred scene at the heart of the work. On a structural level, Leopold is able to retain the usual concerto expectation to write this movement in the dominant key, the primary notes of which are not available on the alphorn. This movement is formed of two melodic components that are commonly found in other Nativity *pastorellas*: the *pastorale* and the *Kindelwiegen*.

The opening phrase is widely used in other music with the title *pastorale*. This motif originates from Italian Christmas traditions, where the local bagpipes (*zampogna*) and flute or double flute (*piffaro*) were commonly played around the crib by the local herdsmen. The gentle motif, with thirds rising from the mediant to the dominant and falling back, set in a rocking triple or compound time and either unaccompanied or supported by a drone bass, is found in many other Christmas works. The opening phrases of Leopold's second movement typically rock to and fro, in the manner of a lullaby. The motif, two violin parts in thirds, is echoed an octave lower by the viola and basso:

Fig. 3.7. Leopold Mozart, *Sinfonia Pastorella*: bars 1–2 of the second movement: violins 1 and 2, viola, basso. Edition HH, ed. Frances Jones.[10]

Italian composers in particular used this *pastorale* motif in their Christmas compositions. Similar music is written by Arcangelo Corelli (1653–1713) in his Concerto Grosso Op. 6, No. 8, composed around 1690. This work is known as his 'Christmas' Concerto because of its subheading '*fatto per la notte di Natale*' (composed for Christmas night). The work culminates in a gentle final movement that is given the title *Pastorale ad libitum*. The *Pastorale*, characteristically in compound time, consists of rocking thirds that move back and forth from the mediant to the dominant over a drone bass:

Fig. 3.8. Corelli, 'Christmas' Concerto: final movement, entitled *Pastorale ad libitum*, bars 1–5. Concertino parts for two violins and cello.[11]

Vivaldi's Concerto *Primavera* (Spring) from *Le Quattro Stagioni* (The Four Seasons) composed in 1723 perhaps reflects the scene at the beginning of the year when the herdsmen are at home in their villages. Vivaldi incorporates various shepherds' motifs in this concerto and includes a movement in compound time that is based on these rocking thirds, set above a *zampogna* drone bass given to the cellos and basses, to which he gives the significant title *Danza Pastorale*. The subheading, '*Di pastoral zampogna al suon festante Danzan Ninfe e Pastor nel tetto amato di primavera*' (the herdsman's bagpipes give a cheerful sound to the dance of the nymphs and shepherds to welcome the spring) describes the scene.

Fig. 3.9. Vivaldi, Concerto *Primavera* from *Le Quattro Stagioni*: second movement: *Danza Pastorale*, bars 1–3.[12]

Johann Sebastian Bach (1685–1750) drew upon the same Italian *pastorale* herdsmen's music. He wrote just one work entitled *Pastorale*: a four-movement piece for organ, BWV 590, in which he incorporates several recognisable *pastorale* elements. The first movement is in compound time, and the first ten bars are supported by a single bass note drone, with passages in rocking thirds:

Fig. 3.10. J. S. Bach, *Pastorale* BWV 590 for organ: first movement, bars 8–10 that includes movement in rocking thirds over a drone bass.[13]

In his *Weihnachts-Oratorium* (Christmas Oratorio) of 1734, Bach depicts the moment of the birth of Jesus with a typical gentle instrumental *pastorale*. This is the only movement in the work without text. Thus, not only does the composer use a musical form familiar to his congregation to depict the Nativity: he also perhaps reminds his listeners that the *pastorale* music itself reflects the scene at the crib, without the need for text. He uses the effect of the singers' devotional silence to observe the sacred moment of the birth of Christ. Rocking thirds are set over a drone accompaniment, in compound time. The sound of the bagpipes is captured with the remarkable scoring of four large members of the oboe family: two oboes d'amore and two oboes da caccia.

Fig. 3.11. J. S. Bach, *Weihnachts-Oratorium* No. 10 *Sinfonia,* parts for 2 oboes d'amore and 2 oboes da caccia, bars 9–13.[14]

There is a substantial Italian repertory of similar Christmas *pastorales*, for example in the works of Giuseppe Torelli, Giuseppe Valentini and Alessandro and Domenico Scarlatti.

The second phrase used by Leopold Mozart in this movement of his *Sinfonia Pastorella* is a quotation of a lullaby with the words *Hajej můj synáčko* (Hush, my dear), known as the crib-rocking lullaby, which is also often quoted in European *pastorella* works.

Fig. 3.12. Šimon Brixi, *Pastorella*, CZ-Pnm VM421, Canto solo bars 35–8.[15]

Fig. 3.13. Leopold Mozart, *Sinfonia Pastorella*: second movement, violin 1, bars 8 and 9. Ed. Frances Jones.

By the mid-1750s this melody was familiar as a Christmas tune in Salzburg: it was one of the seasonal melodies played daily each December from 1753 on a mechanical organ in the precincts of Salzburg castle. The carol had been arranged for this purpose by Johann Ernst Eberlin and was subsequently published by Leopold Mozart in 1759 in a collection of all the melodies played by that organ, entitled *Morning and evening melodic and harmonic performances from the inner courtyard of the Salzburg Residential Palace, or: Twelve Pieces for the Piano, of which one is played daily on the so-called musical organ, morning and evening, at Salzburg Castle.*[16]

Fig. 3.14. The mechanical organ in Salzburg Castle, built in 1502, still plays the melodies of Eberlin. Photo: Frances Jones.[17]

Leopold gives this melody the title *Das Wiegenlied* (The Cradle Song) and the designation of the month of Christ's birth, *Für den Christmonat*. The description *Das Wiegenlied* is significant. This melody had long been associated with the widespread practice of crib-rocking, *Kindelwiegen*, where rustic musicians performed around the crib in church at Christmas while worshippers came to rock a representation of the baby Jesus in its crib. The practice originated in Italy.

Fig. 3.15. Leopold Mozart, *Der Morgen und der Abend … No. 12: Das Wiegenlied: für den Christmonat*, bars 1–6.[18]

It is not only Leopold Mozart in this *Sinfonia Pastorella* who juxtaposed the rocking *piffaro* music in thirds with the crib-rocking melody. In Bach's *Pastorale* for organ BWV 590, described earlier, with *pastorale* elements in the first movement, the fourth movement begins with the crib-rocking melody:

Fig. 3.16. J. S. Bach, *Pastorale* BWV 590: fourth movement, bars 1–2, right hand, the crib-rocking melody.[19]

George Frideric Handel (1685–1759) used the crib-rocking lullaby theme in his opera *Il Pastor Fido* (1712), based on Guarini's text. Here he indulges in the word-play of The Faithful Shepherd with musical reference to the Christmas Nativity scene although the narrative has no connection with Christmas. In the celebrations at the end of the opera, the final dance, which is in simple ABA form, uses as its B theme a quotation of this peaceful lullaby; it may have been intended to be recognised by his audience as the gentle shepherds' melody. In this movement and elsewhere, Handel reverses the elements of the melody and begins with the rising scale that otherwise forms the second half of the motif. In this opera the melody has the character of a soothing musical equivalent of 'and they all lived happily ever after' (a box has been inserted to identify the phrase):

Fig. 3.17. The crib-rocking lullaby theme used in the final dance of Handel's *Il Pastor Fido*.[20]

An instrumental 'Pastoral Symphony' also marks the moment of the birth of the Christ child in Handel's *Messiah* of 1741. The interlude includes a number of the pastoral elements mentioned above, although it is unlikely that the title 'Pastoral Symphony' has any of the connotations for the audience of today that would have been the case in the 1740s. Indeed it is unclear at what stage the title 'Pastoral Symphony' was first used, as only the heading *Pifa* appears above this movement in the editions of The Handel Society (1850) and Chrysander (1892). However, in the second edition of Grove's *A Dictionary of Music and Musicians*, issued around the same time in 1889, the movement is described in two columns of text under the heading 'Pastoral Symphony', which indicates that the title must have been in popular use by then. In Chrysander's 1892 facsimile reproduction of the manuscript, Handel's contents page describes the movement thus: 'A symphony to prepare for the following annunciation by the Angel, marked 'Pifa', i.e. *pifferari*, in imitation of the music with which at Christmas Calabrian shepherds in Rome celebrated the birth of the Saviour'.[21]

Handel again begins with the rising scale, followed by the falling one. He intensifies the pastoral atmosphere with an accompaniment in thirds, a compound time signature, a quiet tonic bagpipe-style drone and the reduced orchestral palette of strings alone. This is the only purely instrumental movement in the main body of the oratorio: again, the reverent silence of the voices directs full aural attention onto the moment of Christ's birth, an atmosphere similarly created by Bach in his *Weihnachts-Oratorium* eight years previously.

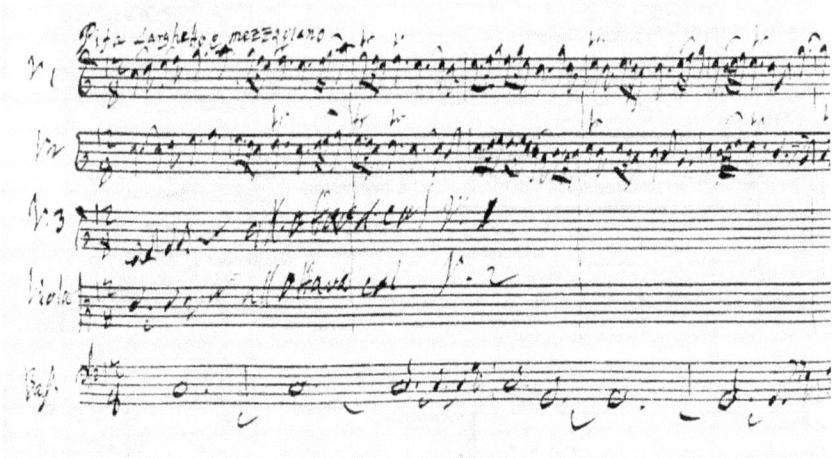

Fig. 3.18. Facsimile of Handel's *Messiah*, No. 13: 'Pastoral Symphony' (*Pifa*), bars 1–3.[22]

A number of these signifiers—the melodic shape of the crib-rocking carol, parallel thirds, compound time and *zampogna*-like drone—appear in other contexts where shepherds are mentioned. When Christ is described as the Good Shepherd, the same musical features can be found, for example in Bach's Cantata BWV 175, *Er rufet sein Schafen mit Namen* (He calls his sheep by name). Handel also incorporates some of these features in the soprano aria in *Messiah*, 'He shall feed his flock like a shepherd' (Air, No. 20) and in his *Ode for the Birthday of Queen Anne* (1713) in stanza 4 for alto solo and chorus, 'Let flocks and herds their fear forget'.

The use of these gentle melodic gestures at the central scene of Leopold's *Sinfonia Pastorella* creates an atmosphere of reverential repose. Although Leopold chose not to use the loud alphorn in his 'lullaby' movement, the alphorn player is nevertheless not only standing quietly among the players during the performance: his symbolic, silent presence at the side of the crib is also signified in the music in two ways. Leopold surrounds his *pastorale* motifs and crib-rocking melody with gentle, triadic horn-call motifs given to the strings throughout this movement, almost as if the alphorn player is present in the stable, but not intruding, just looking on in wonder. In addition, the crib-rocking melody appears in a different form. Two versions of this music were commonly used in the seventeenth and eighteenth century: alongside the flowing melody seen above, a second version often occurs, which opens with the text *Resonet in Laudibus* or *Joseph Lieber, Joseph mein*. This follows the same contours as the melody already seen, but is triadic:

Fig. 3.19. Two permutations of the crib-rocking melody, the flowing form and the triadic form.

Although these are generally considered to be versions of the same tune, the fundamental difference is clear: one can be played on an alphorn and the other cannot. When a *piffaro* or flute player is at the crib, the flowing version could be played; when a herdsman with a horn is present, he could only play the triadic version. Leopold's alphorn player stands quietly by while the gentle version of his melody is played by others.

Third Movement

For the third movement of this *Sinfonia Pastorella*, Leopold uses as his main motif a joyful Christmas carol that has the opening text *Joseph adstabit cugnas agitabit* (Joseph stands by and rocks the cradle), otherwise *Es hat sich halt eröffnet*, a carol that originates from Swabia in southern Germany. Leopold gives the melody an anacrusis and uses it as a recurring rondo theme played on the alphorn. There is, though, discrepancy between the various manuscripts: sometimes the drone-like accompaniment is pulsed in the manner of a hurdy-gurdy, in other versions it is held like the drone of the bagpipe. This melody resembles a horn call, and it features in other Christmas *pastorellas*:

Fig. 3.20. Extract from an anonymous Polish *pastorella*, (F.L.), 1699 PL-Wtm 17.ii, bars 3–37. Its text is translated: 'Joseph will stand by and rock the cradle, heaven will smile and the sun will banish the coldness'.[23]

Fig. 3.21. Leopold Mozart, *Sinfonia Pastorella*: third movement, bars 64–72. Alphorn in
G, violins 1 and 2, viola, basso. Ed. Frances Jones.

In Bach's organ *Pastorale* BWV 590, mentioned above, in which he uses
rocking thirds of the *pastorale* and the flowing crib-rocking lullaby, the first
section opens with similar cheerful horn calls, one voice echoing the other, set
above a bagpipe-like drone bass held on the pedal.

Fig. 3.22. J. S. Bach, *Pastorale* BWV 590, bars 1–2.[24]

Leopold's third movement is an extensive lively celebratory dance with a
strong pulse, in triple time. Towards the close of the work, the dynamics for the
whole ensemble are brought down to *piano* and then *pianissimo*, which could
perhaps represent the baby Jesus falling asleep, or the musicians' retreat from
the stable to leave the Holy Family in peace.

Fig. 3.23. Leopold Mozart *Sinfonia Pastorella* for alphorn and strings. Alphorn part from the manuscript of the Prince of Hohenlohe-Bartenstein.[25]

Rustic signifiers

There are a number of other rustic features that Leopold incorporates into his *Sinfonia Pastorella* for alphorn and strings, besides his use of a drone-like accompaniment and recognised Christmas melodic material. Some of these are general allusions to folk traditions, and some are specific to the alphorn. Other features of folk music are perhaps not unexpected: Christmastide is still today a time when people from the community might dust off their instruments to participate in the annual festivities. The involvement of other folk players, alongside the actual herdsman, the alphorn player, might be expected. Leopold makes some musical references to this.

He decorates many of his motifs in this work with the exuberant rhythm now referred to as the Scotch snap, or Lombard rhythm (see Fig. 3.4 (f) on p. 106).

He uses this idea many times in both the first and second movements. It is a rhythmic motif that was particularly associated with the rustic and therefore with Christmas music: it features in a similar vein in one of the Christmas melodies played daily each December from 1753 on the mechanical organ in the inner yard of Salzburg Castle, mentioned earlier. The piece with the title '*Für den Wintermonat*' (for the Winter Month, i.e. December) includes the Scotch snap in bars 3 and 6:

Fig. 3.24. *Menueto, 'Für den Wintermonat'. No. 11 from Leopold Mozart, Der Morgen und der Abend ... It features the Scotch snap in bars 3 and 6.*[26]

Leopold enjoyed the rural associations of this rhythm so much that in a letter concerning another of his rustic-style compositions, he explained that the exuberance of this motif should be heightened with a vocal cry too: 'At the beginning is the March, where at bars 19 and 21 of the first section , and bars 27 and 29 of the second section , they must shout in tempo after these notes'.[27] It is still usual today in the Alpine folk tradition for a virtuoso performance to be rounded off with a vocal whoop.

The style of accompaniment for the solo passages in this work is also of interest. There is much use of static tonic or dominant harmony that reproduces the effect of the drone of either a set of bagpipes or a hurdy-gurdy. Leopold uses the two different effects here. The first movement opens with a rhythmic *tutti* for strings. When the alphorn player begins, while one part plays along with the alphorn figuration, the other string parts comprise long held notes. This drone effect could represent the fact that most bagpipes have no means of rhythmic articulation; it may otherwise represent the sudden suspense of movement when the shepherds hear the alphorn call, or it could be a reminder of a peaceful pastoral landscape as the shepherds watch their sheep before hurrying to Bethlehem.

In other sections of the work, Leopold's drone effect pulsates on each beat, in replication of the rhythmic playing of the drone strings of a hurdy-gurdy. The repeated use of the pulsed drone in the last movement gives momentum and energy to the dance-like rhythms.

Two characteristics specific to the alphorn are enjoyed in this work: the 'alphorn *fa*' and the short high note added at the end of a performance. There are many references in this work to the 'alphorn *fa*', the out-of-tune 11th harmonic that lies halfway between a perfect fourth and an augmented fourth above the tonic on a natural horn. As noted earlier, the use of the scale with the raised fourth, sometimes called a 'Lydian fourth', is a common signifier for rustic music. Here it appears in the first bar of the work (see Fig 3.4 (f), p. 106), where Leopold not only writes the raised fourth degree of the scale but follows this with the lowered version in close proximity, which highlights the feature. In the third movement, he writes some passages for the orchestra where the strings repeatedly mimic the 'strange' note, adjusting it both upwards (Fig. 3.25, marked *y*) and downwards (marked *z*) for maximum effect:

Fig. 3.25. Leopold Mozart, *Sinfonia Pastorella*: third movement, bars 94–103, string parts. The unusual 'alphorn *fa*' is imitated by violins 1, 2 and basso with the juxtaposition of two different notes at *y* and *z*. Ed. Frances Jones.

American horn enthusiast Marvin McCoy's 1978 publication of this work includes an interesting interpretation of this particular passage. There are recordings of the work performed on a 10ft hosepipe (for example, Dennis Brain plays the final movement, 1956, Hoffnung's Music Festivals, EMI SLS870). With the availability of the intermediate harmonics on this length of tubing, the soloist can sound the 'alphorn *fa*' (harmonic no. 11) simultaneously with the strings at the places marked *y* and *z*. McCoy notates these intermediate harmonics in his publication: they are not present on any of the European manuscripts found in this investigation. It is likely that McCoy's transcription was made by ear from a sound recording, because he selected the wrong note values for the first and second movements (in both cases he wrote the notes as double their original length).

A further unusual phenomenon that is a feature of alphorn music appears at the end of the alphorn part in both the first and the third movements of Leopold's *Sinfonia Pastorella*: a final flick up to the dominant, notated as a grace note after the last main note.

Fig. 3.26. The end of the first movement of Leopold Mozart's *Sinfonia Pastorella*, alphorn part, copy from Stift Lambach.[28]

The feature has also been noted in the *pastorella* of Petipeský (see p. 83) and is seen in a number of the transcriptions of *Kühreien*, for example in the collections of 1805 and 1812 and the material from Appenzell (see Chapter 4); it remains a common feature that rounds off an alphorn performance today. This additional note is consistently present at the end of the alphorn part in both of the alphorn movements in all six of the *Sinfonia Pastorella* manuscripts. In two instances, though, the note written is not the dominant but the mediant (the Berlin copy at the end of the first movement and the Vienna copy at the end of the third movement), which might be copyists' errors, or may suggest that it was merely intended to be an unspecified higher harmonic. These flicked notes are such an unusual phenomenon that the modern editions of McCoy and Janetzky omitted them altogether, while the version edited by Broy has omitted the one at the end of the first movement and altered the one in the last movement to a written high C, an octave above the main final note, with the marking [*sic*] despite the clear G in the Öttingen version upon which this version is based. There can be no doubt that Leopold included it because he heard it played by itinerant alphorn players and that he wished to convey its rustic energy at the end of each movement of this work; to my knowledge, it is not found elsewhere in the canon of Western notated repertoire other than in direct transcriptions of alphorn music.

Motivic similarity in subsequent works

Leopold Mozart's *Sinfonia Pastorella* for alphorn and strings provides a classic example of instrumental Christmas music of the middle of the eighteenth century, and it is invaluable as documentation of the characteristic features and style of the music played on an alphorn in the vicinity of Salzburg at that time. A direct influence might be identifiable in two works written by his son. At the age of ten, the young Wolfgang was commissioned to write some music for performance at the celebrations for the accession of William V at The Hague in 1766. The result was *Galimathias Musicum*, K. 32, a light-hearted collection of 18 movements based on popular music of the time. He includes two *pastorellas*, each set over a drone bass. The first uses the flowing crib-rocking lullaby, *Hajej můj synáčko*, with which he was familiar from its daily appearance played on the mechanical organ every December in Salzburg, noted earlier; the second makes prominent use of references to the 'alphorn *fa*' with both the scale with the raised fourth and the juxtaposition of the raised fourth with the lowered one. He uses the same melody, *Joseph adstabit*, that is used in the third movement of his father's *Sinfonia Pastorella*, and much of the motivic content is similar to that used in both the first and the third movements of Leopold's composition. Here the strong rustic dance pulse in triple time can be seen again, the arpeggiating horn calls, the underlying pulsed drones of the hurdy-gurdy and the final fade to *piano*, then *pianissimo* as the music perhaps drifts off into the distance.

Fig. 3.27. Wolfgang Amadeus Mozart, *Galimathias Musicum*, fourth movement, *Pastorella*, bars 18–38, scored for 2 oboes and strings.[29]

Wolfgang also used herdsmen's music in his Symphony No. 19, K. 132, written in Salzburg in July 1772 when he was 16 years old. The opening phrases of the crib-rocking lullaby *Hajej můj synáčko* repeatedly appear in the second violin part, which at times are followed in thirds by the viola part. There are also phrases from *Nězábudka pri potôčku*, motifs that resemble horn calls and repeated bass notes reminiscent of a hurdy-gurdy drone in this work. It is not known why Wolfgang should quote these Christmas motifs in a work written in mid-summer: it might have been a lullaby for a child in a different context, or intended for a later Christmas performance.

Fig. 3.28. W. A. Mozart, Symphony No. 19, second movement, *Andante*, bars 33–56. The crib-rocking lullaby is quoted in the second violin part, among a number of other *pastorella* features. It is scored for 2 oboes, 2 horns and strings.[30]

This repertoire of musical allusions in the *pastorella* had become a significant element in the eighteenth-century composer's palette. Two later works are mentioned here as examples of the importance, not specifically of Leopold's work, but of the genre of which it is a classic example.

Beethoven's Symphony No. 6, 'Pastoral' (*Pastoral-Sinfonie oder Erinnerung an das Landleben*) of 1808 incorporates many allusions to the countryside, with bird calls, a murmuring brook, peasants' gatherings, bagpipe-like drone effects, a storm and rustic horn calls. Scholarship has additionally revealed Beethoven's use of actual folk melodies in the work.[31] A look below the surface, though, reveals something more fundamental than these. His initial title was *Sinfonia Pastorella*; however, this was later altered because of its direct connotations with the Church. This title, though, is highly significant: Beethoven creates a full symphony with material drawn from the *pastorella* tradition.[32] Many of his *pastorella* motifs, initially presented in a peaceful context, are subsequently transformed into disturbing or agitated music to portray his thunderstorm.

Beethoven first uses material from the crib-rocking lullaby *Hajej můj synáčko* at the start of the second movement, entitled *Szene am Bach*. He does not yet quote the full lullaby melody, rather he combines the opening contour (the dominant rising to the submediant, followed by a descending scale) with typical *pastorale* references to shepherds, gentle rocking thirds and compound time, to depict a peaceful pastoral scene. The second violins, doubled at the octave by a solo muted cello, play a version of the lullaby phrase; violas and a second solo muted cello move in parallel thirds in the style of a *piffaro*. The pastoral setting is enhanced with a tonic octave drone provided by two horns. Alongside these musical allusions to shepherds, the title *Szene am Bach* also conveys the image of gently flowing water. The motif is developed into a string semiquaver accompaniment figure that first appears in bar 7 and is subsequently used as a backdrop in a number of passages in the movement.

Fig. 3.29. Beethoven, 'Pastoral' Symphony, second movement, *Andante molto moto*, bars 1–3.[33]

Beethoven opens the third movement of his 'Pastoral' Symphony, *Lustiges Zusammensein in der Landleute* (Peasants' Merrymaking), with the notes of *Nězábudka pri potôčku*. Initially, he uses the Italian version with an up-beat, presented *pianissimo* and *staccato* by the strings. The motif is used in both F major and D major (bar 33) and appears eleven times, interspersed with an arpeggio phrase that resembles a herdsman's horn call. It rises to a joyous *fortissimo* by bar 53.

Fig. 3.30. Beethoven, 'Pastoral' Symphony, opening phrase of the third movement, violin 1.

Although Beethoven's fourth movement, *Gewitter. Sturm* (Thunderstorm) remains one of the most remarkable depictions of a storm in the entire canon of composed repertoire, much of its effect is lost on audiences of today who do not recognise that the thematic material of the entire movement comprises transformations of the two shepherds' Christmas melodies already presented: the gentle *pastorella* crib-rocking lullaby *Hajej můj synačko* and the carol *Nězábudka pri potôčku*. Beethoven's development of this material into his storm would have made the atmosphere all the more unsettling for contemporary audiences.

He introduces the thunderstorm with an ominous *pianissimo* rumble of tremolo cello and bass, then the melodic shape of the opening of *Hajej můj synačko* appears in bar 3, given to the second violins, *pianissimo* and *staccato*, in the dark key of D flat major. He replaces its customary triple dance metre with 4/4 although the metronome mark is in minims: this pushes accentuation onto different notes of the melody that highlight the raised fourth or 'alphorn *fa*'. He then extracts the interval and the resultant tritone, known as 'the devil in music' (*diabolus in musica*), is played in the first violins two bars later, which reinforces its sinister quality. The *Hajej můj synačko* lullaby melody is later mutated into the minor, with wild distorted outbursts, to become the nightmare music of Beethoven's great, swirling storm.

Fig. 3.31. Beethoven, 'Pastoral' Symphony, fourth movement, bars 1–6, beginning of the storm. The *Hajej* motif is played by violin 2 and the highlighted tritone is given to violin 1.

The opening notes of *Nězábudka pri potôčku* first appear at bar 35 in the composer's depiction of the storm. Here Beethoven does not use the version with a gentle upbeat as he does earlier: he builds a striking phrase from the opening motif (a falling fourth followed by an upward step) which he presents six times. The motif is transformed into the minor and presented with a persistent *sforzando* accentuation on *tutti* strings, with menacing effect.

Fig. 3.32. Beethoven, 'Pastoral' Symphony, fourth movement, *Allegro*, bars 35–39, violin 1.

Once his storm is spent, Beethoven transforms the *Hajej můj synáčko* lullaby theme again, this time into a beautiful prayer-like chorale given to the oboe with scoring reminiscent of an organ. While the melody gently descends to settle on its tonic for the beginning of the final movement, *Hirtengesang. Frohe und dankbare Gefühle nach dem Sturm* (Herdsman's song. Joyful and thankful feelings after the storm), at the same time Beethoven extends the rising line on the flute as if to soar up into the heavens taking all troubles with it:

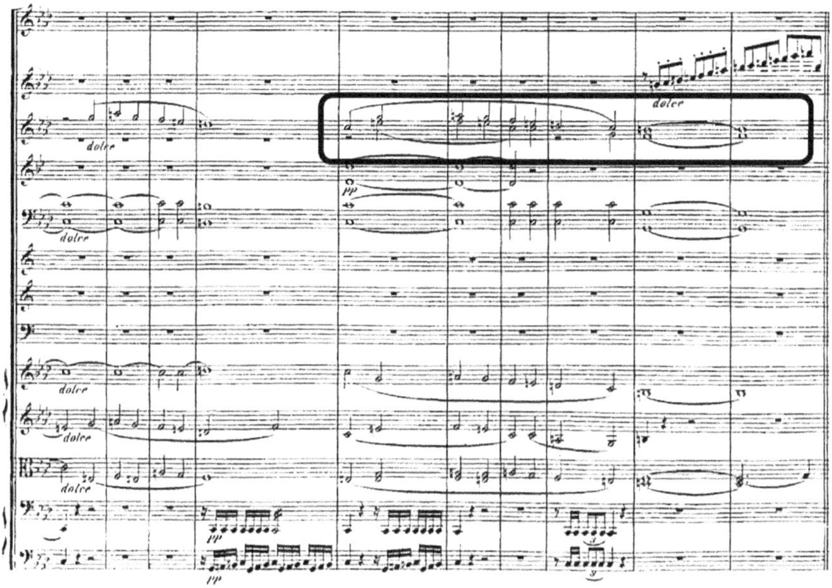

Fig. 3.33. Beethoven, 'Pastoral' Symphony, fourth movement bars 146–155, the *Hajej můj synáčko* theme returns at the end of the storm.

As the crib-rocking melody is thus brought to rest, Beethoven introduces the third *pastorella* motif used as the theme for the final movement in Leopold's *Sinfonia Pastorella*: the lively *Joseph adstabit* melody. Once again, however, Beethoven reverses the mood of this theme. Instead of an energetic joy, it has the character of peace and reflection. It is played on a lone clarinet and given an answering call played on the horn.

Fig. 3.34. Beethoven, 'Pastoral' Symphony, final movement wind parts, bars 1–9.

Thus Beethoven's quotations of the three *pastorella* carols echo the three movements of Leopold's *Sinfonia Pastorella*. Whereas Leopold structured his work in concerto form, Beethoven gives the same material, in the same sequence, full symphonic treatment.

A different example was composed at a later date as the result of the upsurge of interest in music from previous eras that began towards the end of the nineteenth century. The German composer Carl Orff (1895–1982) had a deep fascination for both the music and the literature of earlier centuries. He drew upon the heritage of the *pastorella* in his *Carmina Burana*, a setting of a collection of mediaeval poems of the same title. Orff chose the characteristic *pastorella* carol motifs, along with other *pastorella* signifiers, as the thematic material for the movement that celebrates the arrival of springtime. It begins with the text *Ecce Gratum* (Behold the pleasant and long-awaited spring). True to the *pastorella* tradition, he opens the movement with a bold statement of the *Nězábudka pri potôčku* theme that opens Leopold's first movement; it is then repeated in hushed tones. This is followed by a variant of the flowing crib-rocking melody, *Hajej můj synačko*. All is set over a *zampogna* drone.

Fig. 3.35. Orff, *Carmina Burana: Ecce Gratum,* quotation of the *Nězábudka pri potôčku*
theme and the flowing crib-rocking melody, set over a bagpipe-like drone.[34]

At the time when it was written, Leopold's *Sinfonia Pastorella* constituted imaginative use of the alphorn. It was a work in which the realism of the shepherds' role in the Nativity was brought into a more refined performance space than was commonly found in the *pastorella*. Unlike in a Czech village, where it invited an audience or congregation into the Christmas scene by giving an actual herdsman a participatory role in telling the Christmas story, this setting is on a different cultural level, more sophisticated, designed for an audience of higher social standing who may have been personally less in touch with country life. The rustic realism of the music is thus more refined than that of the Czech village *pastorella*, the alphorn is given more sophisticated music and the work has more substance.

To an eighteenth-century audience, the *pastorella* was a recognised part of the annual musical calendar. Today it is being rediscovered, but is still familiar to few. The allusions to the Christmas narrative in works such as this pass largely unnoticed, because the host of references to the Nativity immediately recognised by an eighteenth-century audience are no longer part of the modern listener's normal aural experience. In the context of the *pastorella*, this work is a typical example of the widespread use of specific material that composers utilised in the genre. It provides an unusual link between the Czech village *pastorella* and the more widespread version, by bringing a folk instrument into the forum of the upper class, non-liturgical performance arena. It displays a higher quality of invention and compositional artistry than many other eighteenth-century works in this genre, and it illustrates how such Christmas material could be effectively moulded into a work of lasting appeal.

Notes

[1] Leopold Mozart, attributed to Pietro Antonio Lorenzoni. https://en.wikipedia.org/wiki/Leopold_Mozart#/media/File:Leopold_Mozart.jpg. Creative Commons CC0 License.

[2] Max Sieffert, ed. *Denkmäler Deutscher Tonkunst*, Vol. 2: *Leopold Mozart Ausgewählte Werke* (Leipzig: Breitkopf & Härtel, 1908), 30: *Monsieur Gignox will ein paar neue Pastorell Synfonien? Ich glaub er meint sie sind immer so fertig, wie das Brod auf dem Laden liegt, denn itzt geschwind solche zu machen hab ich nicht allemal Zeit. Und diess muss er selbst glauben, weil er meint ich hätte nicht einmal Zeit einen Brief von ihm durchzulesen, wissen sie, ich hab zwar eine nagelneue Pastorell Synfonie: allein, ich sage es aufrichtig, ich gieb sie nicht gerne her; denn ich dachte sie nach Wallerstein nebst anderen Stücken zuschicken. Ich dachte sie also recht wohl anzubringen. Es ist ein Hirten Horn und 2 Flauto traversi obligat dabey. Soll ich es denn schicken? Basta! Ich will es mit nächster Post schikken; nur bitte um alles nichts zu melden, dassich es geschickt habe: denn sonst ist es bei dem Wagner, und durch sein Geschwätze beym H.v.Rheling aus. Sie wissen meine Umstände.*

[3] Full details of this analysis are available from the author on frances@AmazingAlphorn.com.

4 Sieffert, ed. *Denkmäler Deutscher Tonkunst*, 30: *Es wären gut, wenn sie auch ein Hackbrettl oder Cymbal darbey hätten, solches müsste der, so es spielet aus der Violinstimme exerciren, und wenn es gut machen will, die Violine und den Bass unter einander setzen …*

5 https://commons.wikimedia.org/wiki/File:Nova_Helvetiae_Tabula_Geographica_01_12.jpg. Creative Commons CC0 License.

6 Robert Rawson, 'Gottfried Finger's Christmas Pastorellas', *Early Music*, Vol. 33, No. 4 (2005), 591–606: b) Linek *Missa Pastoralis*, CZ-Pnm18 f.61; c) Anon (F.L.), *Pastorella*, Lowicz, 1699, PL-Wtfc 17.ii; d) Finger *Pastorelle*, Durham Cathedral Library Ms M197; e) Biber *Pastorella*, A-Wm Cod.726, ff.160v-161v. Reproduced with kind permission of Oxford University Press.

7 Antonio Vivaldi, Concerto in D *La Pastorella* RV95, No. 29.

8 This is a pastoral tragicomedy written by the Italian poet Battista Guarini, published in Ferrara in 1590. It was a popular source of inspiration for many composers including Handel, Marenzio, Monteverdi and Schütz.

9 Antonio Vivaldi (Chédeville), Six Sonatas *Il Pastor Fido*, Op. 13 (Paris: Boivin, c.1737).

10 All extracts from Leopold Mozart, *Sinfonia Pastorella for Alphorn and Strings*, ed. Frances Jones, (Oxford: Edition HH, 2014), are reproduced with kind permission of Per Hartmann.

11 Arcangelo Corelli, *Concerto Grosso in G minor 'Fatto per la Notte di Natale'*, Op. 6, No. 8 (Leipzig: Kahnt, 1913).

12 Antonio Vivaldi, *Le quattro stagioni: da Il cimento dell'armonia e dell'inventione*, Op. 8, ed. Paul Everett and Michael Talbot (Milan: Ricordi, 2010), 14. Reproduced with kind permission of Michael Talbot.

13 Johann Sebastian Bach, *Pastorale* in F major, BWV 590, *Bach-Gesellschaft Ausgabe* (Leipzig: Breitkopf & Härtel, 1891), Vol. 38, 135. https://imslp.org/wiki/Pastorale_in_F_major,_BWV_590_(Bach,_Johann_Sebastian).

14 Johann Sebastian Bach, *Bach-Gesellschaft Ausgabe* (Leipzig: Breitkopf & Härtel, 1856), Vol. 5, 51.

15 Rawson, 'Finger's Pastorellas', 601.

16 Leopold Mozart, *Der Morgen und der Abend der Innwohnern der hochfürstl. Residenz-Stadt Salzburg melodisch und harmonisch angekündigt. Oder: Zwölf Musikstücke für das Clavier, davon eine täglich in der Vestung Hohensalzburg auf dem sogenannten Hornnwerke Morgens und Abends gespielt wird.* (Augsburg: Lotter, 1759). https://imslp.org/wiki/Der_Morgen_und_der_Abend_(Mozart,_Leopold).

17 Inclusion of the photograph with kind permission of the Salzburger Burgen und Schlösser Betriebsführung.

18 *Der Morgen und der Abend*, No. 12.

19 Johann Sebastian Bach, *Bach-Gesellschaft Ausgabe* (Leipzig: Breitkopf & Härtel, 1891), Vol. 38, 132.

20 Georg Frideric Handel, *Il Pastor Fido* in *Collected Works*, ed. Chrysander (Leipzig: Breitkopf & Härtel, 1892), Vol. 30, 84.

21 George Frideric Handel, *Messiah*, ed. Chrysander (Hamburg: Strumper, 1892), p. 10: *Eine Symphonie zur Einleitung der folgenden Verkündigung des Engels, überschrieben 'Pifa', das ist* Pifferari*, als Nachahmung der Musik, mit welcher Kalabrische Hirten zur Weihnachtszeit in Rom die Geburt des Heilands feiern.* https://imslp.org/wiki/Messiah,_HWV_56_(Handel,_George_Frideric).

22 Ibid., 69.

23 Rawson, 'Finger's Pastorellas', 599.

24 Johann Sebastian Bach, *Bach-Gesellschaft Ausgabe* (Leipzig: Breitkopf & Härtel, 1891), Vol. 38, 135.

25 Reproduced with kind permission of the Hohenlohe-Zentralarchiv Neuenstein, ID: HZAN Ba 120 Bü 161.

26 Leopold Mozart, *Der Morgen und der Abend.*

27 Sieffert, ed. *Denkmäler Deutscher Tonkunst*, 30: *Anfangs ist der Marche, welchem man bei 19ten und 21ten Takte des ersten Theils,*(musical quotation) *und beim 27ten und 29ten des zweyten Theiles* (musical quotation) *a tempo nach diesen Noten jauchzen muss.*

28 Reproduced with kind permission of the Bayerischen Staatlichen Bibliotheken, ID: 4 Cod mus 64 (früher MG II 420), 17.

29 Wolfgang Amadeus Mozart, *Galimathias Musicum, Wolfgang Amadeus Mozarts Werke* Series XXIV, Supplemente (Leipzig: Breitkopf & Härtel, 1886), Vol. 1, 8. https://imslp.org/wiki/Galimathias_musicum,_K.32_(Mozart,_Wolfgang_Amadeus).

30 Wolfgang Amadeus Mozart, *Symphony No. 19, Wolfgang Amadeus Mozarts Werke* Series VIII, Sinfonien, (Leipzig: Breitkopf & Härtel, 1880), Vol. 1, 8. https://imslp.org/wiki/Symphony_No.19_in_E-flat_major,_K.132_(Mozart,_Wolfgang_Amadeus).

31 For example, in Béla Bartók, *The Relationship of Folk Song to the Development of the Art Music of our Time, Béla Bartók Essays* ed. Benjamin Suchoff, (London: Faber, 1992), 327–8.

32 See Frances Jones, 'The Influence of the Christmas Pastorella on Beethoven's 'Pastoral' Symphony', *The Consort* Vol. 72, Summer 2016, 90–108.

33 Ludwig van Beethoven, *Symphony No. 6, Ludwig van Beethovens Werke, Serie 1: Sinfonien* (Leipzig: Breitkopf & Härtel, c.1863), 26, and the following two facsimile extracts, 54, 65 and 66. https://imslp.org/wiki/Symphony_No.6,_Op.68_(Beethoven,_Ludwig_van).

34 Carl Orff, *Carmina Burana* (Mainz: Schott, 1937), 28–9, voice, pianos and string parts. Reproduced with kind permission of Schott Music Ltd. All Rights Reserved.

Chapter 4

'That Air': The Appenzell *Kühreien*

'…That air, which instantly and irresistibly excites the Swiss, when in a foreign land, the *maladie du pais …*'[1]

The *Kühreien* (cow procession music) from Appenzell, a sparsely-populated, mountainous canton in the east of Switzerland, is above all other sources of alphorn music the most widely documented. It is the most known and discussed by the Swiss, by tourists to their country and by those who have heard about the music elsewhere; it is therefore the material that has been the most widely quoted by composers.

Fig. 4.1. Herdsmen still move cattle to the high pastures in a *Kühreien* for the summer months. Urnäsch, Appenzell. Photo: Marcel Steiner.[2]

There are many elements that the various transcriptions of the Appenzell material have in common, and the title refers to this motivic content, rather than to a definitive fixed piece of music. As noted earlier, any written version of a *Kühreien* was originally just one transcription of an improvised set of motifs, whereby after an initial call to collect the cattle from their stalls, there is a free collection of motifs that were used to call individual cows on the journey from the villages in the valleys to the high summer pastures as required. The variety of music and text found in the transcriptions of this particular *Kühreien* material from Appenzell is a reflection of the function of this style of music, and thus melodies reproduced as 'the Appenzell *Kühreien*' differ substantially from one version to another.[3]

Although almost every written version of 'the Appenzell *Kühreien*' is different, there are several features that define this music. Fig. 4.2 shows the earliest known printed version, in Georg Rhaw (or Rhau)'s collection of music *Bicinia Gallica, Latina, Germanica et Quaedam Fugae* (Gallic, Latin and German Duets and Four Fugues), published in Wittenberg, Saxony, in 1545. Rhaw was a music teacher, performer, composer and publisher. He was one of J. S. Bach's predecessors as Kantor at St. Thomas's, Leipzig, and like Bach, he was also Music Master at the

Thomasschule. Thus his connection with the church was close; indeed he was a friend of Martin Luther, who wrote in the Preface to one of Rhaw's publications that music serves theology, and stands next to theology as the highest art.[4]

Fig. 4.2. *Der Appenzeller Kureyen* reproduced in Rhaw's *Bicinia Gallica, Latina, Germanica et Quaedam Fugae, Inferior Vox.*[5]

According to its preface, *Bicinia Gallica* is a collection of traditional and specially composed music compiled for his students, to assist with teaching the art of polyphonic writing. It takes the form of two part-books, an upper voice book and a lower voice book. The music from Appenzell quoted by Rhaw runs for three pages.

He uses it as the lower voice in a two-part composition and writes a florid upper line based on the Appenzell material to create an elaborate polyphonic work.

Even at this date, there is indication that the *Kühreien* had an associated text. It is not known at what period this assimilation of the *Kühreien* into repertoire for the voice became commonplace, but the counter-melody set above the Appenzell *Kühreien* in Rhaw's collection of 1545, shown below in Fig. 4.3, is given the description '*lobelobe*' (cf. German *Lobe*: praise, rejoice). This is a word that not only appears in other transcriptions of this *Kühreien* material: it also features in the texts of many *Kühreien* from other parts of Switzerland. Rhaw's use of this word indicates that such lyrics were already associated with this music at that time. Rhaw's choice of spelling for the word *Kühreien* is different in the upper voice book (*Kureien*) from the lower voice book (*Kureyen*): this may be an error or merely a reflection that spelling of Swiss dialect words is not, even today, standardised.

Fig. 4.3. Opening of the *Superior Vox* part written in counterpoint to the alphorn melody from Appenzell in Rhaw's *Bicinia Gallica, Latina, Germanica et Quaedam Fugae*. It bears the descriptive heading '*Der Appenzeller Kureien Lobelobe*'.[6]

The earliest known transcript of Appenzell *Kühreien* music to appear with text occurs in a handwritten volume of 60 songs, the personal songbook of Maria Josepha Barbara Brogerin of Appenzell, dated 1730. Maria Brogerin was a Franciscan sister in the convent of St. Mary of the Angels in Appenzell, a Capuchin foundation established in 1420. Maria (1704–c.1775) was one of seventeen children; she came from the local village of Rapisau (now Flucht) and was professed in 1722. One of her younger sisters also entered the convent and served several terms as its mother superior.

Fig. 4.4. Convent of St. Mary of the Angels, Appenzell. Johann Ulrich Fitzi, c.1829.[7]

All but one of the pieces in Brogerin's *Liederbüchlein* (Little Songbook) are simple song tunes with many verses, some solo and some in two parts, both sacred and secular. The final melody, though, is a version of the local *Kühreien*, with similar musical contours to the version quoted by Rhaw 185 years previously.

Fig. 4.5. Appenzell *Küh Reien* with text in Maria Josepha Barbara Brogerin's *Liederbüchlein* of 1730.[8]

The text, with repeated words or syllables omitted, reads:[9]

Weder ia, loba!	I am walking, *loba*! [rejoice!]
Gotts nama alsama,	in God's name, all together,
die junga, die alta,	the young, the old,
die äna, alsama, loba	the rest, all together, *loba*
Köda Gotts nama alsama, loba	come in God's name all together, *loba*
Weni era fä a pfiffa a,	When I go with my pipe
so köd alsama zua a schlicha,	all together they are charmed by the call,
wohl zua, do zua,	for their wellbeing,
trib ia Gotts nama,	I drive them in God's name,
wohl zua, beser zua,	their well-being, a better time,
höbsch sönds und frey,	lovely and free
holdseelig dor zua loba,	full of joy to be there, *loba*,
b'hüets Gott alsama, loba.	to the summer chalets, in God's name, *loba*.
Wäss wohl, wen mir singa vergoth,	I sing through the long journey
wen zwo wiega i der stuba stoth,	to the meadows from the cowshed,
wen der ma mit füsta drischlot,	no more is the wind blowing
und der wend zuo	through all the holes
alla löchra ia blost. loba.	in your draughty stalls. *loba*.
Trib mer ia, Gotts nama:	I will guide you, in God's name:
die hinckat, die stinckat,	lame one, smelly one,
die g'scheget, die g'fleckhet,	dappled one, speckled one,
die glazet, die blatzet,	one without a top-knot, the two-coloured one,
schwantzeri, tantzeri,	wavy tail, dancer,
glintzeri, blintzeri,	glistening one, blinker,
d'lehneri, d'freneri,	leaning one, disfigured one,
d'hossleri, d'mosleri,	the one from Hossler, the one from Mosler,
d'horeri, d'schoreri,	the hairy one, the one that scratches,
s'halb örli unds mörli,	the one with half an ear, the black one,
s'ä äugli, s'trüfäugli,	the one-eyed one, the one with a weeping eye,
die erst galt und die alt,	the one not yet milked and the old one,
s'krombä und die ä,	the crooked one and the other,
der gross bauch und die rauch,	the big belly and the smoky one,
d'läng bäneri,	the long-boned one,
d'hag läneri,	the one that rubs against the post,
trib ia, wohl zua, wohl zua, bas zua,	I will guide and look after you all,
loba.	*loba*.
Sed das i g'weibet ha,	Since I married
ha i kä brodt me ka,	I have bread with me,

sed das i g'weibet ha,	Since I married
ha i kä glückh me ka.	I am happy.
Trib mer ia	Following me
die g'schiltata vier,	I have the four blotchy ones,
si schlichet hüna noa mit am stier.	and at the back is the bull.
Wohl zua, do zua, bas zua	I will guide you all
loba.	*loba.*
Wens ada wohl gott	Under God's guidance
und nimer stil stoth,	we do not stand still,
so ist jo grota, grota, loba.	but keep moving, *loba.*
Ist käna lütha bas as ösra küa,	And for the well-being of our cows,
sie trinckhit us dem bach	they drink from the brook
und möget trüa.	and gain life.

Another typical transcription of the Appenzell *Kühreien* is found in Sigismund von Wagner's *Acht Schweizer-Kühreien, mit Musik und Text* of 1805: this version was further reproduced in the series of collections of *Kühreien* that appeared thereafter, although there are slight changes to the text in later appearances. In the *Sammlung von Schweizer Kühreihen und alten Volksliedern* published in Bern in 1812 under the editorship of Gottlieb Jakob Kuhn, it appears thus:

Fig. 4.6. The *Kühreihen* of the Appenzellers, *Sammlung von Schweizer Kühreihen und alten Volkliedern*, second edition, 1812.[10]

The Text

A comparison of the 1730 text with that of Wagner's 1805 version reveals that the second is largely a transcription of the first, although some significant alterations have been made:

Brogerin text of 1730	**Wagner text of 1805**
Weder ia, loba!	*Wänder iha, Loba!*
Gotts nama alsama,	*Allsamma mit Namma,*
die junga, die alta, die äna,	*die Alten, die Jungen, die Alten*
alsama, loba	*Alsamma, Loba!*
Köda Gotts nama alsama, loba	*Chönd allesamma, Loba!*
Weni era fä a pfiffa a,	*Wenne anam Be ha pfiffa!*
so köd alsama zua a schlicha,	*So chönd allsamma zuha schlicha.*
wohl zua, do zua, trib ia Gotts nama,	*Wol zuha, da zuha; trieb iha allsamma,*
wohl zua, beser zua,	*wohl zuha, beß'r zuha,*
höbsch sönds und frey,	*hüpsch sinds, und frey,*
holdseelig dor zua loba,	*holdselig dazu, Loba!*
b'hüets Gott alsama, loba.	
Wäss wohl, wen mir singa vergoth,	*Wäß wohl wemmer z'singa vergaht,*
wen zwo wiega i der stuba stoth,	*wenn zwo Wiega i der Stuba staht,*
wen der ma mit füsta drischlot,	*wenn der Ma mit Fäusta dri schlath*
und der wend	*und der Wind*
zuo alla löchra ia blost. loba.	*zu alla Löchra inna blast, Loba!*
Trib mer ia, Gotts nama:	*Trieb iha, iha allsamma,*
die hinckat, die stinckat,	*die Hinket, die Stinket,*
die g'scheget, die g'fleckht,	*die Bläzet, die G'scheket,*
die glazet, die blatzet,	*die Blasset, die G'fleket,*
schwantzeri, tantzeri,	*die Schwanzere, Tanzere,*
glintzeri, blintzeri,	*Glinzere, Blinzere,*
d'lehneri, d'freneri,	*d'Lehnere, d'Fehnere,*
d'hossleri, d'mosleri,	*d'Haslere, d'Schmalzere,*
d'horeri, d'schoreri,	*d'Mosere,*
s'halb örli unds mörli,	*d'Halböhrli, s'Mörli,*
s'ä äugli, s'trüfäugli,	*Sääugli, s'Tröfäugli,*
die erst galt und die alt,	*die erst Gäl,*
s'krombä und die ä,	*und die Altschrombä*
der gross bauch und die rauch,	*und die ä der Großbuch, und die Rauch,*
d'läng bäneri, d'hag läneri,	*d'Längbänere, d'Haglenere;*
trib ia, wohl zua,	*Trieb iha, wol zuha,*
wohl zua, bas zua, loba.	*da zuha, bas zuha, Loba!*
Sed das i g'weibet ha,	*Seit daß i g'wybet ha,*
ha i kä brodt me ka,	*ha i kä Brod me g'ha,*
sed das i g'weibet ha,	*seit daß i g'wybet ha,*
ha i kä glückh me ka.	*ha i kä Glück me g'ha! Loba!*
Trib mer ia die g'schiltata vier,	
si schlichet hüna noa mit am stier.	
Wohl zua, do zua, bas zua loba.	
Wens ada wohl gott	*Wenns a so wohl gaht,*
und nimer stil stoth,	*und niena stillstaht,*

so ist jo grota,	*so isch ja grotha,*
grota, loba.	*grotha Loba!*
Ist käna lütha bas	*S'ist käne Lütha bas*
as ösra küa,	*als usra Kühah;*
sie trinckhit us dem bach	*Sie trinket uss em Bach,*
und möget trüa.	*und möget trüjah!*

The relationship between these texts of the Appenzell *Kühreien* and the alphorn is intriguing. The alphorn evolved so that the herdsman could carry out his work: the alphorn's call is much louder than that of a human voice, and thus it can be used for communication over a substantially greater distance. For this, the words are not relevant. Yet the music here fits the words perfectly. Moreover, the notes to which the text is set are restricted to those playable on an alphorn, and when the *Kühreien* is sung, the voice uses the unique intonation of the 'alphorn *fa*' (see p. 20). This creates a fascinating symbiosis and gives rise to the question as to which came first. Perhaps the herdsman was accompanied on his journey by a companion who sang along; alternatively, a vocal version could have been created in imitation of the alphorn's music and sung by those left behind in the village when the herdsman was away, to pass the time or while otherwise occupied.

The texts provide valuable information about the process of the *Kühreien*. An examination of the words in Brogerin's *Liederbüchlein* reveals a number of separate features, which follow the sections in the music. The opening text describes how the herdsman will gather the animals, to lead them to the mountains where, after spending the winter confined to their stalls, they will enjoy the freedom of the mountain pastures. He expresses his pleasure to be free in the mountains again and repeatedly calls upon God in thanks and praise.

After the opening section, the passages of repeating motifs use several textual elements that are also commonly found in *Kühreien* from other regions of Switzerland. The repeated '*lo, lo, lo*' etc. is a wordless vocalisation, much as 'la, la, la' is found in English: it might be considered the vocal equivalent of a nonchalant whistle. The word '*loba*' is particularly associated with a *Kühreien* and can be seen in most transcriptions that occur with text; indeed its association with this type of music has already been seen, with the use of the word by Rhaw in 1545 to identify his Appenzell transcription as *Kühreien* music. The word occurs with a variety of spellings including *Lobe!, Loba!, Lioba!, Lhoba!, lobela!* or *Liauba!* It is a common call used by a Swiss cowherd when looking after his animals.

The next section of the text is a list of the animals in the care of the herdsman. This may well be merely a checklist so that he can be sure that no animals go missing on the journey or in the mountain pastures. Often in the *Kühreien*, as here, though, it is not a list of the actual names of the animals. Names are found recorded in other places, for example on a painting reproduced as a postcard in the Appenzell region. Milking cows, like dogs, are given names by their owners as they are kept for many years, whereas pigs or geese, that are only reared for slaughter, generally are not given names.

Fig. 4.7. Late nineteenth-century postcard from Appenzell (Guggenheim & Co., Zürich) that shows the cows as they descend from the high pastures at the end of the summer, with their names. The style of clothing, the farmhouse and the white goats are all typical of the Appenzell region.

The rhythmic use of motifs in a *Kühreien* may reflect the rhythm of walking; names may also appear in a rhyming pattern to help the herdsman to remember which animals he must look after. Most colourfully, though, in Brogerin's text the herdsman enumerates the animals in his care with his own descriptions of the cows, like 'smelly one', 'lame one', 'the one that scratches', 'the one with a weeping eye' etc., rather than with their actual names, presumably either for his own amusement, or as a more practical *aide-memoire*.

To what extent the list of animals in Brogerin's version of the Appenzell *Kühreien* is a list of the specific animals taken up to the mountain pastures in one particular year cannot be known. It might be so, or it might be a version sung to a young child on a grandfather's knee, in recollection of the old man's favourite animals and choice descriptions from his former days as a herdsman. It is possible to imagine an element of collation in such a scenario and that the repeat of the rhythmic litany of amusing descriptions of the animals could delight a young child many times over. Thus might such a text evolve from something merely functional into an item of folklore. That this may have become the case here is suggested by the similarity of the text in Brogerin's version with that of 75 years later, in the version of this *Kühreien* in the printed collections that first appeared in 1805. The similarity between the two versions of the text indicates that it had at some stage evolved from its free improvisatory origins into a fairly fixed version: this may indeed have happened even before Brogerin's version was written down.

There are, however, a number of small but significant differences between Brogerin's and Wagner's texts (see the direct comparison on p. 139). The words are rewritten in a Bernese version of Swiss German, with revised spellings and some vowels adjusted from those that reflect the Appenzell dialect. As had become normal for German script, upper case letters are now inserted for the nouns, and the ß is incorporated. A difficulty has arisen, though, in that several Appenzell dialect words have been mistranslated by the author who was not familiar with the local linguistic nuances. For example, '*die erst Galt*', which in the Appenzell dialect means the young cow before she has produced her first milk, has been translated as '*die erste Gäl*' which has no such meaning. In the list of individual cows, '*die alt, s'krombä*' (the old one, the crooked legged one) has been combined into a word with no meaning '*die Altschrombä*'. In addition, in an attempt to avoid conflicting religious sensitivities, the text has been altered to remove all the references to God that appear in the 1730 version. '*Gotts nama alsama*' (in God's name, all together) has been replaced with '*Allsamma, mit Namma*' (all together, with their names). Similar phrases replace every other reference to God in the earlier text. It is not known whether these alterations were made by Wagner, or whether a secular version existed before 1805.

Musical characteristics

With regard to the musical content, the opening phrase of this *Kühreien* material has two different versions. The rising line from tonic to dominant sometimes includes the supertonic, and sometimes does not. The consistent features of the opening are the initial tonic, the mediant, the subdominant and the dominant. The rhythm is variable: Rhaw's version lingers on the initial note, whereas the other two examples given here do not. Other rhythms will be encountered in subsequent examples. Indeed freedom from rhythmic constraint is a fundamental feature of the music that a herdsman plays to his cattle (see a letter written by Viotti reproduced on p. 158).

After this rising motif, in Rhaw's version the dominant note is repeated, with longer and shorter notes, before the music descends to the tonic again by way of a number of half-closes on the supertonic and the lower dominant. The first section settles back on the tonic in Fig. 4.2 on line 4, with a short repeated closing phrase. In the two later versions quoted above, there is some immediate elaboration of the upper dominant before the descent concludes the phrase in a much shorter time-span than in Rhaw's version. The amount and style of elaboration at this point in the various transcriptions of this *Kühreien* material is very varied; in some cases, there is none. Time spent on or around the dominant, after an initial rising passage, could reflect that at times the cattle can be assembled for the journey quickly, while sometimes this is a more lengthy process.

The beginning of the next section of this music reflects that the cattle have gathered and the journey into the mountains is about to begin. This is marked with a double bar in the transcriptions of Brogerin and Wagner/Kuhn (Fig. 4.5 line 2, and Fig. 4.6 at the end of line 1), but is not so clearly identified by Rhaw. It is the start of a series of repeating motivic cells used to call the animals on the journey. The choice of motif, the number of different cells included and the number of times each cell is repeated are different in almost every transcription. Some of these motifs appear in many transcriptions; some are unique to one version. One that is common is the three-note motif seen after the first double bar in both the Brogerin and the Wagner/Kuhn transcriptions. It often appears either with the rhythm shown by Brogerin, with all notes of equal length, or with the rhythm shown by Wagner/Kuhn, with the first note of the three-note cells elongated each time. A section normally ends with a paused note; a new motif is sometimes in a new pulse and in the two later transcriptions above, is signalled with a double bar. Sometimes the opening idea returns in between the motivic sections, sometimes it appears just at the end, sometimes it does not return. In some instances a recurrence is identical to the opening version, on other occasions it is a variant of that.

This *Kühreien* music, then, was known not only in Appenzell: it was also familiar to a composer in Leipzig in 1545, and it was included in a collection of Swiss music published in Bern in 1805. A version of the Appenzell *Kühreien* was requested by Princess Anne, later Queen Anne of England (1665–1714), with whom it was apparently a great favourite: it was said to have been used in services in the Queen's Chapel.[11]

Fig. 4.8. Transcript of the copy of the Appenzell *Kühreien* that was sent to Princess Anne of England in the late seventeenth century.[12]

Association with Homesickness

Other sources indicate not only that this music was known elsewhere, but also that it had acquired a special status in the minds of the Swiss. In 1710, the German doctor and medical writer Theodor Zwinger wrote in his *Dissertationem Medicarum Selectorum* a detailed account of the illness of *pothopatridalgia* (homesickness), a serious condition which, he stated, could cause death in severe cases. Zwinger observed that Swiss mercenaries working in foreign lands could be overcome by this condition when hearing the Appenzell *Kühreien* and he records that for this reason the singing of the melody and the playing of the alphorn among the troops was banned.

> ... those who hear it, while away from home, soldiers, reminded of the delights of their homelands, are immediately afflicted with this illness, especially when among others of their countrymen, to whom it is naturally very painful. When brought before a Military Tribunal, some are so affected by the longing for their home that they may die of a burning fever. In order to prevent this happening any more, it was forbidden by a strict law to sing this song, known in the local speech as the *Kuh-Reyen*, or to play the alphorn. For those who are curious, it is reproduced here, in musical notation, so that the reader can judge for himself whether this is an effect intrinsic to the music, or whether it is something that rests in the minds of the Swiss.[13]

Zwinger reproduces in the book a version of this *Kühreien* (see Fig. 4.9), with the identical opening of the version quoted by Rhaw, so that the reader can judge for himself whether the tune has peculiar properties or whether its power lay purely in the minds of those for whom it had special associations. So even before the time of Brogerin, this melodic material appears to have acquired the status of the Swiss national tune. Although the original purpose of the music was still referred to by the title *Kühreien*, it was the melodic characteristics, independent of its text and its association with the alphorn, that were for the Swiss a symbol of their identity. Zwinger reports as a separate observation that the alphorn itself invoked an equally powerful response as a reminder of the Swiss homeland such that in certain situations it was forbidden too.

The opening phrase in Zwinger's transcription reveals its origins as an alphorn melody with the presence of the 'alphorn *fa*'. It has been noted that in the 'scale' played by an alphorn on the natural harmonics nos. 8, 9, 10, 11 and 12, the 'alphorn *fa*' (no. 11) is sharper than a perfect fourth above its tonic (harmonic no. 8). Thus this alphorn scale has a characteristic sound that is dictated by the fact that it is the natural acoustic product a long tube. The sharp fourth degree of the scale is not a feature of other instruments, and it has been seen that composers choose to incorporate the scale with an augmented fourth as a signifier of this rustic sound. Zwinger also includes in his transcription the final 'flicked' high note with which an alphorn player sometimes ends a performance. This has been seen in transcriptions of alphorn music in other contexts (for example p. 83 and p. 120), but it does not appear in the versions of the Appenzell *Kühreien* of Rhaw, Brogerin or Wagner; Zwinger's source must therefore have been a live performance or another written version of the melody.

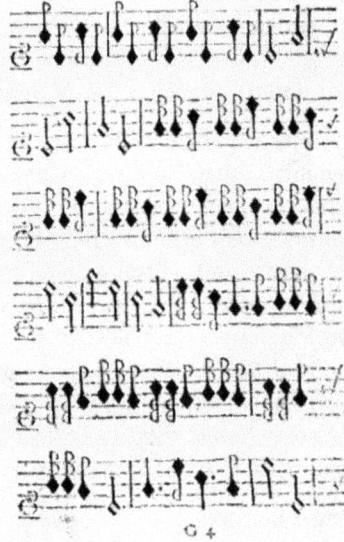

Fig. 4.9. *Cantilena Helvetica der Kühe-Reyen dicta,* the Appenzell *Kühreien,* quoted under 'Homesickness' in Zwinger's *Dissertationem Medicarum Selectorum,* 1710.[14]

The Swiss writer Jean-Jacques Rousseau in his *Dictionnaire de Musique* (1768) also commented on the phenomenon of homesickness caused among the Swiss abroad upon hearing 'the celebrated *Rans des Vaches*': here he uses the French term for the *Kühreien* (procession or row of cows). Rousseau too reported that when Swiss mercenaries were employed abroad, it was forbidden on pain of death to play, whistle or sing the tune because it caused those who heard it to burst into tears, to desert or even die, so much did it arouse in them a longing to see their country again.

> I have attached here the celebrated *Rans-des-Vaches*, this Air so loved by the Swiss that it was forbidden on pain of death to play it among the soldiers, because it caused them to give up their arms, desert or die when they heard it, arousing in them such desire to see their homeland again. One searches in vain in this tune for the strong energy capable of producing such astonishing effects. These reactions, which do not affect others, arise only in those used to the way of life, the memories, the thousand circumstances recalled by this tune in those who hear it, and their memory of their country, their former pleasures, their youth, and all the facets of their lives, provokes in them a deep sadness at what they have lost. Thus the music does not bring them to this circumstance as music, but as a signal to the memory. This Air, although still the same one, does not produce the same effect any more as it used to among the Swiss, because they are no longer familiar with that simple way of life, and they are not reminded of something that they have lost.[15]

Fig. 4.10. *Air Suisse appelé le Rans des Vaches*, the Appenzell *Kühreien* reproduced in Rousseau's *Dictionnaire de Musique*, 1768.

The music of the *Ranz des Vaches* (a term that also appears with many spellings) reproduced in Rousseau's *Dictionnaire de Musique* is similar to, but not exactly the same as, that quoted by Zwinger 58 years earlier. It is a different version, thus drawn from another different source. Although the opening notes are the same as in the music identified as Appenzell *Kühreien* material by Rhau and Zwinger, and it retains all the characteristics of alphorn music, Rousseau not only gives it the French Swiss version of its title, he describes it as a melody played on a *cornemuse* (old French for horn and bag, in other words, the bagpipe). Thus it is no longer defined either by its canton, its linguistic roots or its origin as an alphorn melody. However, like Zwinger, Rousseau does reproduce the final high 'flicked note' that is characteristic of alphorn playing.

Rousseau's comments about this music reflect a markedly different situation from that of Zwinger. It is written two generations later, and Rousseau's text speaks of this effect of homesickness as one in the past: he observes that the melody no longer holds the power that it used to with Swiss mercenaries stationed abroad. A profound change had occurred in the use of the alphorn and indeed the entire musical world in a large part of Switzerland in the period between the writing of Zwinger and that of Rousseau: much of the country had come under the influence of the Protestant Reformation.

Until the middle of the sixteenth century, the herdsman in the mountains was, of necessity, an alphorn player. In large tracts of the country there then followed a gradual change of fortune for the alphorn and the way of life that was dependent upon it. The Reformation, under the leadership of Ulrich Zwingli (1484–1531) in the east of the country and John Calvin (1509–1564) in the west, took hold in Switzerland and the reformers declared that musical instruments were tools of the devil. Following decisions made at several Synods towards the end of the sixteenth century, instruments—including church organs—were systematically destroyed. As with many other areas of Europe, around two-thirds of Switzerland was eventually to become Protestant, and in these regions the alphorn died out. Only in areas that remained Roman Catholic did the instrument survive: the high mountain regions of central Switzerland, Ticino and part of Appenzell.

The writings of Zwinger and Rousseau thus reflect the state of the alphorn in Swiss culture both before and after this new situation. Zwinger wrote at a poignant time: alphorns were no longer heard in many regions of Switzerland, but older people would still have remembered its sound from their childhood. The effect of knowing that this music was no longer played in their mountains and the memory of the heartbreak caused by the destruction of the instruments and the way of life that was dependent on it, could easily have made it unbearable for Swiss abroad to hear the famous Appenzell *Kühreien*. By the time of Rousseau's publication, it appears that this effect was no longer felt so deeply by subsequent generations of Swiss who had grown up under the influence of the Reformation.

The decline of the alphorn in the Swiss psyche was also the result of the increasing urbanisation and industrialisation of the Swiss Confederation. Farming practices were of necessity forced to change and during the course of the eighteenth century more and more Swiss either emigrated or moved into the fast-growing towns and cities. In the past it had been a daily routine in mountain communities to listen out for the signal 'all is well' from the herdsman at nightfall; this ceased to be part of the lives of successive generations of Swiss for whom a pastoral way of life was no longer familiar.

Sometimes, non-Swiss were at a loss to fully understand the reported power of the *Kühreien* in the minds of the Swiss. Learned British travellers were acquainted with reports of the phenomenon; for example, James Boswell and Samuel Johnson referred to Rousseau's comments about homesickness caused among Swiss soldiers by the sound of the Appenzell music. Boswell muses over this in his diary of their travels (1777) and attempts to find parallels in his own experience:

> Much of the effect of musick, I am satisfied, is owing to the association of ideas. That air, † [the footnote contains a translation of Rousseau's text] which instantly and irresistibly excites the Swiss, when in a foreign land, the *maladie du pais*, has, I am told, no intrinsick power of sound. And I know from my own experience, that Scotch reels, though brisk, make me melancholy, because I used to hear them in my early years, at a time when Mr. Pitt called for soldiers "from the mountains of the north," and numbers of brave Highlanders were going abroad, never to return. Whereas airs in "The Beggar's Opera," many of which are soft, never fail to render me gay, because they are associated with the warm sensations and high spirits of London.[16]

William Wordsworth wrote a sonnet on the subject in 1820, in an anthology of poetry entitled *Memorials of a Tour on the Continent*. Unaware of the true depth of resonance of this music in the history of the Swiss people, he expresses more scepticism about the reported profundity of its effect on them:

On hearing the *Ranz des Vaches* on the top of the Pass of St Gothard.

> I listen – but no faculty of mine
> Avails those modulations to detect,
> Which, heard in foreign lands, the Swiss affect
> With tenderest passion; leaving him to pine
> (So fame reports) and die, his sweet-breathed kine
> Remembering, and green Alpine pastures decked

With vernal flowers. Yet may we not reject
The tale as fabulous. Here while I recline,
Mindful how others by this simple Strain
Are moved, for me – upon this Mountain named
Of God himself from dread pre-eminence –
Aspiring thoughts, by memory reclaimed,
Yield to the Music's touching influence;
And joys of distant home my heart enchain.[17]

New Lyrics

It was perhaps inevitable that at some stage, new words would be given to this music to reflect the emotion of homesickness. By the end of the eighteenth century, 'the Appenzell *Kühreien*' was becoming known with just such a text, in French. Benjamin Laborde, in *L'essai sur la Musique Ancienne et Moderne* written in Paris in 1780, quoted the 'famous' Appenzell music with the following lyric:

Quand reverrai-je en un jour	When will I see again one day
Tous les objets de mon amour:	All the objects of my love:
Nos claire ruisseaux,	Our clear streams,
Nos coteaux,	Our hills,
Nos hameaux,	Our villages,
Nos montagnes?	Our mountains?
Et l'ornement des nos compaignes?	And the beauty of our countryside?
La si gentil le sabeau	The gentle touch of our shoes
A l'ombre d'un ormeau,	In the shade of an elm,
Quand danserai-je	When I will dance
au son du chalumeau?	to the sound of the pipe?
Mon pere,	My father,
Ma mere,	My mother,
Mon frere,	My brother,
Ma soeur,	My sister,
Mes agneaux,	My lambs,
Mes troupeaux,	My herds,
Ma bergere,	My shepherdess,
Quand reverrai-je en un jour,	When will I see again one day
Tous les objets de mon amour.	All the objects of my love.

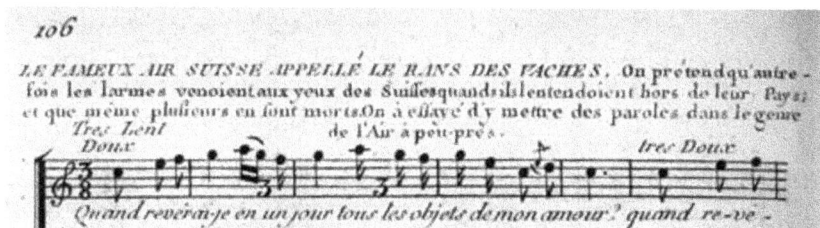

Fig. 4.11. Appenzell music with text that begins '*Quand reverrai-je*' in Laborde's *L'essai sur la Musique Ancienne et Moderne* written in Paris in 1780, bars 1–5.[18]

This version is included in the *Acht Schweizer-Kühreihen* of 1805. Kuhn in the introduction to his subsequent *Sammlung* of 1812 quotes Laborde as the source, but there is some discussion as to whether he was in fact the author of these lyrics.

The circumstances that led to such a text were described by Robert John Thornton in *Philosophy of Medicine, or Medical Extracts on the Nature of Health* in 1797. He describes the music not with reference to its origins, but as an observer who recognises its evocative simplicity:

> That the passion for one's country is increased by absence, is particularly manifested by the natives of Switzerland. They were so affected by a little air, expressive of their situation, that it is affirmed by several, that it once excited so exquisite a solicitude, that it was therefore prohibited to be played in France upon pain of death. … [the above lyrics are quoted] … In this air the images are all rural and simple, and in the highest degree affecting. The music is also remarkable for its simplicity, and sudden transition of measure, varying frequently from Allegro to Andante. When this little air was played or sung to the Swiss soldiers, they would express sighs and tears, and would not unfrequently [*sic*] desert in the impulse of the moment; and such as shewed silent dejection, and scorned so base a procedure, fell martyrs to their own feelings, by a disease called Nostalgia.[19]

Within Switzerland, however, the Appenzell *Kühreien* had also been reinvented. Alongside its inclusion in the 1805 and subsequent collections in two versions, the one closely related to that of Brogerin and the setting with the text '*Quand reverrai-je*' from Laborde, there is a third version with a further new text, given the title '*Ran* [*sic*] *de Vaches des Ormonts*'. Despite this caption that gives its source as a region in the west of Switzerland (far from Appenzell which is the easternmost canton), the music of this too comprises features that identify its source as Appenzell *Kühreien* material. However, it has yet another text that tells a story based in the hills of Colombettes, in the region of Ormont, on the edge of the Gruyère mountains in the canton of Fribourg. The text is in the local French patois.

Fig. 4.12. *Ran de Vaches des Ormonts*, in *Sammlung von Schweizer Kühreihen und alten Volkliedern*, 1812.[20]

The text of the song opens with material similar in sentiment to that of its Appenzell counterpart:

Les Armaillis dé Colombetta	The herdsmen of Colombette
De bon matin sé sont leva,	Rise early in the morning
Ah! Ah! Lioba, Lioba, portaria.	Ah! Ah! Rejoice, rejoice, milking.
Lioba, Lioba, portaria.	Rejoice, rejoice, milking.
Veni dé tote, petite, grozze,	Come all of you, little, big,
E blianz é néré,	The white and black,
d'zou véné autré,	all you others come,
Dezo stou tzano,	Come under the oak tree,
yio, yie, tario,	you, you, wait,
Dezo stou trimblio,	Come under the rustling leaves,
yio, yie, trinzo!	you, you to be milked.
Lioba, lioba portaria.	Rejoice, rejoice, milking.
Lioba, lioba portaria.	Rejoice, rejoice, milking.[21]

It continues with 19 verses. The music is formalised into two repeating refrains based on the two versions of the opening rising music, and verses set to the motivic passages. It tells the story of a cowherd, a priest and a pretty young girl. *Armaillis* is a local Swiss French dialect word for cowherds (Latin: *armentum*, herd). In the subsequent edition of the *Sammlung von Schweizer Kühreihen und alten Volksliedern* of 1818, the title of the song reads *Ranz des Vaches des Alpes de Gruyère ou du Canton de Frybourg*, a reflection of some of the variety of descriptions of the location in which it is set.

This song, with some alteration to spellings and minor melodic detail, appeared in a number of contemporary sources. In a publication by brothers Louis and Philippe-Sirice Bridel, *La Conservateur Suisse ou Recueil Complet des Étrennes Helvétiennes* (1813), for example, it is written thus:

Fig. 4.13. Opening refrain and first verse of the *Ranz des Vaches des Ormonds* [sic], version from *La Conservateur Suisse ou Recueil Complet des Étrennes Helvétiennes.*[22]

Similar music is also found with the source given as the Jura mountains in the canton of Vaud and Simplon in the canton of Valais.[23] Thus the music of the German-speaking, easternmost canton of the Swiss Confederation had become adopted by the inhabitants of the French-speaking western part. The French term *Ranz des Vaches* for this music was to become as common as the German term *Kühreien*.

Through this song, the old Appenzell alphorn calls were popularised in an unusual circumstance. Since 1797, a *Fête des Vignerons* (Winegrowers' Festival) has been held approximately every 20 years in Vevey, some 25 miles from Colombettes, on Lake Geneva. At the *Fête* of 1819, the herdsmen mounted a small dramatic interlude, together with their cattle:

> The herd stopped, the farmers removed their caps and replaced them
> with berets made of leather; after rolling up their sleeves they milked the
> cows and imitated the process of making cheese, all the time singing in
> chorus some verses of the *Ranz des Vaches*.[24]

Following its first appearance at the Vevey wine festival of 1819, the singing of this *Ranz* became a ritual part of the proceedings. The American writer James Fenimore Cooper, author of the novel *Last of the Mohicans*, wrote a moving account of the second Festival of 1833. The programme for the festival included the text of *Les Armaillis de Colombettes*, and the communal singing of the melody assumed an aura of solemnity and deep-felt rootedness in the land and the country:

> No sooner had the herdsmen and milkmaids sung the first two stanzas, than a deep silence descended on the crowd; then, as the verses of the singers rose in the air, numerous echoes mounted in the crowd as they repeated the simple music; and the cry *Liauba! Liauba!* rang out simultaneously from thousands of voices as if directing child-like vows to the mountains. The final verses united in a general outburst of exuberant enthusiasm.[25]

Fig. 4.14. Herdsmen with their cattle enter the arena at the *Fête des Vignerons*, Vevey, 2019, in preparation for the singing of the *Ranz des Vaches*. Photo: Frances Jones.

Today in Switzerland this version of the music has acquired the status of an anthem to be sung at national festivals and private celebrations, at formal events and casual gatherings, sung either by massed crowds or as a solo, in unison or harmony, sometimes with instrumental or even orchestral accompaniment. It features on many CD recordings of Swiss music.

So the old Appenzell *Kühreien* had taken on two different roles. Within Switzerland, it became—and to some extent still is—the best-loved national song. Its text tells a story of life and love in a typical Swiss mountain setting. Outside Switzerland, it has different lyrics: those of homesickness for the Swiss landscape and pastoral way of life. The melody was still played on the alphorn too. In 1840 the anonymous author of an article entitled 'On the National Songs and Music of Switzerland' in the London journal *The New Monthly Magazine and Humorist* not only describes his experience of the alphorn and the 'alphorn *fa*'. He also gives a quotation of the opening of the famous Swiss melody:

> Its sound resembles that of a muffled trumpet; but it is much more powerful, rude, and penetrating, especially in the higher notes of the scale, which scale in an Alp-horn of five feet would be nearly that of a B flat trumpet; and of ten feet that of the common French-horn in B flat basso; the upper F of both the trumpet and the French-horn being rather sharper than the fourth of the scale should be; but the F of the Alp-horn is even more imperfect, being, in fact, almost an F sharp. It is, indeed, to this very imperfection in the formation of the natural and the sharp notes, that the very peculiar and highly-characteristic effect of the instrument (when heard under its appropriate circumstance of time and place) is in great measure attributable. In the following passage, for instance, in which the notes marked with an asterisk would in strictness be F natural, the effect of the peculiar melody requires that the F's should be sharp or very nearly so.

> … As a termination to his "*Kühreihe*," the performer usually selects this plaintive and peculiar note, on which he dwells with long and expressive emphasis, and its effect on the hearers is indescribably singular and impressive, more especially when heard from afar, as it breaks upon the silence of the evening, and is reverberated in softened and varied tones from the surrounding hills. Towards sunset, in the summer months, these "*Kühreien*" may be heard, sounding from different points of the higher lands, on which the *chalets** [a footnote describes the mountain huts where the herdsman and his cattle slept and where cheese was made] or extensive sheds for the shelter of the cattle at night, are situated …[26]

The author further comments on the ability of the cows to recognise their own *Kühreien*:

> ... it is not a little curious to observe the sagacity with which the leaders, or *Dreichalkühe* of the various herds, which during the day have been indiscriminately scattered over the pasturages of the lower plain, recognise and obey this signal of recall; each particular herd dividing from the rest, and slowly filing off in the direction of its own herdsman, the sound of whose horn, or perhaps his particular method of instrumentation, they appear to be capable of distinguishing. Such at least was the effect produced on our minds by this Alpestral scene, which we have frequently witnessed in mountain districts.[27]

In contrast to the musings of Wordsworth quoted earlier, this detailed description demonstrates that visitors from abroad could indeed be profoundly affected by this melody when it was heard in an appropriate context.

The Appenzell *Kühreien* in concert works

The next phase of the development of the Appenzell *Kühreien* was its increasing incorporation into formal, composed music as a recognisable melodic signifier, by non-Swiss composers who came into contact either with the melody, or with its effect on Swiss people abroad, or both. In some cases, the music was simply a transcription for piano, or voice and piano, while in others it was used as the basis of a Fantasie or a set of variations. Sometimes the characteristic melodic shapes were quoted for a specific reason in larger works. There follows an exploration of a selection of these compositions.

Muzio Clementi (1752–1832) was a key figure in the development of a technique specific to the piano in contrast to that of the harpsichord. Much of his output as a composer was designed as teaching material for this new instrument that incorporated an exploration of its tonal capabilities. Clementi lived in London for much of his life where he developed a successful publishing and piano-building business; he also travelled widely throughout Europe and stayed in Switzerland on several occasions. In 1797 he published Six Sonatinas, Op. 36: the second movement of Sonatina No. 5 has the title *Air Suisse* and is a decorative version of the Appenzell *Kühreien*. The main rising theme is preceded and followed with sections based on the familiar three-note repeating motifs. Clementi incorporates typical *Kühreien* echo effects and a *rallentando* to a pause; his simple folk-like accompaniment in places resembles a rustic drone.

Fig. 4.15. Clementi, Six Sonatinas No. 5: *Air Suisse*, bars 23–34.[28]

Alongside Clementi, fellow Italian Giovanni Battista Viotti (1755–1824) was also an active figure in the musical life of London at this time. Clementi and Viotti were together instrumental in the foundation of the Philharmonic Society and the Royal Academy of Music. In the same year as the publication of Clementi's Sonatinas, above, Viotti spent some time in Switzerland. While walking in the canton of Vaud, he was so struck by the sound of an alphorn playing the 'famous' *Ranz des Vaches* that he wrote the following letter to his London landlady, Mrs Chinnery. He describes the magical effect of the music and its setting, its form and its impact.

> I was walking alone, towards the end of the day... I descended the valleys and traversed the heights. At length chance brought me to a valley which, on arousing from my waking dream, I discovered to be full of delight. It reminded me of one of those wonderful retreats so beautifully described by Gesner: flowers, meadows, small streams, all united to form a picture of perfect harmony. There, without being tired, I sat against a rock ... While thus sitting, wrapped in this slumber of the soul, sounds broke upon my ear which were sometimes hurried, sometimes prolonged and sustained, and which were softly repeated by the echoes around. I found they came from a mountain-horn, and their effect was heightened by a plaintive female voice ... and a procession of cows was descending calmly down the mountain. Struck as if by enchantment, I started from my reverie, listened with breathless attention, and learnt, or rather engraved upon my memory, the Ranz des Vaches which I enclose ... in order to understand all its beauties, you ought to be transported to the scene in which I heard it, and to feel all the excitement that such a moment inspired.[29]

Viotti described the experience more than once: in another letter, after a description of the occasion on which he heard the music, he elaborated on the music itself, with the explanation that the music must not be structured or be given any pulse if it is to be authentic and retain its charm and character:

> This *Rans des Vaches* is not the one that we know from our friend Jean-Jaques [Rousseau] ... I transcribed the notes without pulse, in other words without bars. The melody needs to be without structure in order to be its authentic self; the least pulse distorts its effect: it is more accurate to leave the sounds hanging in the air, as you cannot determine the time it takes for them to resound from one mountain to another. This is the feeling and the thought that brings authenticity, not pulse and rhythmic phrases. This *Rans des Vaches* put into bars becomes unnatural and loses its simplicity; therefore, to play it as I heard it, your imagination must take you to where it was born, and those in England must direct all their mental powers to being in Switzerland. This is how in some ravishing moments I have played it on my violin, so that people can hear it well.[30]

Fig. 4.16. Walkers gather to enjoy the sound of the alphorn as it reverberates in the landscape near La Dôle, Canton Vaud. The author plays with Bryony Stahel.
Photo: Martin Jones.

Fig. 4.17. *Ranz des Vaches* written down by Viotti in the canton of Vaud, transcription for violin.[31]

This melody bears the recognisable contours and phrases of the Appenzell *Kühreien*, but is sufficiently different from it that Viotti composed two quite different works that appear to reflect the two versions:

Fig. 4.18. Viotti, Violin Concerto No. 9, bars 1–2, which show influence from the *Ranz des Vaches* from Vaud.[32]

Fig. 4.19. Viotti, Serenade for piano with violin obbligato and cello, bars 1–5, which more closely resembles the earlier versions of the Appenzell *Kühreien*.[33]

While Clementi and Viotti were working in London, Paris was embroiled in the turmoil of the French Revolution (1789–1799). Two substantial works that incorporate the Appenzell *Kühreien* were written in Paris during this time. Both tell a significant story within the context of that political struggle, although each work uses the Swiss music for a different purpose.

André Grétry (1741–1813) set a French version of the story of William Tell in 1791. The libretto was created by Michel-Jean Sedaine, based on a play *Guillaume Tell* by Paris dramatist Antoine-Marin Lemierre. The leaders of the *Nouveau Regime* were determined to turn the nation away from the frivolity and artifice of the operas of the former aristocracy: they established a new set of musical styles with such themes as military pride, heroism against tyranny or celebration of peasant life. The story of the Swiss hero William Tell, who reputedly outwitted oppressors from the House of Habsburg in 1307, provided an ideal script. Two operas were written in Paris after the abolition of the monarchy based on this story: that of André Grétry, and another by Gioachino Rossini in 1829 (examined later, p. 209). Grétry's score opens with instructions that the stage should be set to show the son of William Tell playing a *Ranz des Vaches* as he stands on a rocky outcrop at sunrise. A procession of cattle should be visible in the distance:

> Act 1. Scene 1. The theatre represents the Swiss mountains at sunrise; a small meadow; in the distance William Tell's son is seen on a crag playing a *Ranz des Vaches*: one can see in the gap in the mountains the pastures of the cows that are passing by.[34]

The music begins in Scene 2, with 40 bars of Appenzell *Kühreien* material to establish the pastoral scene. The melody is given to the clarinet. Grétry uses the opening rising phrase, marked *Adagio*, which he alternates with interjections of the three-note motivic cells in *Allegro* tempo, in reflection of the character of the early transcriptions of the Appenzell *Kühreien*. Grétry varies the accompaniment for each section. Rippling string semiquavers support the opening phrase whereas short flourishes and held notes accompany the first triple-time passage. The subsequent sections are similarly marked by changes in the style of the accompaniment. The final triple metre section is accompanied with the imaginative instrumentation of a long bass note held on the violas, while the basso is given a quiet dominant marked *sontflute* (flautando). Each section ends with an atmospheric paused note. The motifs are supported by notes on a cow-horn in C: there are three differently pitched cows' horns required in the work. The typical alphorn final high 'flicked' note is present at the end of a number of the sections.

GUILLAUME TELL.

ACTE PREMIER.

SCENE PREMIERE

Le Théâtre Represente les montagnes de la Suisse, le lever de
l'aurore; un petit Pâtre; le fils de Guillaume Tell, est vu sur la -
pointe d'un rocher dans le lointain il joue le Rhans des Vaches:
On voit dans les entre deux des montagnes des Pâtres des Vaches
qui passent.

SCENE II.

Fig. 4.20. Music of the Appenzell *Kühreien* in the opening pages from the score of Grétry's opera *Guillaume Tell*, 1791.[35]

A second work written in Paris three years later that quotes the *Kühreien* from Appenzell is a one-act opera entitled *La Triomphe de la République, ou Le Camp de Grand Pré*, composed by François-Joseph Gossec (1734–1829). He had arrived in Paris in 1751 at the age of 17, where he became a student of Rameau. By his early twenties, he was already a key figure in Paris as a conductor, composer and teacher. As conductor of the *Garde Nationale*, he was an important musical figure in the French Revolution. Gossec's opera, written in 1794, celebrated a major victory during the Revolution. His original title was *Le Triomphe de la Liberté et La Trêve Interrompue* (The Triumph of Liberty and the Broken Truce), but this title was altered following the defeat of the monarchy in September 1792 to *Le Triomphe de la République, ou Le Camp de Grand Pré*. The libretto by Marie-Joseph Chénier describes the events at what proved to be a decisive battle at Grand Pré in 1792: fighting, waiting for news and the celebration of victory. Many foreign mercenaries fought in the Revolution, both for the King and for the revolutionaries; Swiss soldiers were particularly renowned for their bravery and skill. The final scene of Gossec's opera depicts the nations as they unite in celebration, through a series of melodies and dances from the various homelands of the soldiers: *Air pour les Polonois, Anglaise ou Bostoniene, Air pour les Suisses 'Rans des Vaches', Grivois, Valsque, Air pour les Negres*, and *Air pour les Savoisiens*, followed by a *Vielle* and a final *Contre Danse*.

Fig. 4.21. Gossec, *Air pour les Suisses Rans des Vaches.* Part of the final scene of *Le Triomphe de la République, ou Le Camp de Grand Pré.*[36]

Gossec's *Rans des Vaches* here quotes the opening rise and fall of the Appenzell melody in three different versions. These are presented very slowly (marked *Adagio*) with a smooth accompaniment that creates an atmosphere of solemnity and reflective calm. In contrast, these alternate with bright arpeggiating phrases in 3/8, marked *Allegro*, which are based on the contrasting three-note motifs commonly seen in other versions of the *Kühreien*. The clarinet is again chosen for the main motif, with the violins given faster dance-like interludes. Gossec additionally imitates the music of the alphorn with the raised fourth, irregular phrase-lengths and the inclusion of a final high 'flicked' note.

As various versions of the Appenzell *Kühreien* became more widely known across Western Europe, it became fashionable for composers to write their own settings of the music. A fine example of the incorporation of this music in a work for piano is a work by the Hungarian composer Franz Liszt (1811–1886). He was well-travelled and wrote much music in which he reflected his feelings about the places he visited. In his preface to *Tagebuch eines Wanderers* (Diary of a Traveller), written in 1836 at the age of 25, Liszt writes eloquently about his motivation for the composition of the work. He explains that he visited many places celebrated for their history or their poetry, but they did not just pass meaninglessly before his eyes—they penetrated his soul. This relationship between him and the places he visited is what he has tried to depict in these compositions. As he began to compose, the images intensified in his mind and organised themselves naturally.

> I recently came to know a number of new regions and places, many renowned for their history and their poetry. I felt the various natural forces and the associated events, not as meaningless images that passed before my eyes, rather as resonances deep within my soul; there arose between them and myself an undoubted and immediate relationship, an indefinable but clear connection, an inexplicable but definite bond. I tried then to create my strongest sensations, my most vivid impressions, in sound. After I started this work, the memories became more and more intense and they formed their own combinations and order …[37]

Tagebuch eines Wanderers comprises 18 piano pieces, some of which were written in Switzerland. They include many references to both alphorn music and yodelling. Alphorn music provides the main thematic material in five of the movements: *Die Tellskapelle,* two of the *Melodieenblüten von den Alpen, Kuhreigen* and *Ein Abend in den Bergen.* Quotations of other alphorn motifs in *Tagebuch eines Wanderers* will be explored in Chapter 5; however, the sixth in the set of *Melodieenblüten von den Alpen* comprises a solemn rendition of the Appenzell *Kühreien.* This is reminiscent not only of the music's early prayer-like connotations, but also of its reverential use at the Vevey Festivals. Liszt marks the statement of the opening phrases *Adagio molto espressivo, semplice* and gives each motif an appropriate pause at the end. The second theme from the *Kühreien* then appears in the tenor voice in 3/8, set with a drone underneath and against an elaboration of the melody in 1/4 in the right hand. After several other sections, the prayer-like *Adagio* section returns to close the movement.

Fig. 4.22. Liszt, *Tagebuch eines Wanderers*. Appenzell *Kühreien* material is the basis of the sixth of his *Melodieenblüten von den Alpen*. Bars 49–80.[38]

It was not uncommon to write Fantasies or sets of variations based on the Appenzell material. Many examples appear in keyboard music, and the melody is used in settings for other instruments too. One example of an extensive *Fantasie* that includes the Appenzell music was written for the harp by Gustavus von Holst (1799–1871). His father Matthias had been a harp player in the Imperial Russian court in St. Petersburg before moving to London as a music teacher; his grandson was the more famous composer Gustav Holst. Gustavus, like Matthias, was also a renowned harp player and teacher who composed much music for his instrument. He extended the family surname to 'von Holst' reputedly to improve his perceived social status in the eyes of his harp and piano students and settled in Cheltenham, where grandson Gustav was raised. (By a strange quirk of history Gustav Holst chose to remove the '*von*' by deed poll in 1918 to anglicise his name in response to anti-German sentiment.)

Gustavus wrote a set of variations for the harp based on music of the Alps, of which the opening pages use material from the Appenzell *Kühreien*. He called the work *Fantasia Tirolese, in which is introduced Tyrolean [sic] Airs and Ranz de Vaches, for the Harp*. The harp is popular in the Tyrol where it is the most common instrument used for accompaniment; it features in paintings on farmhouses and frequently appears still today in Austrian folk music groups. Despite the fact that Tyrol is in Austria (and part of northern Italy) and that the *Ranz des Vaches* is a Swiss phenomenon, Gustavus von Holst treats both the location and the melody as a unified 'Alpine' source of inspiration. He had the work published privately in London around 1826, and it is dedicated to the harpist Miss Speid.

Fig. 4.23. Painting on the wall of a chalet in the Austrian Tyrol. Photo: Frances Jones.

Gustavus provides detail for pedal changes and fingerings, and creates his atmosphere with the use of many special effects that can be achieved on the instrument, for example with the marking 'near the sounding board'; he also includes instructions to use swell-box louvres (*soupapes*) in the pillar of the harp, newly invented by the Parisian harp-maker Erard, with the indication 'From this mark ⊕ until this *, the swell pedal should be opened and closed after each note, so as to produce a reverberation of sound, or echo'. The final two long notes in the excerpt below also have the marking that the louvres should be opened and closed several times to create an atmospheric impression of reverberation for the *Ranz des Vaches* theme. This section is in a rocking triple time and has the subtitle *Pastorale*.

Fig. 4.24. The opening page of Gustavus von Holst's *Fantasia Tirolese* for the harp.[39]

Many salon pieces based on the now popular *Ranz des Vaches* were published with elaborate illustrations on the cover, although occasionally the artist employed to produce the drawing appears to have had scant knowledge of the background to the music. For example, a *Fantaisie sur le Ranz des Vaches* for solo piano by Louis Niedermeyer was printed by Pacini, the publisher of Rossini's operas in Paris. The illustration, by Parisian lithographer Langlamé, shows a wonderful depiction of a herdsman with an alphorn, although his familiarity with the flamboyant world of Italian opera, rather than the scenario of the *Ranz des Vaches*, is reflected in the stance and attire of the herdsman!

Fig. 4.25. *Fantaisie sur le Ranz des Vaches* for piano, by Louis Niedermeyer, lithograph on the cover.[40]

Vocal settings of the famous Swiss melody sometimes had new lyrics that reflected the music's origins in new ways. One such song is from the pen of Giacomo Meyerbeer (1791–1864), who travelled and studied throughout Europe and eventually settled in Paris. Meyerbeer used alphorn motifs in a number of his works, and he wrote a setting of the *Ranz des Vaches d'Appenzell* for soprano and piano in 1840. The title is *Chanson Suisse: Fais Sonner la Clochette: Ranz des Vaches d'Appenzell* (Swiss Song: Sound your little Bell: *Kühreien* from Appenzell).

The chorus carries the subheading '*Cri pour rappeler le troupeau*' (Cry for calling the herd). This is a strain of lyrics independent of the surge of interest in the melody at the Vevey wine festivals in the west of Switzerland: the text here is by the French dramatist Eugène Scribe who wrote libretti for Verdi and Rossini. It tells of a stranger who tries to entice a herdsman away from his rural way of life in Appenzell to earn his fortune elsewhere. Meyerbeer sets the chorus to Appenzell *Kühreien* music, against static or slow-moving harmony. He uses the version of the opening phrase with the raised fourth degree of the scale.

Fig. 4.26. Meyerbeer, Chorus to *Chanson Suisse: Fais Sonner la Clochette: Ranz des Vaches d'Appenzell*.[41]

Le Berger:

 Voici donc le soir,
 je vais la revoir,
 Mes vaches chéries
 Quittons les prairies,
 On m'attend déjà!

 Ah! Fais sonner ta clochette
 mon gentil troupeau,
 afin que Jeannette
 m'entende plûstôt.

 Mais de ce rocher
 Qui vois-je approcher?
 Étranger, sans doute,
 Tu cherches ta route?
 Jean te conduira!
 Ah! Fais sonner...

L'étranger:

 Voudrais-tu, berger,
 de destin changer?
 Si tu veux me suivre
 Gaiment tu peux vivre.

Le Berger:

 Moi quitter cela?

 Ah! Fais sonner ...

 Voi donc ce beau ciel,
 Le ciel d'Appenzell!
 Là c'est ma patrie,
 Là ma douce amie
 Souvent me chanta.

 Ah! Fais sonner ...

L'étranger:

 Tu peux au retour
 L'enrichir un jour,
 Tiens voici d'avance
 Cent écus de France.

Herdsman:

 Here in the evening
 I make my return,
 My lovely cows
 leave the meadows,
 They wait for me already!

 Ah! Sound your little bell
 my gentle herd,
 so that Jeannette
 Will hear me soon.

 But by that rock
 Who do I see approaching?
 A stranger, undoubtedly,
 Are you looking for your way?
 Jean will lead you.
 Ah! Sound your little bell . . .

Stranger:

 Herdsman, would you like
 to change your destiny?
 If you wish to follow me
 You could have a gay life.

Herdsman:

 Me leave this?

 Ah! Sound your little bell . . .

 Look at the beautiful sky,
 The sky of Appenzell!
 Here is my homeland,
 Here my gentle friend
 Who often sings to me.

 Ah! Sound your little bell . . .

Stranger:

 You could return
 Rich, one day,
 Take here an advance
 of a hundred French écus.

Le berger:	Herdsman:
Eh! Quoi les voilà?	Hey! What are these?
Ah! notre fortune est faite,	Ah! Our fortune is made,
Quittons le hameau,	We will leave the village,
Adieu mon Jeannette,	Goodbye my Jeannette,
Adieu mon troupeau.	Goodbye my herd.

L'étranger:	Stranger:
Les voilà	Here we are
Quittons le hameau	We will leave the village
partons . . .	Let us go . . .

Le berger:	Herdsman:
Mais, quel bruit	But what is this sound
dont mon coeur frémit,	That beats in my heart,
j'entends leur clochettes	I hear the cowbells
dont le son répète,	and the sound repeats,
tu nous fuis, ingrat!	you flee away, ungrateful!
Tiens, reprends ta richesse.	Come, take back your riches.
Je reste au hameau	I will stay in the village
avec ma maîtresse	with my sweetheart
avec mon troupeau.	with my herds.

L'étranger:	Stranger:
Tu restes au hameau?	You are staying in the village?
Eh, quoi, tu restes?	Hey, why do you stay?
Partons, viens!	Leave! Come!
Si tu veux me suivre	If you follow me
Gaiment tu peux vivre,	Gay your life can be,
Eh quoi! eh quoi!	Hey what? What?
Tu restes au hameau?	You are staying in the village?

An example of the Appenzell music used in a song setting where the text focuses on the source of the material, the alphorn, is a work by Richard Strauss (1864–1949). He was steeped in the world of the horn throughout his early life, as his father Franz was for 50 years the leading French horn player in Germany. Richard wrote most evocatively for the horn and was particularly skilled in the use of the instrument as a symbol of the landscape.[42] The subject matter of this song, entitled *Alphorn*, Op. 16, for soprano, French horn and piano, is highlighted by the use of both the *Kühreien* music from Appenzell and by the inclusion of a part for *obbligato* French horn. It was written in 1876 when Richard was twelve years old and is dedicated to his father.

The text, by the poet and psychologist Justinus Kerner, reflects on the haunting qualities of the sound of the alphorn. Strauss gives many alphorn-like phrases to the horn and opens with the characteristic strains of the Appenzell *Kühreien*, set over a still, quiet backdrop.

Ein Alphorn hör' ich schallen,	I hear an alphorn calling
Das mich von hinnen ruft,	But know not whence its sound:
Tönt es aus wald'gen Hallen?	From crag or woodland falling,
Tönt es aus blauer Luft?	From azure skies around,
Tönt es von Bergeshöhe,	From peak or flower-strewn hollow
Aus blumenreichen Thal?	Whence comes the haunting strain?
Wo ich nur geh' und stehe,	I walk and stand and follow
Hör ich'sin süßer Qual.	And feel the sweetest pain.
Bei Spiel und frohem Reigen,	For I am called up yonder
Einsam mit mir allein,	To paths and meadows high,
Tönt's, ohne je zu schweigen,	And as alone I wander
Tönt tief ins Herz hinein.	The endless sound seems nigh.
Noch nie hab'ich gefunden	For ever I'm enraptured
Den Ort, woher es schallt,	By such sweet music made,
Und nimmer wird gesunden	A homesick heart is captured:
Dies Herz, bis es verhallt.	Those echoes never fade.[43]

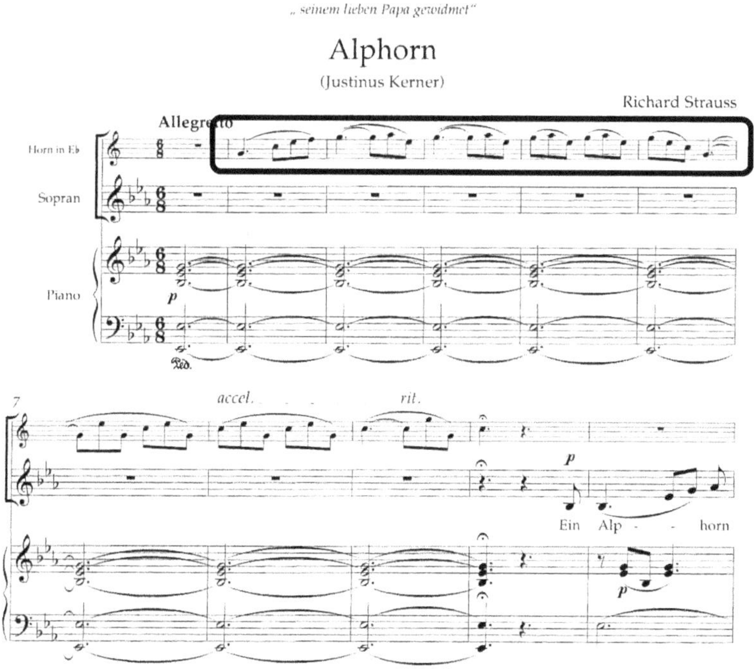

Fig. 4.27. The Appenzell motif opens Strauss's setting of Kerner's text *Alphorn*, Op. 16. Bars 1–11.[44]

Home, Sweet Home

The *Kühreien* from Appenzell was to experience a further transformation, one that would have a dramatic impact on the English-speaking world. This was its reincarnation with a text on the subject of homesickness in the English language, as the now much-loved song *Home, Sweet Home*. The song sold 100,000 copies in its first year of publication.

It was the work of composer Sir Henry Rowley Bishop (1786–1855). He was asked by the London publishing house Goulding, D'Almaine, Potter & Company to compile a collection of *Melodies of Various Nations* which was completed in 1821. Bishop wrote piano accompaniments and Thomas Bayly added lyrics to each of the melodies. Switzerland was represented by the Appenzell *Kühreien*, but there is an anomaly in the designation. Although Bishop's melody has the characteristic opening rising and falling phrase of the famous Appenzell tune and is given a poignant text that reflects the sentiments of nostalgia for the homeland, it has the appellation 'Sicilian'. It will become clear from its music, its text and from Bishop's later reference to the melody as the *Ranz des Vaches* (see below) that it is likely that the handwriting was misread by the printer and the original designation was 'Swiss' or 'Switzerland'.

Bishop uses both versions of the opening phrase here that signify the Appenzell *Kühreien*: the climb from tonic to dominant without the supertonic opens the piano introduction, whereas the full rising line from tonic to dominant opens the vocal line. The first line of the lyric 'To the home of my childhood', used as its title in the collection, immediately sets the stage for the emotional content of the rest of the song. Bishop is meticulous in his instruction as to the required mood for the piece, providing five indications *Larghetto, Sostenuto, Affettuoso, Soave e legatissimo* at the beginning.

There are four verses; the first gives an indication of the sentiment throughout:

> To the home of my childhood in sorrow I came,
> And I fondly expected to find it the same –
> Full of sunshine and joy, as I thought it to be
> In the days when the world was all sunshine to me:
> Those scenes were unalter'd by time, and I stood
> Looking down on the village half hid by the wood;
> That happy abode, where I us'd to possess
> A father's affection, a mother's caress.

Two years later, Bishop arranged the song for inclusion in his opera *Clari, or The Maid of Milan*, which was performed at the Theatre Royal, Covent Garden. The libretto for the opera was a play written by the American actor and dramatist John Payne, and the entire plot revolves around the theme of homesickness. Alongside the new title for this melody, *Home, Sweet Home*, Bishop adds the information that it was 'adapted from a national melody and arranged by Henry R. Bishop, 1823'.

Fig. 4.28. Bishop, *Melodies of Various Nations*: 'Sicilian' melody that opens with the shape of the Appenzell *Kühreien*.[45]

Its lyrics now transfer the connotations of homesickness, with which the Swiss melody was associated, to the American hearth and the song reappears at telling moments throughout the work. John Payne's version of the text reads:

Mid pleasures and palaces though we may roam,
Be it ever so humble, there's no place like home.
A charm from the skies seems to hallow us there,
Which seek thro' the world, is ne'er met with elsewhere.
Home, home, sweet sweet home,
There's no place like home, there's no place like home.

I gaze on the moon as I tread the drear wild,
And feel that my mother now thinks of her child;
As she looks on that moon from our own cottage door,
Thro' the woodbine whose fragrance shall cheer me no more.
Home, home, sweet sweet home,
There's no place like home, there's no place like home.

An exile from home, splendour dazzles in vain,
Oh, give me my lowly thatched cottage again;
The birds singing gaily that came at my call:
Give me them and that peace of mind, dearer than all.
Home, home, sweet sweet home,
There's no place like home, there's no place like home.[46]

The song became so popular that Bishop used it again in a sequel to *Clari*, another opera significantly entitled *Home, Sweet Home or the Ranz des Vaches*, which was produced at Covent Garden and in New York in 1829.

The song now exists in several slightly different versions, both in musical detail and in its lyrics. As with the old *Kühreien* and the version in Bishop's collection of *Melodies of Various Nations*, the opening is heard today both with the supertonic present and without.

Fig. 4.29. The opening of the melody *Home, Sweet Home* by Henry Rowley Bishop, based on the Appenzell *Kühreien*.

Despite its roots as a Swiss melody, it was quickly embraced both as a quintessential English song by the English and as an American song by Americans. It was to become the most widely sung and reproduced tune of its time. In particular, it was adopted both by soldiers while away from home and by their families left behind. The number of stitchwork pictures of English cottages, with the accompanying text *Home, Sweet Home*, hanging above living-room fireplaces throughout England and the Americas a century ago, pays homage to the widespread popularity of this melody in the English-speaking world and its adoption into our 'folk' tradition.

Irwin Silber, in *Songs of the Civil War*, describes the extraordinary effect that this song had upon soldiers on both sides of the American Civil War (1861–1865): that the opposing armies stopped fighting each other in order to join in singing this song together, with its sentiment of homesickness deeply felt by everyone present. He writes:

> On a clear, starlit night along the banks of the Potomac River, while two mighty armies faced each other in the darkness from opposite sides of the river, the loneliness and heartaches and suffering of men at war overflowed into song. There were martial songs and patriotic songs and sentimental songs, first from one side and then from the other. And then, one of the armies took up the yearning refrain of "Home, Sweet Home," and suddenly the sweet strains of the melody familiar to all Americans came drifting through the air from both sides of the Potomac. The two armies, locked in fierce and mortal combat, had stopped their killing for the length of a song, to share a common emotion.
>
> It was only proper and appropriate that this musical unity should be achieved with one of the most popular songs ever written … "Home, Sweet Home" quickly became the first genuine American "hit" – American despite its British composer because of the widespread popularity and commercial success which it enjoyed in the United States.[47]

In a remarkable repetition of events, this melody had become so widely loved that, as in Europe 150 years earlier, when it was forbidden for Swiss mercenary soldiers serving abroad to play or sing the Appenzell *Kühreien* lest the soldiers sicken, desert or die of nostalgia, now under the title of *Home Sweet Home* it was once again to become the subject of the same restriction. It is recorded in documents pertaining to the American Civil War that in fear of mass desertion from the Union Army in the winter of 1862–63, orders were given to forbid Federal bands from playing the melody, such was its power to induce homesickness among the troops.[48]

The old Appenzell *Kühreien* music was the subject of one further bizarre twist of fortune: the return of *Home, Sweet Home* to the French language in the form of an English melody. The popularity in nineteenth-century Paris of transcriptions and Fantasies based on the famous Swiss *Ranz des Vaches*, both those identified by the text that opens '*Les Armaillis de Colombettes*' and that which begins '*Quand reverrai-je*' has been noted. Alongside these, though, Fantasies and sets of variations subsequently appear that are based on the melody of *Home, Sweet*

Home, now cited as an English melody. An example is an extensive set of Variations entitled *Hom! Sweet Hom! [sic], Melodie Anglaise, Variée pour le hautbois avec l'accompagnement du piano* by Gustav Vogt (1781–1870). He was professor of oboe for 52 years at the Conservatoire National de Musique in Paris. It was customary for the professor to compose an annual *Morceau de Concours*, the work to be performed successfully for a student to graduate: *Hom! Sweet Hom!* was the work written for the oboe for this purpose in 1865.

Fig. 4.30. Title page of *Hom! Sweet Hom!, Melodie Anglaise*, for oboe and piano by Gustav Vogt.[49]

Thus the humble music played on an alphorn at some distant and now forgotten time by a herdsman to his cows in the mountains in the secluded Swiss canton of Appenzell has evolved and developed in a remarkable manner. The beauty of the Appenzell landscape, captured in the music, endowed its strains with such powerful feelings of nostalgia that those innocent motifs have come to represent these feelings across the globe and still creates the same effect today.

Removed from its source instrument, the alphorn, from its text that describes the joy of the herdsman free at last to take his cattle into the mountains after their winter confinement, the amusing descriptions of the animals in his care, the repeated calls of '*Lobe!*' to God protect them in the summer pastures—removed from the mountains, from Switzerland, from the Alps and even from Europe, this innocent melody has taken on many new meanings and new connotations.

Fig. 4.31. A timeless scene: cows still graze peacefully in the high Alpine pasture in Appenzell. Photo: Frances Jones.

That this melody has become an unofficial Swiss national song and that it brings tears to the eyes of Swiss in the UK when I play it on the alphorn at Swiss events is not so remarkable. That it should have appeared in a German counterpoint exercise book, in a medical dictionary, in services in Queen Anne's Chapel and been quoted by numerous composers in order to represent an Alpine landscape, is more surprising. That its connotations of homesickness have been absorbed by other cultures, though, is an extraordinary tribute to the power and longevity of these simple Swiss herdsmen's calls played long ago in the remote mountains and valleys of Appenzell.

Notes

[1] James Boswell, *Life of Samuel Johnson* (Dublin: Cross, 1792), Vol. 3, 198.

[2] Reproduced by kind permission of Appenzellerland Tourismus AR. Copyright Marcel Steiner.

[3] Georg Rhau, *Bicinia Gallica, Latina, Germanica et Quaedam Fugae* (Wittenberg, self-published, 1545). https://imslp.org/wiki/Bicinia_gallica,_latina,_germanica,_Tomus_2_(Rhau,_Georg).

[4] Martin Luther, Preface to Georg Rhau (or Rhaw)'s *Symphoniae Iucundae* (Wittenberg, self-published, 1538).

[5] Georg Rhau, *Bicinia Gallica, Latina, Germanica et Quaedam Fugae* (Wittenberg, self-published, 1545), Lower voice book. https://imslp.org/wiki/Bicinia_gallica,_latina,_germanica,_Tomus_2_(Rhau,_Georg).

[6] Georg Rhau, *Bicinia Gallica, Latina, Germanica et Quaedam Fugae* (Wittenberg, self-published, 1545), Upper voice book. https://imslp.org/wiki/Bicinia_gallica,_latina,_germanica,_Tomus_1_(Rhau,_Georg).

[7] Reproduced with kind permission of the Kantonsbibliothek Appenzell Ausserrhoden, Trogen, Switzerland.

[8] Maria Josepha Barbara Brogerin, *Liederbüchlein* (1730). Photos: Martin Jones. Reproduced with kind permission of Roothuus Gonten, Zentrum für Appenzeller und Toggenburger Volksmusik.

[9] Translated by the author with the help of Joe Manser, curator, Roothuus Gonten, 21 July 2009. All further translations are my own unless otherwise stated.

[10] Kuhn, ed. *Sammlung von Schweizer Kühreihen und alten Volkliedern, nach ihren bekannten Melodien in Musik gesetzt* (Bern: Burgdorfer, 1812), 17–19. Universitätsbibliothek Basel. https://www.e-rara.ch/bau_1/doi/10.3931/e-rara-50794. Public Domain Mark 1.0.

[11] Louis and Philippe-Sirice Bridel, *Conservateur Suisse ou Recueil Complet des Étrennes Helvétiennes* (Lausanne: Knab, 1813), Vol. 1, 429.

[12] 'On the Ranz des Vaches', *The Harmonicon* (London: Pinnock, 1824), Vol. 2, 39. No author given. In my opinion, the minim D flat in the penultimate bar should be an E flat.

[13] Theodorus Zwinger, *Dissertationem Medicarum Selectorum* (Basel: Koenig, 1710), 102–106: ... *audientes, qui recenter e Patria advenerunt, Milites, refricata patriarum deliciarum memoria protinus hoc Morbo corripiuntur, praesertim si jam alteratum alias sanguinem adepti, vel tristitiae cuidam naturaliter obnoxii fuerint. Cumque Tribuni Militum vidissent, plures hac ratione ad repetendae Patriae desiderium stimulari, aliquos etiam impetrata hinc Febri ardente mortuos esse, severa lege prohibere coacti sunt, ne quis amplius Cantilenam istam, quam vernacula lingua den Kühe-Reyen nuncupare consueverunt, sive Ore sibilando, sive Fistulam inflando canere sustineret. Curiosis vero heic sistere voluimus Lectoribus Cantilenam notis musicis expressam, quo ipsimet de effectu ejus in Mentes Helvetiorum judicare, si velint, queant.* https://commons.wikimedia.org/wiki/File:Le_Ranz_des_Vaches_de_Zwinger.png. Creative Commons CC0 License.

[14] Ibid.

[15] Jean-Jacques Rousseau, *Dictionnaire de Musique* (Paris: Duchesne, 1768), 315: *J'ai ajoûté dans la même Planche le célèbre Rans-des-Vaches, cet Air si chéri des Suisses qu'il fut defend sous peine de mort de le jouer dans leurs Troupes, parce qu'il faisoit fondre en larmes, deserter ou mourir ceux qui l'entendoient, tant il excitoit en eux l'ardent desir de revoir leur pays. On chercheroit en vain dans cet Air les accens énergiques capables de produire de si étonnans effets. Ces effets, qui n'ont aucun lieu sur les étrangers, ne viennent que de l'habitude, des souvenirs, de mille circonstances qui, retracées par cet Air à ceux qui l'entendent, & leur rappellant leur pays, leurs anciens plaisirs, leur jeunesse, & toutes leurs façons de vivre, excitent en eux une douleur amere d'avoir perdu tout cela. La musique alors n'agie point précisément comme musique, mais comme signe mémoratif. Cet Air, quoique toujours le même, ne produit plus aujourd'hui les mêmes effets qu'il produisoit ci-devant sur les Suisses; parce qu'ayant perdu le goût de leur première simplicité, ils ne la regrettent plus quand on la leur rappelle.* https://imslp.org/wiki/Dictionnaire_de_musique_(Rousseau,_Jean-Jacques).

[16] James Boswell, *Life of Samuel Johnson* (Dublin: Cross, 1792), Vol. 3, 198.

[17] William Wordsworth, *Memorials of a Tour on the Continent*, Sonnet 21 (London: Longman, 1822).

[18] Benjamin Laborde, *L'essai sur la Musique Ancienne et Moderne* (Paris: Pierre, 1780), Vol. 2, Book IV, Chapter 12, Appendix *Des Chansons*, 106. https://digital.nls.uk/special-collections-of-printed-music/archive/94670340. Creative Commons Attribution 4.0 International Licence.

[19] Robert John Thornton, *Philosophy of Medicine, or Medical Extracts on the Nature of Health* (London: Johnson, 1797), Vol. 4, 860–1.

[20] Kuhn, ed. *Sammlung* of 1812, 47.

[21] Author's translation, from the French version provided by Louis and Philippe-Sirice Bridel in *Conservateur Suisse ou Recueil Complet des Étrennes Helvétiennes* (Lausanne: Knab, 1813), Vol. 1, 425–7.

[22] Ibid., Appendix. In other sources, in the first bar of the final line, the second note is G.

[23] Johann Rudolf Wyss, ed. *Sammlung von Schweizer Kühreihen und Volksliedern*, fourth edition (Bern: Burgdorfer, 1826), 91, 99.

[24] *Description de la Fête des Vignerons Célébrée à Vevey, le 5 août 1819* (Vevey: Loertscher, 1819): *La troupe arrêtée, les figurants ôteront leurs chapeaux qu'ils remplaceront par la barrette de cuir; après avoir retroussé leurs manches, ils s'occuperont à traire les vaches et à imiter l'operation de faire le fromage, tout cela en chantant en chour quelques couplets du Ranz des vaches.*

[25] James Fenimore Cooper, *Le Bourreau de Berne, ou L'Abbaye des Vignerons* (Paris: Gosselin, 1839), 25: *Les pâtres et les laitières n'eurent pas plutôt dit les deux premiers versets, qu'un profond silence se fit dans la foule; puis, à mesure que les strophes du choeur s'élevaient dans l'air, de nombreux échos partant de la foule répétaient les notes sauvages; et à l'exclamation Liauba! Liauba!, des milliers de voix partirent simultanément comme pour adresser aux montagnes les voeux de leurs enfants. Les derniers vers se confondirent dans un élan général d'enthousiasme.*

[26] 'On the National Songs and Music of Switzerland', *The New Monthly Magazine and Humorist* ed. Theodore Hook (London: Colburn, 1840), Vol. 59, 369–70. No author given.

[27] Ibid.

[28] Muzio Clementi, *Six Sonatinas* Op. 36 (New York: Schirmer, 1904), 22. https://imslp.org/wiki/6_Piano_Sonatinas,_Op.36_(Clementi,_Muzio).

29 English text quoted in 'Ranz des Vaches', *The Music Box* ed. Arthur W. J. G. Ord-Hume (London: The Musical Box Society of Great Britain, 1969), Vol. 4, No. 1, 55–6. No translator acknowledged.

30 Manuscript in the Collection of papers of or relating to Giovanni Battista Viotti, Royal College of Music Library, London, ms. 41 18, 26 June 1792: *Ce* Rans des vaches *n'est ni celui que notre ami J. Jaques nous a fait connaitre ... J'ai crû devoir les notes sans rhitme, c'est a dire sans mesure. Il est des cas ou la mélodie veut être sans gêne pour être elle, elle seule; la moindre mesure derangissit son éffet; cela est ci vrai, que les sons prolongeant dans l'éspace, on ne sauroit déterminer le temps qui leur faut pour arriver d'une montagne à l'autre. C'est donc le sentiment et la pensée qui doivent plutôt ne transporter à la verité de son éxécution que le rhitme et une cadence mesurée. Ce* Rans des Vaches *en mesure servit dénaturé et perdroit de sa simplicité; Ainsi pour le rendre dans son veritable sens et tel que je l'ai entendù, il faut que l'imagination vous transporte là ou il est né, et tout en l'éxécutant en Angleterre reunir toutes ses facultés pour le sentir en Suisse. C'est ainsi que dans quelques moments ravissans, je l'ai éxécuté sur mon violon, la meilleur des Amis l'entendoit.*

31 Giovanni Battista Viotti, Félix Huet *Étude sur les différentes écoles se violon depuis Corelli jusqu'à Baillot* (Châlons-sur-Marne: F. Thouille, 1880), 97. https://fr.wikisource.org/wiki/Page:Huet_-_étude_sur_les_différentes_écoles_de_violon.djvu/109.
Creative Commons Attribution 4.0 International license.

32 Chappell White, *Viotti, Thematic Catalogue* (New York: Pendragon Press, 1985).

33 Ibid.

34 *Acte Premier. Scene Premiere. Le Théâtre Représente les montagnes de la Suisse, le lever de l'aurore; un petit Pâtre; le fils de Guillaume Tell, est vu sur la pointe d'un rocher dans le lointain il joue le Rhans des Vaches: On voit dans les entre deux des montagnes des Pâtres des Vaches qui passent.*

35 André Grétry, *Guillaume Tell* (Paris: Huguet, 1791), 1–2. https://imslp.org/wiki/Guillaume_Tell_(Grétry,_André_Ernest_Modeste).

36 François-Joseph Gossec, *Le Triomphe de la République, ou Le Camp de Grand Pré* (Paris: Huguet, 1794), 191–3. https://imslp.org/wiki/Le_triomphe_de_la_République,_RH_618_ (Gossec,_François_Joseph).

37 Franz Liszt, *Pianofortewerke*, Vol. 4 (Leipzig: Breitkopf & Härtel, 1916), Vorwort: *Nachdem ich in der letzten Zeit viele neue Länder neue und verschiedenartige Gegenden, viele durch die Geschichte und die Dichtkunst verklärte Orte kennen gelernte, nachdem ich empfunden habe, dass die mannigfaltigen Erscheinungen der Natur und die Vorgänge in derselben nicht wie eindruckslose Bilder an meinen Augen vorüberzogen, sondern dass sie in meiner Seele tiefe Empfindungen hervorreifen – entstanden zwischen ihnen und mir zwar undeutliche aber doch unmittelbare Beziehungen, ein unbestimmtes aber doch vorhandenes Verhältnis, eine unerklärliche aber vorhandene Verbindung. Ich versuch dann, in Töneneinige meiner stärksten Empfindungen, meiner lebhaftesten Eindrücke wiederzugeben. Nachdem ich diese Arbeit begonnen hatte, verdichteten sich die Erinnerungen mehr und mehr, verbanden und ordneten sich naturgemass die Bilder und die Ideen ...*
https://imslp.org/wiki/Album_d'un_voyageur,_S.156_(Liszt,_Franz).

38 Ibid., 97.

39 Gustavus von Holst, *Fantasia Tirolese, in which is introduced Tyrolean Airs and Ranz de Vaches, for the Harp* (London: self-published, c.1826). Reproduced with kind permission of the British Library, copyright The British Library Board, ref: h173 (c) 6 p002.

[40] Louis Niedermeyer, *Fantaisie sur le Ranz des Vaches* (Paris: Pacini, no date). Reproduced with kind permission of the Bibliothèque de Conservatoire de Musique, Genève.

[41] Giacomo Meyerbeer, *40 Mélodies à une et plusiers voix* (Paris: Brandus, c.1849), 218. https://imslp.org/wiki/Le_ranz-des-vâches_d'Appenzell_(Meyerbeer,_Giacomo).

[42] Other works in which Strauss incorporates alphorn motifs will be examined in Chapter 5.

[43] Translation by Robert Baker-Glenn / Frances Jones.

[44] Richard Strauss, *Alphorn* (Mainz: Schott, 1995). Reproduced with kind permission of Schott Music Limited. All rights reserved.

[45] Henry Rowley Bishop, *Melodies of Various Nations* (London: Goulding, D'Almaine, Potter & Co, 1921), 69. Reproduced with kind permission of the British Library, copyright The British Library Board, ref: h1423.1,2,3 p69.

[46] Barbara Duncan, 'Home Sweet Home', *University of Rochester Bulletin*, Vol. 4, No. 2 (Winter 1949) (reprint, no page numbers).

[47] Irwin Silber, *Songs of the Civil War* (New York: Columbia University Press, 1960), 120–1.

[48] Wayne Erbsen, *Rousing Songs and True Tales of the Civil War* (Asheville, NC: Native Ground Books, 1999), 42.

[49] Reproduced with kind permission of the Bibliothèque Nationale, Paris, ms. 14098.

Chapter 5

Alphorn Motifs in Romantic Repertoire

This chapter expands on the theme of the use of alphorn calls in concert works beyond the quotations of the Christmas music of the *pastorella* and the music of the Appenzell *Kühreien*: it explores a variety of other types of alphorn motif used in music for the concert hall, the theatre, the church or the salon, as a metaphor for the mountains or its inhabitants. The rise of tourism in the Alps, and the specific cultivation of the alphorn as an aural and visual representation of the mountain landscape, begins to play a key role.

Alpine Tourism

Tourism until the end of the eighteenth century was a pastime for the rich. The Grand Tour evolved in the latter part of the seventeenth century, whereby young northern-European aristocrats spent months, or even years, in exploration of the Classical heritage of Italy and the culture of other major European centres. In general, the Alps were regarded merely as a barrier to be negotiated *en route* to the Mediterranean: an alternative to an equally feared sea journey. These sentiments are expressed, for example, by Walter Scott who wrote in 1829 in his novel *Anna of Geierstein or the Maiden of the Mist* of the fears of travellers who crossed the mountains:

> It was not an age in which the beauties or grandeur of a landscape made much impression either on the minds of those who travelled through the country, or who resided in it. To the latter, the objects, however dignified, were familiar, and associated with daily habits and with daily toil; and the former saw, perhaps, more terror than beauty in the wild region through which they passed, and were rather solicitous to get safe to their night's quarters, than to comment on the grandeur of the scenes which lay between them and their place of rest.[1]

A gradual change of attitude towards the mountains and their inhabitants developed during the eighteenth century, partly in the wake of the publication of a text written by Swiss scientist and author Albrecht von Haller (1708–1777). At the age of 21, Haller spent some time in the high Alps to undertake a survey of the plants to be found there. He was inspired by his visits to write an epic poem, *Die Alpen*, which was published in 1732. Through 490 verses, he describes the beauty of the mountain landscape and the simple honesty of its people. He includes a description of the herdsman with his alphorn leading his cows to the pastures and contrasts these rural scenes with the corruption and decadence of city dwellers. The poem was widely read: it ran to nine reprints during Haller's lifetime and was translated into English, French, Italian and Latin. The Alps might no longer be seen as a difficult region to be tolerated: it could be a source of delight, where one might experience the wild and absorb the beauty and wonder of nature.

As a result of the industrial revolution, a new middle class was emerging in Europe, with a redistribution of wealth that was not dependent upon heredity or noble birth. The successful entrepreneur could amass a personal fortune and was increasingly able to support a lifestyle that included leisure time and financial independence. A new type of gentleman, educated and with time on his hands, might be interested in travelling and exploring the world around him. There was now an opportunity for a visit to the Alps, and a tourist could come across the sound of the alphorn played by herdsmen during daily routines in the mountains.

The British were among the earliest and the most intrepid in their excursions into the Alpine wilderness. An account of one such experience in 1741 in the region around Chamonix at the foot of Mont Blanc was given by Thomas Roscoe in 1830:

> Near St. Maurice [*sic*] is the celebrated valley of Chamouni [*sic*], which, with Mont Blanc and its glaciers, and the still more wonderful Mer de Glace, are the most surprising natural curiosities ever witnessed in this or any other country. This extraordinary valley, strange as it may appear, was wholly unknown to the inhabitants of the country till the year 1741, when it was *discovered* [original italics] by two adventurous English travellers, who explored the valley, ascended the Montanvert [*sic*] to the Mer de Glace, penetrating those recesses where human voice was never before heard, and treading paths before unvisited, except by the chamois and by the goat of the rocks. It was a singular instance of enterprise, and it deserves to be recorded, that although within eighteen leagues of the city of Geneva, it was reserved for the adventure and courage of Englishmen to disclose to the world the hidden wonders of the Alps. An immense block of granite on the Montanvert, on which the adventurous travellers dined, is called, to this day, "*la pierre des Anglais.*"[2]

Lack of knowledge of the dangers of their surroundings, though, at first caused considerable problems not only for the visitors but also for the local guides employed to assist them. Walter Scott is one of many writers who gives graphic descriptions of the dangerous situations in which early explorers placed themselves and their guides through recklessness, arrogance, bravura and inexperience of mountain conditions.

   Independent travel across Europe was greatly assisted at the beginning of the nineteenth century by developments in road and rail transport. A substantial project of European road-building was launched on the instructions of Napoleon and soon the 'diligence', or public stagecoach, provided a new level of convenience and relative comfort for a traveller on a limited budget. In addition, the emergence of a Europe-wide system of railways that began in the 1820s was to have a further major impact on travel. Three primary regions of the Alps were now opened up to tourism: the area around Chamonix and Mont Blanc in the south-west, the Jungfrau region in the heart of the Alps known as the Bernese Oberland and the picturesque northern city of Lucerne with its surrounding lakes and peaks.

Fig. 5.1. Stunning mountain vistas have attracted visitors to the Alps in ever-increasing numbers since the middle of the eighteenth century.
Interlaken and the Bernese Oberland from Niesen. Photo: Frances Jones.

   The educated classes were able to read about the travels of others in published material. Descriptions of people and experiences in the mountains, often including references to the alphorn, began to appear in articles, newspapers, published diaries, poems and novels. For example, the French traveller George Tarenne, in a volume written in 1813, describes his impressions of an alphorn that he heard played on Mount Pilatus which rises to the west of Lucerne:

The herdsmen of Mount Pilatus in the canton of Lucerne, the least civilised people in the whole of Switzerland, usually played the melody, without words, on a large trumpet of the Alps, called an alphorn, with a long conical curved shape which magnifies and prolongs the sound, so that you can sometimes hear it more than two leagues away. This melody is also used to sound the alarm against local and foreign enemies. It is extremely beautiful on the horn during the night: its plaintive languishing phrases penetrate the soul.[3]

Two British poets, Lord Byron and Percy Bysshe Shelley, both wrote about the sound of the alphorn after spending the summer of 1816 together with friends in Switzerland. Byron records in his diaries that they came across *Ranz des Vaches* both in the mountains and at informal entertainments. Byron set an epic three-act poem, *Manfred*, in the high Alps around the Jungfrau: the descriptions of Alpine scenes in Acts 1 and 2 resemble those found in his Alpine journal of September 1816. He explains in a letter: 'I wrote a sort of mad drama, for the sake of introducing Alpine scenery and descriptions'. One scene describes the protagonist's feelings on hearing the herdsman's horn:

Hark! the note,
        [The Shepherd's pipe in the distance is heard.]
The natural music of the mountain reed
(For here the patriarchal days are not
A pastoral fable) pipes in the liberal air,
Mix'd with the sweet bells of the sauntering herd;
My soul would drink those echoes.[4]

Shelley also recalls the Swiss landscape and the herdsman's horn in his poem *Adonais*, written in 1821 upon receipt of the news of the death of their friend and fellow poet John Keats:

Lost Echo sits amid the voiceless mountains,
And feeds her grief with his remembered lay,
And will no more reply to winds or fountains,
Or amorous birds perched on the young green spray,
Or herdsman's horn, or bell at closing day; ...[5]

The English writer John Murray published *A Glance at some of the Beauties and Sublimities of Switzerland* in 1829. He includes a description of the delight he felt on hearing a herdsman with an alphorn on the road to Chamonix:

On the main road our delighted ear was charmed with a fine musical echo, produced from the blowing of a horn, composed of pieces of common wood, roughly put together, with five iron hoops: this musical instrument was from three to four feet long, the mouth-piece about four inches circumference, and the opening at the further extremity eight to ten inches. This rude horn was employed by one of the shepherds of the Alps to collect together his wandering flock, and summon them from the mountains. The sound, at first loud and full, vibrated from rock to rock, until its tones were so softened as to be heard only as a distant murmur, that gradually died away upon the astonished but delighted ear, though, in its last sigh, the tone and note were perfect and distinct.[6]

Murray also describes the use of the alphorn at sunset. This might have been for one of two reasons. As noted earlier, it was a fundamental part of the daily summer routine that the herdsman would play a melody on his alphorn each evening at nightfall, in order to let the people in the valley below know that all was well. However, it appears that Murray may also have known about the *Alpsegen* or *Betruf*, which is still heard in Catholic cantons today. This is a prayer, sung at nightfall from a high place in the mountains at full voice, with amplification provided by the funnel that was used in milking. The lyrics and melody, unique to every occasion, are personal and heartfelt. An *Alpsegen* calls to God, to Mary, to Jesus and generally to some other relevant or local saints, to protect the mountain people and their animals through the night. Murray records that he heard the sound of the alphorn as if in evening prayer:

> There was a wild romance in its notes, which was characteristic in a very high degree all round. This instrument is about eight feet long and its farther extremity rests on the ground. It is used among the mountains not merely for the herdsmen's call, but as an invocation for the solemnities of religion. As soon as the sun has shed his last ray on the snowy summit of the loftiest range, the Alpine shepherd from some elevated point, trumpets forth 'Praise God the Lord,' while the echoes in the caves of the everlasting hills, roused from their slumbers at the sacred name of God, repeat 'Praise God the Lord'. Distant horns on lower plains now catch the watch-word, and distant mountains ring again with the solemn sound 'Praise God the Lord,' and other echoes bounding from other rocks, reply 'God the Lord'. A solemn pause succeeds; with uncovered head and on bended knee, the shepherd's prayer ascends on high. At the close of this evening sacrifice, offered in the temple not made with hands, the Alpine horn sounds long and loud and shrill, 'good night,' repeated by other horns; while a thousand 'good nights' are reverberated around, and the curtain of Heaven closes on the shepherds and their flocks.[7]

A new facility was to appear in the 1830s: the travellers' guide-book. This was written for those with the desire and the time to explore new places, but on a more moderate budget than the aristocratic travellers of earlier times. John Murray produced the first comprehensive guide-book to Switzerland for the

English-speaking traveller, *A Hand-Book for Travellers in Switzerland, Savoy and Piedmont*, which he published in 1838. According to the Preface, its content was based on the experience of four separate visits to the country. In his introduction, he explains the phenomenon of the *Ranz des Vaches* to his readers. He mentions that it caused homesickness among the Swiss abroad and that 'almost every valley has an air of its own, but the original air is said to be that of Appenzell'. His references to both yodel and the alphorn reflect his own encounters in his visits to the mountains. He writes of the *Kühreien* and describes the instrument, its echoes and its use at evening-time:

> The name *Ranz des Vaches* (Germ. *Kuh-reihen*), literally *cow-rows*, is obviously derived from the order in which the cows march home at milking-time, in obedience to the shepherd's call, communicated by the voice, or through the *Alp-horn*, a simple tube of wood, wound round with bark 5 or 6 feet long, admitting of but slight modulation, yet very melodious when caught up and prolonged by the mountain echoes … The traveller in the Alps will have frequent opportunities of hearing both the music of the horn and the songs of the cow-herds and dairy-maids; … In some of the remoter pastoral districts of Switzerland, from which the ancient simplicity of manners is not altogether banished, the Alp-horn supplies, on the higher pastures, where no church is near, the place of the vesper-bell. The cow-herd, posted on the highest peak, as soon as the sun has set, pours forth the 4 or 5 first notes of the Psalm "Praise God the Lord;" the same notes are repeated from distant Alps, and all within hearing, uncovering their heads and bending their knees, repeat their evening orison, after which the cattle are penned in their stalls, and the shepherds betake themselves to rest.[8]

Interest in Switzerland was cultivated by the English press. It has already been noted that in 1840 an article appeared in *The New Monthly Magazine and Humorist*, a publication that flourished in London between 1814 and 1884. The anonymous article entitled 'On National Songs and Music of Switzerland' gives a contemporary view of the impact of Swiss music, in particular the *Ranz des Vaches*, on the visitor:

> To those amongst our readers who have chanced to hear the Ranz-des-Vaches in its native glory – in the wild passes of Appenzell, or the sylvan seclusion of the Emmenthal, how many a scene of grandeur and sublimity – of sweetness and tranquillity – of soul-stirring excitement, and overpowering but delicious melancholy – will its very name conjure back to recollection: the far-spreading gloom of the Alpine forest – the foam and roar of the mountain torrent – the many-tinted glacier sparkling in the last rays of sunset, like glow-worms in darkened foliage

– the distant thunder of the avalanche – the deep-toned carillon of the grave leader of the struggling herd, in contrast with the silvery tinkling of the lively and sportive goat – the joyous "*Hoh hoh*" of the herdsman echoing afar, its well-known sound greeted by the loud bellow and the shrill bleat – such are amongst the recollections which vibrate at the mention of the "*Küh-reihe*".[9]

Fig. 5.2. Alphorn played to call cows to their stall at the end of the day. Allières, Canton Vaud. Nicolas Marie Joseph Chapuy, c.1840.[10]

Karl Baedeker (1801–1859) and his heirs expanded on Murray's concept of guide-books, and with numerous reprints and updates, the Baedeker guide-books are still in use today. After tackling Holland, Belgium and his native Germany, Baedeker first produced a guide-book for Switzerland in 1844, for German readers, based entirely on his own journeys and experiences. It was first printed in English in 1863 and has since run to 39 revised editions. The Preface to the first English edition of Baedeker's guide-book to Switzerland provides a snapshot of the state of tourism and travel at the time and includes advice about how to make a journey without an entourage of servants:

> … to render the traveller as independent as possible of the extraneous services of guides, domestiques de place, voituriers and inn-keepers, and enable him to realize to the fullest extent the exquisite and rational enjoyment of which this magnificent country is a fruitful source. Since the great increase of late years in the facilities for travel afforded by the wide extension of railways, the number of travellers on the Continent generally has enormously increased, of which no country has been the witness in a more marked degree than Switzerland.[11]

A serialised diary was another way in which a literate public could share in the wonder of the Alpine experience. In 1874, a London weekly newspaper *The Graphic* ran an 11-part serialised diary column of a trip taken by newlyweds John and Nelly Wood, entitled 'An Autumn Tour of Switzerland'. Detailed sketches illustrated the scenes in all but one of the issues. The couple wrote with enthusiasm about their travels, their wonder at the dramatic scenery and the people they met, their impressions of the hospitality they found and a range of new experiences they encountered, including the sounding of the alphorn.[12]

Visitors and the Alphorn

Increasingly during the nineteenth century, the instrument came to be played specifically for tourists, as Switzerland sought to create unusual experiences for its new visitors. Part of this cultivated image was a performance on an alphorn for travellers at prominent tourist locations, and it will be seen that this was often how composers became aware of the instrument. The inclusion of an alphorn motif in a composed concert work in the nineteenth or twentieth century was therefore in no small part due to the deliberate promotion of the instrument by the Swiss, with the sound of the alphorn used by a composer to conjure up an image of the mountains that it had been commandeered to represent.

The presence of the alphorn played specifically for tourists is noted by many writers. At the Giessbach Falls, on Lake Brienz below the Jungfrau massif, Murray describes performances of traditional Swiss music given to tourists by the local schoolmaster, Johann Kehrli, who owned the land around the falls, with his family (see Fig. 5.3). They were renowned for their musical ability, in singing and alphorn playing:

> The cottage opposite the Falls is inhabited by the schoolmaster of Brienz, whose family and himself are celebrated as the best choristers of native airs in Switzerland. He is now a patriarch of 64 and most of his children are married; but he is training his grand-children to the same profession of songsters. The concert, accompanied by the Alpine horn, with which travellers are saluted on their departure, is very sweet.[13]

In his description of the area around the foot of the Wetterhorn, a steep-faced peak alongside the Jungfrau, Murray prepares the readers of his *Hand-Book* for the experience of the alphorn player and the extraordinary qualities of the echoes that rebound off the cliffs:

> Upon the slope in front of the Wetterhorn is usually stationed one who blows the *alpine horn*, a rude tube of wood, 6 or 8 feet long. The traveller should on no account omit to stop and listen. A few seconds after the horn has ceased, the few and simple notes of the instrument are caught up and repeated by the echoes of the vast cliff of the Wetterhorn, and

return to the ear refined and softened, yet perfectly distinct, as it were an aerial concert warbling among the crags.[14]

Der Giefsbach und die Sängerfamilie auf seiner Alpe
1 Vater Johann Kehrli _ Kinder 2 Bäbi 3 Hansi 4 Gritli 5 Köbi 6 Heinz

Fig. 5.3. Johann Kehrli and his family Bäbi, Hansi, Gritli, Köbi and Heinz, entertain tourists at the Giessbach Falls. Engraving by Peter Carl Geissler, c.1830.[15]

Baedeker also enjoyed the sounds of the alphorn at the foot of the Wetterhorn and describes the beauty of its echoes for his readers:

The Alphorn (an instrument from 6ft. to 8ft. in length, of bark or wood) is often sounded from the opposite slope while tourists are passing. Its simple notes are re-echoed a few seconds later from the precipices of the Wetterhorn, the effect of which is extremely pleasing.[16]

Vue du Wetterhorn, Schrekhorn, Finsteraarhorn
et des deux glaciers du Grindelwald.

Fig. 5.4. Visitors hear an alphorn by the Wetterhorn, Bernese Oberland. Hand-coloured
etching c.1840 by Rudolf Dikenmann.[17]

At the foot of the Jungfrau is the dramatic flat-bottomed valley of
Lauterbrunnen, with vertical limestone cliffs that face each other for four miles
along its entire length. It is a place renowned for alphorn echoes: these are
described by the Victorian diarist Jemima Morrell, in her account of a visit there
on the first tour of Switzerland to be organised by Thomas Cook in 1863:

> In the sward was stationed a man and some boys with a horn. It is a
> wooden tube from five to six feet long bound round with split withies of
> willow. This he rested on a wedge-shaped hollow trough, and blew as we
> approached. He must have practised long to emit such a flow of mellow,
> sonorous sounds from so unmusical-looking an instrument. The notes
> died away in softest cadence, which notes were taken up by the
> mountains and reverberated by them again and again. We had scarcely
> a moment's interval to remark on their sweetness, when the rocks
> echoed the notes in fainter strains, another pause and we heard their
> vibrations still lingering among the cliffs till they expired in but a
> musical sigh.[18]

Fig. 5.5. Alphorn player by the Staubbach waterfall, Lauterbrunnen. William Henry Bartlett, 1834.[19]

Travellers often describe a peak that rises to the east of Lucerne, the Rigi. Many comments are made about the use of the alphorn there and the visitors of various nationalities who gathered at the top to view the sunrise. There was an opportunity to spend the night in lodgings near the summit in order to watch the dawn, and a wooden belvedere was built at the top that could be climbed for an even higher viewpoint. Carl Maria von Weber (1786–1826) wrote in a letter of a visit to the Rigi Kulm (summit) in September 1811:

> 7th. I got up at 3am in order to climb the Kulm … I reached the summit in ¾ hour and was very hot when I got there, although it was cold, so the fire that was made by our guide was very welcome. At 5.30 there was a glorious sunrise, at first the sun appeared above one peak and the glacier had a golden glow; it was a wonderful reward for my exertions. It was indescribable.[20]

Fig. 5.6. *Der Rigi-Kulm*, by Franz Niklaus König, c.1810, shows the viewing platform and an alphorn player, centre, at sunset. Watercolour on translucent paper, for back-lighting. Kunstmuseum, Bern.[21]

In 1816 the first hotel was built at the top of the peak, and there are many accounts that tell of the alphorn used to waken the guests in time to see the sunrise. Alexandre Dumas (1802–1870), French novelist and dramatist famed for *Les Trois Mousquetaires* (The Three Musketeers), journeyed throughout Europe and wrote extensively about his experiences. In his *Impressions de Voyage: Suisse* of 1834 he too describes a visit to the Rigi Kulm. To mingle with the international tourists at the hotel was, he felt, like walking into the Tower of Babel: there were 27 visitors of 11 different nationalities, all gathered to view the sunrise from the summit; the proprietor played them a *Ranz des Vaches* on the alphorn and explained how it caused homesickness when played to the Swiss abroad.[22]

John Murray in his *Hand-Book* of 1838 ensures that his readers are prepared for the use of the alphorn in the Rigikulm Hotel to waken the guests in time to venture out to watch the sunrise from the belvedere:

> … whether the inmate have slept or not, he, together with the whole household, is roused about an hour before sunrise, by the strange sounds of a long wooden horn, which is played until every particle of sleep is dispelled from the household. Then commences a general stir and everybody hastens out with shivering limbs and half-open eyes to gaze at the glorious prospect of a sunrise from the Righi [*sic*].[23]

A new 130-bed hotel was built on the Kulm in 1848 and porters were provided to carry not only luggage but sedan chairs for the visitors up to the summit. By the last third of the century, engineers had begun to construct a series of funicular and cog railways in Switzerland to assist with access to high vantage points and to satisfy a thirst for the ultimate Alpine holiday experience. The first of these to be completed, in 1871, ascends to the summit of the Rigi. By 1875 a new hotel that could accommodate 300 guests was built there and the continued use of the alphorn to waken the guests was by now considered an integral part of the Rigi experience.

An author who wrote about the alphorn on the Rigi in a novel was the American author Samuel Langhorne Clemens (1835–1910), who used the pseudonym Mark Twain. He travelled through much of central and southern Europe and drew on these experiences for his novel *A Tramp Abroad*, which he published in 1880. Having decided to walk up to the top of the Rigi, the protagonist in the novel also describes the sounding of the alphorn to rouse the guests of the Rigikulm Hotel from their sleep in time to see the sunrise:

> We found by this guide-book that in the hotels on the summit the tourist is not left to trust to luck for his sunrise, but is roused betimes by a man who goes through the halls with a great Alpine horn, blowing blasts that would raise the dead ... We were so sodden with fatigue that we never stirred nor turned over till the blooming blasts of the Alpine horn aroused us.[24]

Alphorn players were not only employed by the hotel to waken its guests. They also positioned themselves to perform from the peak at dawn and dusk: a good player would provide an unforgettable experience as the sounds echoed over the lakes and mountains that fan out all around the Rigi. He would expect a few coins in return. The illustration in the first edition of Twain's *A Tramp Abroad* shows an interesting amplification box through which the bell of the alphorn was played (Fig. 5.7).

It would appear, though, that the player at the Rigikulm was having a bad day when Baedeker made his visit in preparation for the 1863 edition of his guide-book. He comments on the playing of the instrument at sunset: 'An indifferent performer on the Alpine Horn awakens the echoes and sorely tries the temper by his ill-timed exertions'.[25] However, by the time of the 1889 version of the guide-book, Baedeker's sons did not write unfavourably of the evening performance. They describe the scene at the Rigikulm thus:

> The Kulm almost always presents a busy scene, but is most thronged in the morning and the evening. The sunset is always the chief attraction. A performer on the Alpine Horn blows the 'retreat' of the orb of day, after which the belvedere is soon deserted. Half-an-hour before sunrise, the Alphorn sounds the reveille. All is again noise and

bustle; the crowded hotels are for the nonce without a tenant; and the summit is thronged with an eager multitude, enveloped in all manner of cloaks and mantles...[26]

WHAT AWAKENED US.

Fig. 5.7. Illustration of the alphorn player at the top of the Rigi by Walter Francis Brown in the first edition of Mark Twain's *A Tramp Abroad*.

The sort of occasions during which a traveller to Switzerland experienced the sound of an alphorn in the mountains is therefore varied, with a range of opportunities, locations and scenarios in which the instrument was heard. This variety of experiences is reflected in the range of different alphorn-inspired motifs that nineteenth-century composers include in their works.

The word 'alphorn' has been used in the texts quoted above to describe instruments that vary considerably from one to another and also from the typical alphorn of today. Nevertheless, the term is consistently used for an instrument that is fundamentally a simple tube of wood, wound round with strips of bark, split willow or something similar. An examination of nineteenth-century paintings, etchings and drawings of alphorns in Switzerland show that the normal length for the alphorn was between four and eight feet: this is the case in artwork produced both by the Swiss and by their visitors.[27]

The length of the instrument has an effect on the music that could be played: a tube of this sort of length is restricted to half a dozen bugle-like arpeggio notes and does not have easy access to the higher harmonics that include the 'alphorn *fa*' (harmonic no. 11). To play the music of the *Kühreien* from Appenzell, for example, a longer horn is needed. It will be noticed that many of the compositions based on the Appenzell material, examined in Chapter 4, refer to vocal versions of the music. An alphorn upon which one could play Appenzell *Kühreien* material would need to have been longer than those generally in use in Switzerland by the nineteenth century. Music heard by nineteenth-century tourists therefore normally used the arpeggio notes of harmonics nos. 3 to 6, and not the scale-like range found in the Appenzell *Kühreien*.

Alphorn motifs in concert works: the social background

In an investigation into the use of an alphorn motif by a composer, three interlinked questions arise: why should a composer wish to incorporate an alphorn motif into a work for concert performance, why is this a desire that matured during the nineteenth century, and upon what grounds could a composer assume that such a quotation would convey some meaning to his audience. The answers lie in the two fundamental changes that had swept across Europe: the industrial revolution and the French Revolution. These were to reorganise western European social structure and distribution of wealth for ever, and each played a significant part in the change in the role of the arts and the lives of composers from the beginning of the nineteenth century too.

The music of the herdsman's horn had little impact on concert music before the French Revolution. Until this time, the arts in western Europe were primarily either a diversion for the ruling classes or a medium for the dissemination of religion. During the age of patronage, the sounds of folk instruments replicated in art music as rustic signifiers were those of the musette and the vielle or hurdy-gurdy, with allusions to the pastoral flute, the chalumeau and the bagpipes. Horns were first introduced into classical music to play fanfares in Italian opera in the 1630s, and for the next 150 years their use in a descriptive context was largely restricted to the depiction of hunting scenes. Unusual situations where the music of herdsmen's horns had been used before the nineteenth century have been examined in the previous chapters: the particular context of Christmas shepherds' music, the rare empathy with rustic musicians shown by a very few composers as exemplified by Leopold Mozart, and the allusions to the *Kühreien* of Appenzell.

The changes in European social structure that began around the turn of the nineteenth century created new living conditions that brought both advantages and disadvantages. Although the rapid growth of cities in the wake of industrialisation meant that a newly emerging middle class now gained education and disposable income, it also meant that for an increasing proportion of the European population, individuals had less and less contact in their daily lives with the natural world. They often lived in a dirty, noisy or pressured urban environment. In addition, the political turbulence of the nineteenth century was deeply disturbing, and many composers, writers and artists created works that reflected troubled times, censorship and deep personal and political struggle. The arts therefore assumed two important roles: the maintenance of public morale through entertainment, and the indirect voicing of political beliefs. These new intentions were particularly marked in Paris during and immediately after the French Revolution, and in the works of German and Austrian composers.

Those who could afford it could take a holiday in a new or unusual place; alternatively, they could go to a concert or the theatre, and the writer, the actor, the painter and the composer increasingly sought to bring the flavour of the natural world into the urban environment. Of all forms of art, music was considered pre-eminent in this endeavour. Although public or 'subscription' concerts had been enjoyed from time to time in a number of regions since the 1740s, the arts now played a major part in city life for a much larger sector of society. The representation of an alternative way of life both provided escapism and allowed artists to ask deep questions of their audiences. Music, literature, drama or art that reflected the world of nature could portray many things. It could represent a place of calm, peace, serenity and tranquillity. It could describe an idealised, lost world of innocence, where the heart was once free. The artist could convey remoteness, strangeness, the fleeting or the intangible. The natural landscape could be a setting for myths and legends, the transcendental and the metaphysical, powerful wild forces, supernatural terror or evil spirits.

The Alps provided a suitably dramatic setting for stories set in an alternative place. Such works would particularly attract references to the alphorn, in paintings, in literature, in drama and especially in music, where the sound of the alphorn provided a perfect symbol of a mountain landscape for the nineteenth-century composer. It could carry the implication of simple beauty, it might represent other-worldliness, or it could have overtones of independence and freedom that resonated deeply with those at the mercy of changing political forces.

Nineteenth-century composers, writers and artists worked together. Some composers, such as Mendelssohn, were also accomplished painters; some, for example Schumann and Wagner, were actively involved in political writing. Poets such as Goethe, Schiller and Byron created epic dramas that could comment on social and political matters when a more direct voice was not possible. Many texts, full of deep personal emotion, raised profound questions; such texts were eagerly set to music that could echo and enhance these sentiments. Composers wrote music with an implied narrative that drew on pre-existing scripts, the work of contemporary writers or ideas of their own. The music of the alphorn features in many such works.

Characteristics of an alphorn motif in a concert work

Various kinds of extra-musical scenes that a composer may wish to portray, for example, that of the hunting horn, posthorn or military bugle, etc., have been mentioned earlier. All these rustic brass instruments are restricted to the notes found in the harmonic series. The trumpet, bugle or posthorn fanfare is rhythmic and arresting. Hunting horn calls are generally energetic: a composer will normally use the 'horse-riding' rhythm of 6/8 and music that depicts hunting horns in the concert hall is often written for two, three or four horns playing together in harmony as in a *cor de chasse* ensemble. Music that represents an alphorn call has different characteristics that will be seen in the selection of works examined below.

An alphorn figure is typically formed from a gently turning major arpeggio-based motif that may include a leap of an octave, because when such notes are played in an environment where there is an echo, these notes linger to create a pleasing chord:

Fig. 5.8. Typical 'turning arpeggio' alphorn motifs.

In contrast to rhythmic or energetic music for the hunting horn or military bugle, alphorn motifs that a composer may have heard in the mountains are free from regular pulse, and often slow and peaceful. In the manner of the *Kühreien*, phrases are often built from repeating cells, of an irregular number of bars, and usually end with a paused note. The melody that represents an alphorn in the orchestra or on the piano is generally a lone voice: it will be presented either unaccompanied, or against a peaceful backdrop of held chords, sometimes with the open fifths of a bagpipe-like drone. Occasionally a composer will provide an echo or simulate a response from another alphorn player in the distance; sometimes there will be a chorus of overlapping echoes as the calls might reverberate and re-echo in the solitude of the mountains. In the examples that follow, such features immediately identify the scene to be portrayed as that of an alphorn, alone in a mountain landscape.

The position of an alphorn motif in relation to preceding and subsequent material is also important: it will be seen that this can be a reflection of the role of the alphorn in the management of cattle in the mountains. As previously noted, for the herdsman tending his animals in the high Alpine pastures, the alphorn was a necessary means of communication to fellow herdsmen and to those in the villages below: the herdsman would play a melody to let others know that 'all was well', for example after a mountain storm and at the end of each day. Thus an alphorn motif in an orchestral work is often found after a stormy passage, in the context of eveningtide, or as an evening prayer. These scenarios have engendered some of the most beautiful alphorn-like writing in the canon of Romantic orchestral and piano music, where reassuring calls of 'all is well' are used to create a particularly profound resonance in the representation of peace after turmoil.

In contrast, a composer may give his alphorn motif a more light-hearted setting, reminiscent of a cheerful herdsman's call from a *pastorella*, or a tourist's simple delight on holiday in a glorious landscape: a carefree spirit of relaxation that the Swiss wished the alphorn to represent. This is more often found in the accompaniment for a song or in piano music with an Alpine setting, and in music written by visitors to the mountains. Here, both alphorn motifs and yodel melodies may be used merely as token symbols of the mountain landscape, to lend a touch of 'authentic' colour to a scene. Music designed to replicate yodel contains scale-based melodic lines alongside the characteristic repeated leaps across the break in the voice, while a typical alphorn motif is restricted to the notes of the arpeggio.

Some composers quote authentic alphorn phrases, while others use a melodic style that resembles music played on an alphorn. Some references may well have been quotations of phrases heard in the mountains by the composer, but which are now no longer recognised. Some might be genuine herding motifs, while others may be alphorn melodies created for tourists to enhance their Swiss holiday experience. It is remarkable that in each case, the composer felt that he could use this imagery as a metaphor and that his audience would understand the landscape or feelings to which he was referring.

Often an alphorn motif is given to the French horn. Many of the composers who included alphorn music in their writing were horn players, or the sons of horn players, factors that will be noted later. These composers appear to have been especially aware of the sound of the horn in the countryside, well-attuned to the use of the horn in the orchestra and particularly interested in the evocative impact of the incorporation of a rustic horn motif in works written for an urban audience. In addition, though, the use of the French horn in itself can be enough of a reference, with an allusion that is subliminal rather than explicit: a reference to the alphorn that derives from its sound as a concept. Schumann described what could be considered as the 'essence of the alphorn' in a comment concerning notes played on orchestral horns in the second movement of Schubert's 'Great' C Major Symphony. Despite the extremely quiet sound required, Schubert creates an echo-like resonance with the specification that two horns be played in unison. The horns do not play a melody, but single notes, *pianissimo* with *diminuendo*. The choice of horns for these notes is evocative, and although no connotations are explicit either in context or in melodic content, Schumann voices a general awareness of the implications of the use of the horn in this context. An alphorn motif is not used: the choice of the horn is enough to create this inference.

> There is also a place there [in the second movement] where a horn calls as if from a distance, that appears to come from another sphere. Here everyone listens with rapt attention, as if a gust from heaven has enveloped the orchestra.[28]

Fig. 5.9. Schubert, Symphony No. 9, second movement, bar 148–158: interplay of string parts with horn calls referred to by Schumann.[29]

More usually, though, the quotation of an alphorn motif on a French horn is explicit. There are occasions when a distant echo will be given to an oboe, cor anglais or clarinet, with the player occasionally actually placed offstage. However, if a composer wished to elaborate on the motif, orchestral hand-horns in use before the adoption of valves in the second half of the nineteenth century were unable to give the composer a full range of notes. Alphorn motifs are therefore not uncommonly allocated to a different instrument. The qualities of an alphorn motif are so distinctive that a reference to its origins is clear even when the motif is not given to an orchestral horn. Many representations of alphorn music occur in music written for the piano, or for voice and piano: the motifs themselves are sufficiently distinctive that the allusion is clear.

Alphorn motifs feature primarily in music written to represent the Swiss Alps: as has been demonstrated, the instrument has been promoted as a symbol of Switzerland since the rise of tourism there. These motifs were adopted by three groups of composers: those who were Swiss, those who spent a substantial period of time in Switzerland and those who visited the country, upon whom the scenery and its culture left an unforgettable impression. Primary sources of inspiration for the composer were texts related to Switzerland or the Swiss:

these include the story of William Tell, Byron's drama *Manfred* and tales that relate to Swiss mercenary soldiers. Further music with alphorn motifs describes the Swiss landscape, without a narrative.

Alphorn music is, however, not only found in relation to depictions of Switzerland. Some composers incorporate alphorn-inspired music from Austria, Bavaria and possibly the French and Italian Alps too: instances will be examined where alphorn-like motifs used by composers from these areas are recognisably different from those found in quotations with a connection to Switzerland. In addition, tourists sometimes view the Alps as a region not defined by national borders; thus works include alphorn-like motifs although they do not refer specifically to Switzerland, for example in Gustavus von Holst's *Fantasie* for harp, described earlier.

Although the alphorn is generally associated with a mountain landscape, alphorn motifs fundamentally represent the life of the herdsman. It has been noted in earlier chapters that the instrument was used by herdsmen beyond the confines of the Alps and examples will be seen in the works below where the metaphor of the alphorn is used for a herdsman although a mountain setting is not implied. A composer sometimes reflects familiarity with the Italian shepherds' Christmas *pastorale*, a gentle call might be given a compound time signature reminiscent of the music used at the Nativity, sometimes with a rustic drone, and music similar to an extended *Ranz des Vaches* will also be found.

A selection of compositions that include alphorn-inspired material

The oratorio *Die Jahreszeiten* (The Seasons) by Josef Haydn (1732–1809), was completed in 1801. Haydn had already referred to Austria's critical political situation in his *Paukenmesse* of 1796, written when Napoleon's armies invaded Styria. He subsequently expressed his feelings in two large-scale oratorios that portrayed two fundamental aspects of life: *Die Schöpfung* (The Creation), completed in 1798, a religious celebration of life, and *Die Jahreszeiten*, a secular portrait of country people, three years later. This second work poignantly describes rural life and the timelessness of annual farming routines. It is not only a celebration of human labour: it is also perhaps a statement of Haydn's belief that mankind must not destroy the very things that sustain life. We shape the landscape, but we also need it and are refreshed by it.

Haydn's text is based on extracts from a set of four poems *The Seasons* published by the Scottish writer James Thomson in 1730. One of Thomson's themes was that the earth not only rewards the honest farmer for his labours: it also provides leisure and pleasure, a place of respite and renewal. The inhabitants of Haydn's text are neither looked down upon nor idealised: rather they are both the custodians of the countryside and the product of it. The characters' response to and interaction with their landscape is at the heart of the work. Haydn relocates the setting of this text from the British countryside to a small Alpine village.

Die Jahreszeiten tells the story of the yearly cycle of farming life. Aria No. 11 is the song that describes the tradition of the *Kühreien*, where the herdsman leads his cattle to pasture at the beginning of summer. Haydn gives Lucas, the herdsman, an *obbligato* solo French horn as an accompanying voice to represent his alphorn, with simple alphorn calls that are very similar to those used almost 50 years before by Leopold Mozart in his *Sinfonia Pastorella*. As Haydn had been brought up in rural eastern Austria, like Leopold it is possible that he also quoted alphorn motifs that he may have heard played by an Austrian herdsman.

Fig. 5.10. Haydn, *Die Jahreszeiten*, Aria No. 11, in which the herdsman, Lucas, sings of taking his animals up to the high pastures, bars 1–6. A substantial *obbligato* part for solo French horn is given alphorn-like motifs.[30]

This movement is set in compound time typical of a *pastorale*. It is created from cheerful calls with a simple accompaniment reminiscent of a rustic drone. Haydn combines these features with the irregular phrase-lengths, reflective pauses and text of a *Ranz des Vaches*, which describes the scene where the herdsman collects the animals at sunrise, ready for the journey to the pastures.

Der muntre Hirt versammelt nun	The cheerful herdsman now gathers
die frohen Herden um sich her;	the happy herds around him;
zur fetten Weid'auf grünen Höh'n	to lead them slowly on their journey
treibet er sie langsam fort.	to the rich green pastures up above.
Nach Osten blikkend steht er dann,	He gazes eastwards
auf sienem Stabe hingelehnt,	and leans on his staff,
zu dehn den ersten Sonnenstrahl,	as the sunrise sends forth its first rays
welchem er entgegen haart.	and gives cheer to his heart.

Seven years later, in 1808, a fellow resident of Vienna, Beethoven (1770–1827), wrote his own depiction of the natural landscape, his Symphony No. 6, *Pastoral-Sinfonie*. The extensive use of Christmas *pastorella* material by Beethoven in this symphony has already been examined in Chapter 3.

Beethoven was at pains to explain that the symphony conveyed feelings aroused when in the countryside, rather than sound paintings of country scenes. He was fond of taking long walks in the country, and Beethoven refers in his letters to his escape from the city [Vienna] for rural retreats. Not only was the work written at a time of intense political and social turmoil: Beethoven was also struggling with the personal torment of increasing deafness. His feelings when walking in the countryside were possibly intensified by the fact that the region's peace was now in question and also because he could no longer hear many of nature's delights.[31]

Like Haydn, Beethoven too was keen to depict real people in the countryside, rather than describe mythical idylls of nymphs and shepherds as had been common before this time. Beethoven includes representations of people, landscapes and the weather in this work. He gives a descriptive title to each movement:

Erwachen heiterer Empfindungen bei der Ankunft dem Lande (Awakening of cheerful feelings on arrival in the countryside);

Szene am Bach (Scene by the brook);

Lustiges Zusammensein in der Landleute (Peasants' merrymaking);

Gewitter. Sturm (Thunderstorm);

Hirtengesang. Frohe und dankbare Gefühle nach dem Sturm (Herdsman's Song. Joyful and thankful feelings after the storm).

Beethoven was not the first composer to write a substantial orchestral work on the theme of nature: there were many such works written before his 'Pastoral' Symphony. Twenty years earlier, a symphony was published by Justin Heinrich Knecht (1752–1817), an organist, theorist and composer working in Württemberg in Germany, entitled *Le Portrait Musical de la Nature, ou Grande Sinfonie (Pastoralsymphonie)* (A Musical Portrait of Nature, or Grand Symphony (Pastoral

Symphony)). Each movement of this symphony carries a descriptive title not unlike those used by Beethoven, and both compositions have five movements.

Despite his assertions to the contrary, Beethoven's music does contain graphic musical descriptions of the scenes specified in his headings, none more so than his representation of a storm. Once Beethoven's storm is spent, he writes peaceful and reassuring alphorn-like calls for the French horn, which grow out of the *pastorella* theme of *Joseph adstabit* played on the clarinet. The new movement, which follows *attacca* from the previous extract, is called *Hirtengesang. Frohe und dankbare Gefühle nach dem Sturm* (Herdsman's Song, Joyful and thankful feelings after the storm) and Beethoven uses the combination of the *Joseph adstabit* theme and typical peaceful horn-call music, in *pastorale* compound time, to create a wonderful epilogue, evocative of the herdsman playing to reassure everyone that all is well after a storm in the mountains (see Fig. 3.34 on p. 126).

Felix Mendelssohn (1809–1847) showed prodigious musical talent from early childhood, and at times he reflected his experiences in his compositions. At the age of 13, in August 1822, he spent two nights with his family on the Rigi mountain above Lucerne. His mother, Lea, wrote in a letter that halfway up to the Kulm they had to seek shelter from a storm and when they finally arrived, they were surrounded by low cloud for an entire day. On the second evening, though, they witnessed a wonderful sunset and were woken the following morning in time to see the sunrise by a call on an alphorn:

> ... the fog dispersed, and we enjoyed the most beautiful sunset in this heavenly region; only the southern mountains continued to be veiled. To wake up on Rigikulm on a lovely morning is striking and highly moving. An hour before sunrise, when the heaven is clear, the alphorn sounds, rousing all the residents of the house with its sharp, piercing tone. Now amid the darkness stirs the liveliest bustle in the narrow quarters ... [32]

Mendelssohn returned to the summit of the Rigi in August 1831 and wrote of the cheerful alphorn, the magnificent views and his happy memories of his previous visit with his family. On this occasion, he stayed at the viewing platform for six hours to absorb the beauty of the scenery:

> For our family, the Rigi is also clearly very special, and again today it has aroused in me a devotion so wonderful, with its pure sunrise, just as it did then. The waning moon, the cheerful alphorn, the long-lasting dawn which allayed the cold, the shadows on the snowy mountains, the white clouds above the Lake of Zug, the clarity and sharpness of the peaks, the slopes in all directions one behind another, the light that emerged gradually on the peaks, the huddled, cold people in their blankets, the Mönch and the Jungfrau - nothing was missing. I could not tear myself away from the sight, and remained a full six hours at the peak, absorbing

the mountain views. I thought that if I come again, something might not be the same, and I wanted to engrave the sight indelibly on my memory.[33]

The young Mendelssohn wrote 12 *Sinfonie* for strings at this time. In the slow movement of his *Sinfonia No. 9*, composed the year after his first visit, he includes gentle alphorn calls. He provides echoes, a quiet drone accompaniment and a *pastorale* 6/8 time signature. The passages appear three times and each ends with an atmospheric pause.

Fig. 5.11. Mendelssohn, *Sinfonia No. 9*, third movement bars 45–51. The staves are for violin 1, violin 2, viola 1, viola 2, cello and bass.[34]

Fig. 5.12. Watercolour of the Rigi, above Lucerne. Painting by Mendelssohn during his third visit to the area, in 1847.[35]

Mendelssohn includes in his diary a transcription of a *Ranz des Chèvres* by Ferdinand Huber that appears in J. B. Gluck's *Les Délices de la Suisse* of 1835.

Franz Schubert (1797–1828) was, like Beethoven and Haydn, a resident of Vienna in his final years. He composed one of his last works, *Der Hirt auf den Felsen* for voice, clarinet and piano in 1828, the year after Beethoven's death. The work has become known in English as *The Shepherd on the Rock*, although *Hirt* means 'herdsman' in German and *Felsen* is more likely here to mean 'crags'. In this setting, the world of the alphorn and the yodel are intertwined, which could suggest an alphorn played by a herdsman in the high pastures alongside a companion who sings. The scene depicted by Schubert was a common romantic subject. It was described by Viotti, for example, and was portrayed in several eighteenth- and nineteenth-century paintings, drawings and engravings.

Fig. 5.13. Title page from the 1812 edition of *Sammlung von Schweizer Kühreihen und alten Volksliedern*, which shows a typical scene of the *Hirt auf dem Felsen*. This is a view in the Bernese Oberland of the Rosenlaui Glacier, the Wellhorn and the Wetterhorn.[36]

The first four stanzas of Schubert's text are a poem *Der Berghirt* (The Mountain Herdsman) by Wilhelm Müller, author of the poems that Schubert had used in *Die Schöne Müllerin* and *Winterreise*. Müller had also died the previous year, aged only 32. The second half of the text is written by another poet, Wilhelmina Christiane von Chézy: this gives the overall song a different tone. The carefree world of yodel and the alphorn is transformed into a scene of loneliness and grief, although at the end of the song, the herdsman looks forward to the joy of freedom from pain. This is a poignant work, written so soon after the deaths of Beethoven and Müller and when Schubert, at the age of 30, had received the news that he himself had not much longer to live. Horn-call motifs, with echoes, are given to the voice, the clarinet and the piano.

Fig. 5.14. Schubert, *Der Hirt auf dem Felsen*, bars 37–56.[37]

The text reads:

Wenn auf dem höchsten Fels ich steh',	When on the highest rock I stand,
ins tiefe Thal hernieder seh',	And down into the valley gaze,
und singe,	And sing,
Fern aus dem tiefen dunkeln Thal,	Far from the deep and misty vale,
schwingt sich empor der Wiederhall	There soars aloft re-echoing sound
der Klüfte.	of ravines.
Je wieter meine Stimme dringt,	My voice, the more it penetrates
je heller sie mir wieder klingt,	The clearer it resounds to me
von unten.	From down below.
Mein Liebchen wohnt so weit von mir,	My darling lives so far from me,
drum sehn' ich mich so heiss nach	Thus ardently I long for her,
ihr hinüber.	Far away.
In tiefem Gram verzehr ich	In deepest grief I waste away
mich mir ist die Freude hin,	All joy from me has fled;
auf Erden mir die Hoffnung	On earth for me all hope is dead
wich ich hier so einsam bin.	So lonely here am I.
So sehnend klang im Wald das Lied,	So ardent sounded forth my song,
so sehnend klang es durch die Nacht,	So ardent sounded in the night,
die Herzen es zum Himmel zieht	Our hearts it draws to Heaven,
mit wunderbarer Macht.	With wonder-working might.
Der Frühling will kommen,	The springtime is coming,
der Frühling meine Freud',	The spring my delight,
nun mach' ich mich fertig	I prepare myself
zum Wandern bereit.	For wandering.[38]

The herdsman on a crag was specified in the opening scene of Grétry's opera *Guillaume Tell* (William Tell) of 1791, described on p. 160. Gioachino Rossini (1792–1868) wrote an opera based on the same story, *Il Guglielmo Tell*, also for a Parisian audience, 38 years after that of Grétry, in 1829. Rossini's opera, and in particular its overture, has achieved greater popularity. The celebration of the exploits of its Swiss peasant hero was a theme in keeping with the post-Revolutionary spirit.

Rossini was very close to his father. In a conversation with Wagner, he explained that in this he found inspiration for the close relationship between the father and son at the heart of the tale of *Il Guglielmo Tell*. Rossini took his version of the text from the German poet and philosopher Friedrich von Schiller, who had written a substantial drama entitled *Wilhelm Tell* in 1804. The *Kühreien* plays an intrinsic role in Schiller's text: he introduces his first three characters singing to a *Kühreien* melody. The opening of the play is set on the shores of Lake Lucerne, and the stage directions specify the mountain scene, with cowbells and the singing of the *Kühreien*.

... Noch ehe der Vorhang aufgeht, hört man den Kuhreihen und das harmonische Geläut der Herdenglocken, welches sich auch bei eröffneter Szene noch eine Zeitlang fortsetßt.

... The *Kühreien*, and the harmonious tinkling of cowbells, continue for some while after the rising of the curtain.

Fischerknabe, singt im Rahn,
Melodie des Kuhreihens,

Fisher boy, sings in his boat,
the melody of the *Kühreien*,

Es lächelt der See, er ladet zum Bade,
Der Knabe schlief ein am grünen Gestade,
Da hört er ein Klingen,
Wie Flöten so süß,
Wie Stimmen der Engel
Im Paradies.
Und wie er erwachet in seliger Lust,
Da spülen die Wasser ihm um die Brust,
Und es ruft aus den Tiefen:
Lieb Knabe, bist mein;
Ich locke den Schläfer,
Ich zieh' ihn herein.

The merry lake invites him to swim,
The boy sleeps on its green shore,
He heard a melody,
Drifting sweetly,
Like the voice of an angel
In paradise.
And he wakens with pleasure,
The waters ripple over his chest;
And a voice from the deep cries:
Dear boy, you are mine;
I call the shepherd,
I draw him in.

Hirte, auf dem Berge,
Variation des Kuhreihens.

Herdsman, on the mountain,
Variation of the *Kühreien*.

Ihr Matten, lebt wohl!
Ihr sonnigen Weiden!
Der Senne muß scheiden,
Der Sommer ist hin.
Wir fahren zu Berg, wir kommen wieder,
Wenn der Kuckuck ruft,
Wenn erwachen die Lieder,
Wenn mit Blumen die Erde sich kleidet neu,
Wenn die Brünnlein fließen im lieblichen Mai.
Ihr Matten, lebt wohl!
Ihr sonnigen Weiden!
Der Senne muß scheiden,
Der Sommer ist hin.

Your meadows come alive!
Your sunny pastures!
The herdsman must leave,
The summer is here.
We go to the hills, we are coming again,
When the cuckoo calls,
When the birds sing,
When the flowers clothe the earth anew,
When the brooks flow in lovely May.
Your meadows come alive!
Your sunny pastures!
The herdsman must leave,
The summer is here.

Alpenjäger, erscheint gegenüber auf der Höhe	Hunter, appearing on the top of a cliff,
des Felsen, zweite Variation	Second variation of the *Kühreien*
Es donnern die Höhen,	There is thunder above,
Es zittert der Steg,	It shakes the bridge,
Nicht grauet dem Schüßen	There is no grip
Auf Schwindlichtem Weg.	On the dangerous path.
Er Schreitet verwegen auf Feldern von Eis,	He calls across the ice fields,
Da pranget kein Frühling,	Where Spring never blossoms,
Da grünet kein Reis;	Where nothing green will grow;
Und unter den Füßen ein neblichtes Meer,	And under his feet a sea of mist,
Erkennt er die Städte der Menschen nicht mehr;	He cannot see the towns any more;
Durch den Riß nur der Wolken	Through the parting clouds
Erblickt er die Welt,	He can glimpse the world,
Tief unter den Wassern	Deep under the water
Das grünende Feld.[39]	Of the green meadows.

Rossini was generous in his use of alphorn themes in *Il Guglielmo Tell* to portray the Swiss landscape, possibly because both he and his father played the French horn. It is significant that Rossini chose turning arpeggio motifs to represent the alphorn, unlike Grétry's choice of the Appenzell *Kühreien*. This might suggest that Rossini considered that motifs played on the alphorn to visitors to the Alps were widely enough recognised as a symbol of Switzerland by the time this work was written.

The end of the second part of this opera features a storm. In the section that follows, Rossini restores the peace of the pastoral scene with a passage entitled *Ranz des Vaches* that opens with an expansive alphorn melody based on a turning arpeggio motif, triplet figures with a bagpipe-like drone accompaniment reminiscent of the local herdsmen playing a *pastorale*. These phrases, also featured in the overture, were originally given to the tenoroon or *alto-fagotto*, but by the time that the score was published the following year, Rossini had re-allocated the tenoroon phrases to the cor anglais. However, he had not yet had the part rewritten in cor anglais notation: despite the words *Corno Inglese*, the music still appears in bass clef to sound an octave higher, as for the tenoroon. It becomes an extensive herdsman's duet, with each phrase echoed an octave higher by the flute.

These motifs combine *pastorale* features with typical *Ranz des Vaches* repeating three-note cells, while five-bar phrases give the impression of a pause at the end of each statement. Yodel figures are introduced later to enhance the rustic scene. It is quoted extensively in the overture to the opera.

Fig. 5.15. Rossini, overture to the opera *Il Guglielmo Tell*, bars 176–183, wind parts. The tenoroon/cor anglais part is on stave 7, echoed by the flute (stave 1). A drone effect is provided by horns, clarinets and bassoons.[40]

A year after the first performance of Rossini's *Il Guglielmo Tell*, another composer working in Paris at that time, Hector Berlioz (1803–1869), completed his *Symphonie fantastique*. According to Berlioz's *Memoires*, before the composition of this work he had been wholly absorbed in reading Goethe's *Faust*. He immediately wrote *Huit Scènes de Faust* (Eight Scenes from Faust), which he later withdrew and refashioned into *Le Damnation de Faust* (The Damnation of Faust) eighteen years later. He recorded that while still under the influence of *Faust*, he wrote his *Symphonie fantastique*, in which the protagonist, after taking opium, experiences a series of visions of his beloved.[41]

At the opening of the third movement of *Symphonie fantastique*, entitled *Scène aux Champs* (Scene in the Meadows), the cor anglais plays *Ranz des Vaches* phrases with distant answering calls provided by an offstage oboe. At the end of the movement, the cor anglais phrases are heard again but receive no response. Berlioz uses the absence of the reply of another herdsman as a statement of loneliness and abandonment. Again, the world of the alphorn and the yodel come together, with vocal calls implied by instrumental arpeggio material. In his own description of this movement in the preface to the symphony, Berlioz refers to this music as a *Ranz des Vaches*, although he does not specify whether the herdsmen are calling to each other with voices or with instruments. He explains that he is using the sounds of the *Ranz des Vaches* at evening time:

> One summer evening in the countryside, a Ranz des Vaches is heard from two herdsmen; the pastoral duet, the gentle rustling of the trees gently shaken by the wind, some recent signs of hope, all combined to fill his heart with an unaccustomed calm to lift his spirits, but she appears once more. His heart is filled with foreboding, what if she deceived him ... One of the

shepherds resumes his simple melody, but the other answers him no more. The sun sets ... distant rolling of thunder ... solitude ... silence ...[42]

It is possible that Berlioz may have come across these alphorn phrases in his childhood. He had grown up in the foothills of the French Alps near Grenoble, and the music of the herdsmen in the nearby Chartreuse mountains could have been the source of Berlioz's motifs, as they bear little resemblance to those found in a Swiss, Bavarian, Austrian or Italian context. He also uses notes found on horns that are longer than those typically quoted at this time.

Fig. 5.16. High pastureland in the Chartreuse mountains. Photo: Frances Jones.

In his renowned treatise on instrumentation and orchestration of 1843, *Grand Traité d'Instrumentation et d'Orchestration Moderne*, Berlioz quotes this example to demonstrate the evocative use of the cor anglais in an echo passage to create a pastoral dialogue:

In the *Adagio* of one of my symphonies, the cor anglais, having repeated the phrases of an oboe an octave lower, as if it were a pastoral dialogue, the voice of a youth and the response of a girl, it restates the phrases (at the end of the movement) with a soft accompaniment of four quiet timpani, and the silence of the rest of the orchestra. The feelings of absence, of being forgotten, of painful solitude which arouse in the souls of some listeners the memory of this forlorn melody, would have only a quarter of its effect if it were played on any instrument other than the cor anglais.[43]

Auf dem Lande.
Scène aux champs.   In the country.

Fig. 5.17. Berlioz, *Symphonie fantastique*, third movement bars 1–6.[44]

The alphorn phrases used by Berlioz in his *Symphonie fantastique* also appear in *Prélude à l'Après-Midi d'un Faune* (Prelude to the Afternoon of a Faun) by fellow Frenchman Claude Debussy (1862–1918). This work, composed in 1894, has a pastoral setting reminiscent of the backdrop to Berlioz's *Scène aux Champs*. It is based on a poem by Stéphane Mallarmé set in ancient Greece that describes the sensuous feelings of a faun (a rural deity with a goat's horns, body and tail but a human head). He plays on his pan-pipes, unsuccessfully chases nymphs, falls asleep and then pursues them in his dreams. Mallarmé disapproved of Debussy's intention to set his poem to music as he felt that his words created their own music in the reader's imagination; however when Debussy played a piano reduction of his score to the poet, the response, after a prolonged silence, was delight at the way in which the composer had captured and enhanced the spirit of the text.[45] Debussy sets the scene in this delicate masterpiece of orchestration with a gentle unaccompanied flute passage that opens with two typical musical references to the pastoral landscape: a repeated flowing panpipe-like phrase, followed by an alphorn motif that closely resembles that heard in Berlioz's work:

Fig. 5.18. Debussy, *Prélude à l'Après-Midi d'un Faune*, bars 1–4. After a repeated panpipe-like phrase, bar 3 is similar to the alphorn call used by Berlioz in his *Symphonie fantastique*.

Berlioz's collection of five pastoral songs, Op. 13, entitled *Fleurs des Landes* (Flowers of the Countryside) was completed three years after his *Symphonie fantastique*, in 1833. The fourth song, *Le Jeune Pâtre Breton* (The young Breton Herdsman), is a trio for voice, French horn and piano; it was later published in a version for voice and orchestra. Berlioz's piano writing here is more complex and multi-layered than that found in Schubert's *Der Hirt auf den Felsen*: perhaps already in this version of the composition Berlioz was thinking of the possibilities that the full orchestra could offer.

Although it has been noted that herdsmen's horns were in use in non-mountainous locations, the scene described in the text bears little relation to Brittany, since the lyrics talk of mountains and valleys and high cliffs that divide them. Nevertheless, the vocal part, horn part and piano accompanying figurations are all based on arpeggiations that a herdsman would play to his animals: almost every bar of the piece contains such alphorn-like motifs. The verses tell of a young cowherd, Luc, who yearns for the company of Anna who tends the goats. The horn *obbligato* begins at verse 2, where the mountains are first described.

Dès que la grive est éveillée,	As soon as the thrush wakens,
Sur cette lande encor mouillée	Upon this damp ground
Je viens m'asseoir	I sit down
Jusques au soir;	Until the evening;
Grand'mère de qui je me cache,	Grandmother from whom I hide
Dit: Loïc aime trop sa vache.	Says: Luc loves his cow too much.
Oh! Nenni da!	It's not that,
Mais j'aime la petite Anna.	But I love little Anna.
A son tour Anna, ma compagne,	In her turn, Anna, my companion,
Conduit derrière la montagne,	Leads behind the mountain,
Près des sureaux,	Near the elder trees,
Ses noirs chevreaux;	Her black goats;
Si la montagne où je m'égare,	If the mountain, where I wander,
Ainsi qu'un grand mur, nous sépare,	Separates us like a great wall,
Sa douce voix	Her sweet voice
Sa voix m'appelle au fond du bois.	Calls me from deep in the woods.
Oh! Sur un air plaintif et tendre,	Oh! A plaintive and tender song
Qu'il est doux au loin de s'entendre,	Although sweet when heard from afar,
Sans même avoir	Isn't the same
L'heure de se voir!	As when I can see you!
De la montagne à la vallée	From the mountain to the valley
La voix par la voix appelée	One voice called by another
Semble un soupir	Is like a sigh
Mêlé d'ennuis et de plaisir.	A mix of care and joy.
Ah! retenez bien votre haleine,	Ah! keep on blowing,
Brise étourdie, et dans la plaine,	Heedless wind, and in the fields,
Parmi les blés	Among the corn
Courez, volez!	Hasten, soar!
Dieu! la méchante a sur son aile	God! the cruel wind beats on its wings
Emporté la voix douce et frêle,	The soft, delicate voice,
La douce voix	The sweet voice
Qui m'appelait au fond du bois.	That calls me from deep in the woods.

Fig. 5.19. Berlioz, *Le Jeune Pâtre Breton* for French horn in E flat, soprano and piano, bars 27–40.[46]

While in *Faust* Goethe took his readers on a deep psychological journey, his libretto for an operetta or *Singspiel* entitled *Jery und Bätely* was a more light-hearted text. The narrative, set in Switzerland, became a source of inspiration for many composers and it gained considerable popularity on the operatic stage in Paris in the nineteenth century. Goethe wrote the story at the end of 1779 after travels in Switzerland during the autumn of that year. He calls on the familiarity of the employment of Swiss soldiers in foreign lands in that a leading character in the narrative is a Swiss mercenary, at home on leave with his fellow servicemen from duties abroad. The story of love and intrigue is set in a dairy farm in the Swiss canton of Appenzell.

Goethe's comments about this story give an insight into visitors' attitudes towards Switzerland at that time, in that he expressed concerns about ongoing interest in the country and wished to take an active role in the promulgation of its picturesque rural delights. He hoped that this text would be set as an opera as quickly as possible, 'at a time when interest in Swiss stories is not yet extinguished ...' and intended it essentially as a diversion where 'actors wear Swiss clothing and speak of cheese and milk'.[47] His crusade was worthwhile and his intention far-reaching: at least ten composers wrote settings of this libretto during the 60 years after it was written. One of these, *Le Chalet* with music by Parisian composer Alphonse Adam, became one of the most widely performed operas of its time. Completed in 1834, using a French translation of Goethe's text created by Eugène Scribe and Anne-Honoré-Joseph Duveyrier, who used the pseudonym Mélesville, it was performed for Queen Victoria at Windsor Castle and by the 1920s attained 1,500 performances at the Opéra-Comique in Paris.

Adam's musical allusions focus on the military connotations of the story rather than its Swiss pastoral setting; however, another setting of the story, by Gaetano Donizetti (1797–1848), does use alphorn-like music to enhance its Swiss flavour. His *Betly, o la Cabanna Svizzera* (Betly, or The Swiss Chalet), uses his own Italian translation of the French libretto and the work was first performed in Naples in 1836. Although the story is set in Appenzell, Donizetti does not quote the local *Kühreien*. Rather, he sets the opening chorus in a gentle *pastorale* 6/8 rhythm. Many turning arpeggio alphorn-like calls are used in the opening number, initially presented on a lone clarinet, with a silent backdrop. They are free from pulse (marked *a piacere*) and end with two atmospheric pauses. Meanwhile, the shy herdsman, Daniale, is instructed to hide (*Daniale di dentro*). The initial alphorn-like music comes to rest before the marking *a tempo* heralds the introduction of the chorus and strings.

These alphorn motifs are not unlike those used by Rossini in his opera *Il Guglielmo Tell*, above. In that both composers are Italian and both replicate the rhythms of the Italian herdsmen's *pastorale*, there is a possibility that this style of alphorn motif, not seen in the work of German, Swiss, French or Austrian composers, derives directly from the playing of Italian herdsmen.

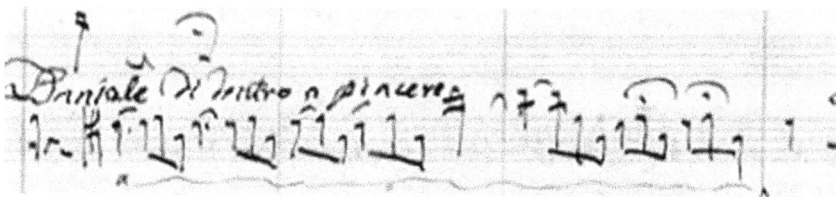

Fig. 5.20. Donizetti, *Betly, o La Capanna Svizzera*. Alphorn-like calls punctuate and accompany the opening chorus. Introduction, bars 102–105, clarinet in A.[48]

Alongside material based on Swiss narratives and references to Alpine scenes or herdsmen, many composers also sought to recreate the effect of a visit to the Alps for their audiences. As mentioned earlier, Franz Liszt wrote three sets of piano pieces entitled *Tagebuch eines Wanderers* (Diary of a Traveller), published in 1842, which include many alphorn-like motifs. He subsequently reworked a number of the pieces and re-issued them as the first book of *Années de Pèlerinage* (Years of Pilgrimage); thus many of the titles of these pieces apply to two quite different versions of Liszt's thoughts. The original versions are discussed here. Liszt's reverential quotation of the music of the Appenzell *Kühreien* in this collection was described earlier; four other instances of

alphorn material in this work illustrate different ways in which Liszt makes use
of alphorn music:

Eindrücke und Poesien:	5. *Die Tellskapelle;*
	11. *Ein Abend in den Bergen;*
Paraphrasen:	1. *Kuhreigen. Aufzug auf die Alp;*
Melodieenblüten von den Alpen:	1.

Die Tellskapelle. William Tell's chapel is on the edge of Lake Lucerne,
reputedly at the place where Tell landed after his escape from his captors during
a storm on the lake. Liszt contrasts two aspects of the warrior's character in his
portrayal: his military skills, and his pride in his mountain homeland.

Fig. 5.21. Contemporary watercolour *Tell's Chapel, Lake Lucerne*, by Joseph Mallord
William Turner, c.1841.[49]

The opening of Liszt's composition reflects the military connotations of the
story, with trumpet-like fanfare motifs marked *marziale;* then he writes the
word *Alphorn* in the score and supplies bright alphorn-like figurations in triple
metre, marked *f* and *energico*. Liszt develops the two motifs throughout the
work, exploiting their similarities and their differences. As in *Le Jeune Pâtre
Breton* by Berlioz, described above, Liszt uses a complex interplay of ideas in
his writing for the piano. He not only attempts to tell a story and recreate scenes
of the Alps on the keyboard: he also brings the sound palette of a range of other
instruments and orchestral colours into the drawing-room in his piano writing.

Fig. 5.22. Liszt, *Tagebuch eines Wanderers: Die Tellskapelle*, bars 1–12.[50]

Ein Abend in den Bergen (An Evening in the Mountains). In this piece, Liszt returns to the solemnity that he created in his composition based on the *Kühreien* of Appenzell, *Melodieenblüten von den Alpen* No. 6, described earlier. In *Ein Abend in den Bergen* he gives the pianist the instructions *dolce religiosamente* and *dolce espressivo*. He creates a beautiful evening stillness with repeating high octave Gs, reminiscent of a shimmering *tremolando* of orchestral violins, then brings in a simple turning arpeggio alphorn motif in the register at which it would be played on an alphorn. He builds the motifs into a tender prayer-like melody reminiscent of the *Alpsegen* or *Betruf*, with the instruction *dolce con sentimento*.

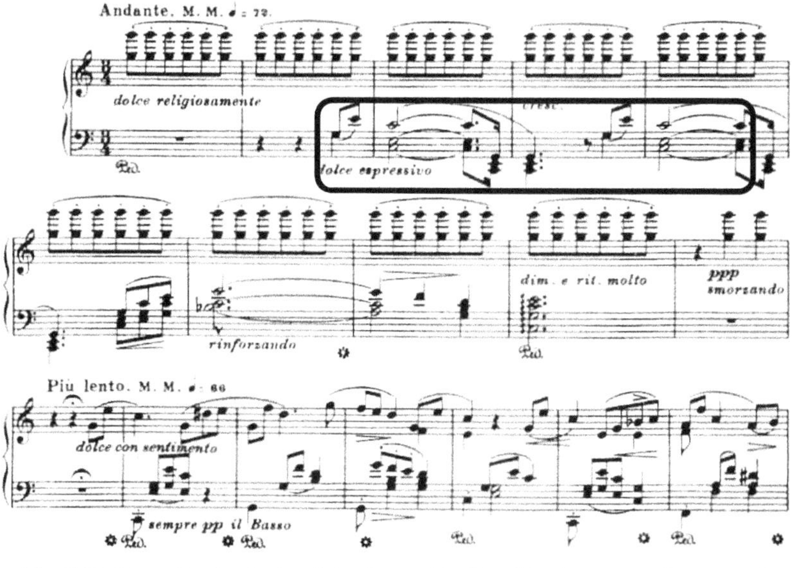

Fig. 5.23. Liszt, *Tagebuch eines Wanderers: Ein Abend in den Bergen*, bars 1–17.[51]

Fig. 5.24. An evening in the mountains. The author, Titlis summit, Switzerland.

Kuhreigen. Aufzug auf die Alp. The third section of Liszt's *Tagebuch eines Wanderers* bears the title *Paraphrasen*. It opens with a piece entitled *Kuhreigen* [*sic*]. *Aufzug auf die Alp*, which is built around an alphorn-style melody that is the opening phrase of a song written by Ferdinand Huber entitled *Kuhreihen im Fruehling zum Aufzug auf die Alp* (Departure of the Cattle Procession in Spring for the Alp) which had appeared in *Les Délices de la Suisse*, a collection of Swiss songs and *Kühreien* published three years previously in 1835. After a cadenza-like introduction, Liszt quotes Huber's melody in its entirety and then builds a series of variations upon it. He includes short phrases in triple time that end with a paused note. The opening, marked *ff*, is repeated as an extended atmospheric echo, marked *ppp*, before the music moves into a series of rhapsodic elaborations of the material.

Fig. 5.25. Liszt, *Tagebuch eines Wanderers: Kuhreigen. Aufzug auf die Alp*, bars 1–27. The piece is based on Huber's *Kuhreihen im Fruehling zum Aufzug auf die Alp*.[52]

Fig. 5.26. Opening bars (1–9) of *Kuhreihen im Fruehling zum Aufzug auf die Alp*, by Huber, from *Les Délices de la Suisse*. The accompanying vignette illustrates the scene.[53]

***Melodieenblüten von den Alpen* No. 1**. There are many alphorn motifs in the nine pieces included under the title *Melodieenblüten von den Alpen*. A complex example is shown below. An alphorn-like arpeggio pattern is established at the top of the left-hand chords. Out of these, rising call figures emerge, which Liszt develops into a cheerful melody.

Fig. 5.27. Liszt, *Tagebuch eines Wanderers*. Alphorn motifs open the first of the *Melodieenblüten von den Alpen*.[54]

Liszt also wrote song settings based on scenes from Schiller's *Wilhelm Tell*. In 1845 he set the three *Kühreien* texts from the opening of the drama under the title *Drei Lieder aus Schillers Wilhelm Tell*. The songs form one continuous work. It is dedicated to the Dutch artist Ary Scheffer, who painted several portraits of leading nineteenth-century intellectuals, including Dickens, Lamartine and Chopin, and completed a painting of Liszt in 1837. The portrait depicts Liszt as one of the magi; thus, the much-fêted composer is elevated to the hierarchy of kings of legendary biblical status.

No. 2 of the set bears the title *Der Hirt*. The text describes the *Kühreien*, or departure of the herdsman with his cattle to the summer pastures. As seen in the opera of Grétry, the words are given by Schiller to William Tell's son.

Ihr Matten, lebt wohl,	Your meadows come alive!
Ihr sonnigen wieden!	Your sunny pastures!
Der Senne muss scheiden,	The herdsman must leave,
Der Sommer ist hin.	The summer is here.
Wir fahren zu Berg,	We go to the hills,
wir kommen wieder,	we are coming again,
wenn der Kukkuck ruft,	when the cuckoo calls,
wen erwachen die Lieder,	when the birds sing,
wen mit Blumen die Erde	when the flowers
sich kleidet neu,	clothe the earth anew,
wenn die Brünnelein fliessen	when the brooks flow
in lieblichen Mai.	in lovely May.

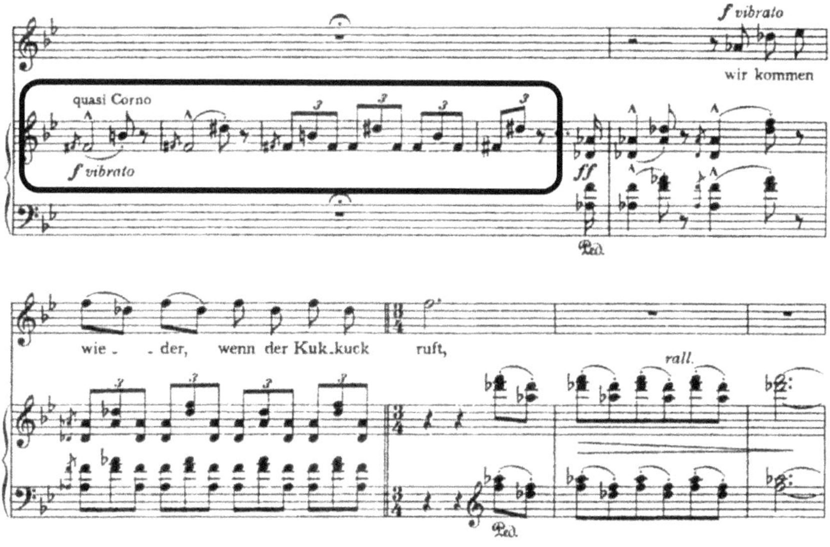

Fig. 5.28. Liszt, *Drei Lieder aus Schillers Wilhelm Tell* No. 2, *Der Hirt*, bars 39–44.[55]

Liszt's setting for voice and piano of the herdsman's song from *Wilhelm Tell* is almost operatic in its complexity, sonorities and approach. The vocal part and the piano accompaniment form an integrated whole reminiscent of a substantial orchestral score, with many different types of textures. At times the piano is in conversation with the voice; at times it takes prominence; indeed, Liszt includes an extensive piano cadenza. He gives his setting the significant tempo indication *Andante Pastorale*. He uses a variety of alphorn motifs, each one many times, and highlights the initial alphorn-like call with the marking *quasi Corno*.

Besides using alphorn-inspired material in his salon pieces, Liszt also incorporated alphorn references in his orchestral music. He creates a beautiful representation of calm after a storm in *Les Préludes*, originally composed in 1848. In contrast to the quotations of alphorn material in the works examined above, here Liszt's awareness of the more substantial range of the longer alphorn, rather than the shorter instrument played to tourists, can be found. He uses harmonics beyond the usual nos. 3, 4, 5 and 6: in this instance nos. 6, 8, 9, 10, 12 and 13. Thus this alphorn-type motif has more of a pentatonic feel, where most of the degrees of the scale are available (for an explanation of the harmonic series, see p. 19).

The work was written as the introduction to a cantata *Les Quatre Elemens*, with words by the poet Joseph Autran. The music subsequently underwent several transformations, including an association with writings of Alphonse de Lamartine instead; however, the piece has no specific narrative, rather it reflects concepts and ideas. Liszt uses many images drawn from nature in this work and a section that describes the storms of life (*allegro tempestuoso)* is returned to calm with a passage that reflects rural innocence, in replication of an alphorn being played in the mountains after a storm to signal that all is well. This section is also headed *Allegretto Pastorale*, and the passage has a typical *pastorale* compound time signature. Liszt provides a carefree alphorn-like melody for the French horn that is repeated and extended by the oboe and then the clarinet. It is set over a *pianissimo* rustic drone in the strings.

Fig. 5.29. Liszt, *Les Préludes*, bars 200–211, *Allegretto Pastorale*, horn, oboe and clarinet parts. An alphorn-like melody gives a rural flavour to the scene.[56]

A third narrative set in Switzerland, alongside that of William Tell and *Jery und Bätley*, attracted the interest of composers: Byron's epic poem *Manfred*. The text is partly autobiographical and partly rooted in ideas found in Goethe's *Faust* (concerning which Byron was accused of plagiarism);[57] there are parallels with several other literary works, including Shakespeare's *Hamlet*. Despite Byron's insistence that it was not intended for stage performance, Robert Schumann (1810–1856) was one of many composers inspired to write incidental music to the poem after a holiday with his family in Switzerland in 1848. It has been suggested that Schumann felt much affinity with the character of Manfred while facing his own fears during his bouts of depression. It is reported that while reading the poem to some friends, Schumann's voice suddenly faltered and he broke down in tears, so that he could read no further.[58]

In the resulting three-act work, for which Schumann retained the title *Manfred*, Scene No. 4 of Act 1 is a *recitative* with the descriptive title *Alpenkühreigen*. The protagonist contemplates suicide at the top of the Jungfrau. He hears distant alphorn music and reflects on his desire to be freed from his mortal self and become just the pure spirit of music itself.

Horch, der Ton!	Hark! the note!
Des Alpenrohrs	The natural music
natürliche Musik –	of the mountain reed –
denn hier ward nicht	for here the days are not
zu blosser Hirtendichtung	of the pastoral poets
die Patriarchenzeit –	and our forefathers –
in freien Lüften	the fresh mountain air
vermählt dem Klinggeläute	mingles with the sweet bells
muntrer Heerden;	of the herd;
die Töne trinkt mein Geist.	my soul would drink those echoes.
O wär'ich doch	Oh, that I were
solch'sansten Klanges	the sightless spirit
ungesch'ner Geist,	of a lovely sound,
lebend'ge Stimme,	a living voice,
athmende Harmonie,	a breathing harmony,
leiblose Wonne,	a bodiless desire
sterbend wie geboren	born and dying
im sel'gen Tone,	with the blessed tone
der mich zeugte![59]	which made me!

In Schumann's setting, Manfred's spoken musings appear against the backdrop of a lone cor anglais playing typical alphorn figures. The scene is introduced with the text: *'Man hört eine Hirtenschalmei in die Ferne und später Heerdengeläute'* (You can hear a herdsman's pipe in the distance and later, a herd on the move). The cor anglais is given slow phrases, then fast ones, then the slow ones return, as in a *Kühreien*. There are motifs marked *echo* and many repeating cells. The score shows how the text is declaimed while the music is played:

Fig. 5.30. Schumann, *Manfred*, Scene 4: *Alpenkühreigen*.[60]

Schumann was not only wrestling with problems of mental health. In May 1849, fighting in the vicinity of his home in Dresden forced Robert and Clara to flee from the neighbourhood. His *Liederalbum für die Jugend* (Song Album for the Young) Op. 79, written around that time, has been described as highly political: in some cases, the choice of poet was a political statement in itself, whereby Schumann expressed his views by setting texts written by those critical of the German state. Schumann conjures up scenes of dream-like innocence, but also of freedom, independence and the search for a better life: he used his art either as a means to escape from the violence and political turmoil that dominated daily life, or to express his feelings without attracting the attention of the censors.

As an example, Song No. 9 bears the title *Des Knaben Berglied* (The Mountain Boy's Song) with a text by Johann Ludwig Uhland who wrote the version of the *Tannhauser* legend upon which Wagner based his music-drama. *Des Knaben Berglied* celebrates the courage of the herding boy, although the text is far from merely a description of the joys of life in the high pastures: the underlying theme is that he is brave and strong and will challenge the storms that threaten his home.

Ich bin vom Berg der Hirtenknab,	I am the herding boy from the mountains,
seh' auf die Schlösser all' herab.	looking down on you from my castle.
Die Sonne strahlt am ersten hier,	The sun's rays strike here first
am längsten weilet sie bei mir,	and linger with me here the longest.
Ich bin der Knab' vom Berge,	I am the boy from the mountains,
vom Berg der Hirtenknab!	I am the mountain boy!
Der berg, der ist mein Eigenthum,	The mountain belongs to me
da zieh'n die Stürme rings herum,	when it draws the storms around,
und heulen sie von Nord und Süd,	and howls from north and south,
so überschallt sie doch mein Lied:	then I drown it with my song:
Ich bin der Knab' vom Berge,	I am the boy from the mountains,
vom Berg der Hirtenknab!	I am the mountain boy!
Sind Blitz und Donner unter mir,	With thunder and lightning below me,
so steh' ich hoch im Blauen hier;	I stay up here in the blue;
ich kenne sie und rufe zu:	I know it and call to it:
lasst meines Vaters Haus in Ruh'!	leave my father's house in peace!
Ich bin der Knab' vom Berge,	I am the boy from the mountains,
vom Berg der Hirtenknab!	I am the mountain boy!
Und wann die Sturmglock' einst erschallt,	And when the storm warning first appears,
manch' Feuer auf den Bergen wallt,	with fire in the mountains,
dann steig' ich nieder, tret' in's Glied	then I climb down, striding out,
und schwing' mein Schwert und sing' mein Lied;	and swing my sword and sing my song:
Ich bin der Knab' vom Berge,	I am the boy from the mountains,
vom Berg der Hirtenknab!	I am the mountain boy!

Schumann's approach to piano accompaniments contrasts with that of Liszt. Whereas it has been seen that Liszt often treated his piano-writing as a salon representation of an orchestral score, it was fundamentally as a pianist that Schumann wrote for the instrument. He had composed little for orchestra before he embarked on his 'year of song', 1840, and he retained this stylistic integrity in his second period of song-writing (1849–50) as demonstrated in this piece.

Schumann's piano introduction to *Des Knaben Berglied* consists of simple alphorn-like turning arpeggio calls. A repeating arpeggio refrain is given to the voice at the end of each verse; this is interspersed with alphorn-like motifs on the piano, which also bring each verse to a close.

Des Knaben Berglied.
(L. Uhland.)

Sehr markirt.   Op. 79 Nr. 9.

1. Ich bin vom Berg der
2. Der Berg, der ist mein
3. Sind Blitz und Don - ner
4. Und wann die Sturm-glock'

1. Hir - ten-knab', seh auf die Schlösser all' her - ab.   Die Son - - ne strahlt am
2. Ei - gen-thum, da zieh'n die Stür-me rings her - um,   und heu - - len sie von
3. un - ter mir, so steh ich hoch im Blau-en hier;   ich ken - - ne sie und
4. einst erschallt, manch Feu - er auf den Ber-gen wallt,   dann steig' ich nie - der,

1. er- sten hier,   am läng - sten wei - let   sie bei mir,
2. Nord und Süd,   so   ü - - berschallt sie doch mein Lied;
3. ru - fe zu: lasst mei - - nes Va - ters Haus in Ruh'!
4. tret' in's Glied   und schwing' mein Schwert und sing' mein Lied;

ich bin der Knab' vom

Ber-ge.   vom Berg der Hir-ten - knab!

Fig. 5.31. Schumann, *Des Knaben Berglied.*[61]

Schumann also included a setting of the *Kühreien* from Schiller's *Wilhelm Tell* in his *Liederalbum für die Jungend,* as song No. 23. He gave the *Kühreien* text the title *Des Sennen Abschied* (The Herdsman's Departure). He again writes alphorn-like interjections between the vocal phrases, although of a different character from those in *Des Knaben Berglied*: these are more haunting and wistful.

Fig. 5.32. Schumann, *Des Sennen Abschied,* bars 24–29.[62]

In his setting of another text, *Die Sennin* (The Milkmaid), the following year, Schumann chooses a different way to feature alphorn music and gives his alphorn motifs a different character. He begins the vocal line with a typical alphorn motif and adopts a persistent, almost menacing alphorn-like figuration for the piano accompaniment. The text that inspired Schumann here draws both cheerful and then sinister meaning from alphorn-like calls. The lyrics of *Die Sennin* were a poem written by Nicolaus Franz Niembsch, eight years older than Schumann, who wrote under the pseudonym of Nicolaus Lenau. With striking similarity to the course of Schumann's life, Lenau suffered from persistent depression and ended his days in a mental asylum.

Die Sennin is one of six of Lenau's texts that Schumann set as his Opus 90 as a tribute following the poet's death. Schumann added a short Requiem, and the set was published with an unusually elaborate cover that included a depiction of a cross and a funeral wreath. The text here initially describes the joyful milkmaid's song as it echoes off the cliffs, such as might be heard in the valley of Lauterbrunnen, at the foot of the Jungfrau (see Fig. 5.39), the setting for Byron's drama *Manfred.* The second half of the text dwells on the effect of death which saddens and silences the grey cliffs:

Schöne Sennin, noch einmal	Beautiful milkmaid, once again
singe deinen Ruf in's Thal,	sing your call in the valley,
dass die frohe Felsensprache	that the cheerful voice of the rocks
deinem hellen Ruf erwache!	may resonate with your light voice!
Horch, o Sennin, wie dein Sang	Hear, oh milkmaid, how your song
in die Brust den Bergen drang,	penetrates the heart of the mountains,
wie dein Wort die Felsenseelen	how with your words the mountain's soul
Freudig fort und fort erzählen!	tells of stronger and stronger joy!
Aber einst, wie Alles flieht,	But then when you depart with your song,
scheidest du mit deinem Lied,	everything disappears,
wenn dich Liebe fortbewogen,	when love has moved you on,

oder dich der Tod entzogen.   or when death has taken you away.
Und verlassen werden stehn.   And there, standing deserted,
Traurig stumm herüber sehn   sad and mute,
dort die graunen Felsenzinnen,   the grey crag pinnacles will look across,
und auf deine Lieder sinnen.   and reflect on your songs.

Die Sennin.

Fig. 5.33. Schumann, *Die Sennin*, bars 1–3.[63]

A second composer who had to flee from Dresden in 1849 was Richard Wagner (1813–1883). He found refuge in Switzerland: this was the first of two extended stays in the country. Wagner had, though, already showed a certain familiarity with the sound of the alphorn. In 1841 he was living in Paris. To support himself, he made arrangements of others' operas, wrote articles and produced small-scale compositions. One of his works includes parts for alphorns: a four-minute musical interlude for chorus and small orchestra for a vaudeville play, *La Descente de la Courtille*, written by Théophile Marion Dumersan. It was first performed at the Théâtre des Variétés in Paris January 1841.

La Courtille was an area at the edge of the city of Paris where Parisians could eat, drink and enjoy themselves without paying tax to the city. Music, dancing and drinking were prominent features of the activities. An alcohol-fuelled procession from here towards the centre of the city, called *La Descente de La Courtille*, was part of the annual calendar, a familiar scene in the Paris Carnival on Ash Wednesday morning for forty years from 1822 until around 1860. There are lively eye-witness descriptions of the procession, and it is the subject of many contemporary paintings, drawings, and etchings. Several composers also wrote salon pieces inspired by the procession, which, together with this two-act theatre entertainment, all contribute to the lasting legacy of this once-popular event.

Wagner's choice of the sound of an unspecified number of unison offstage alphorns in F to open his interlude *La Descente de la Courtille* sets the scene with an appropriate lack of sophistication. There are two low announcement notes. Snare drum and trumpets then enter, with a hint of the lively dance-like material to come, then after further alphorn entonement, the music proper begins. As

Wagner does not include a tuba in the score, the alphorns provide occasional bass notes while the chorus sings of the progress of the jolly procession.

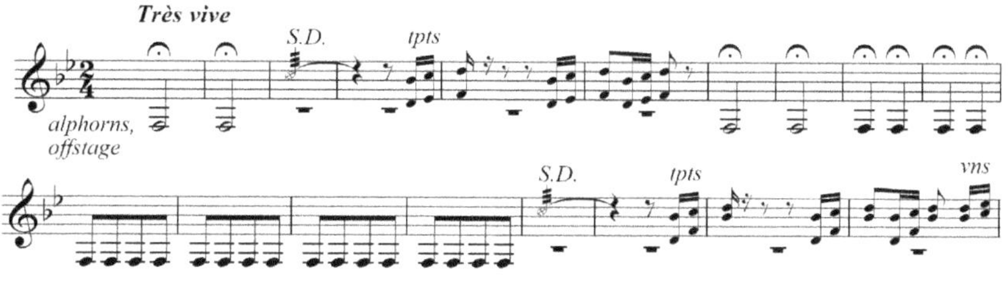

Fig. 5.34. Wagner, *La Descente de la Courtille*, bars 1–18.

Once in Switzerland, Wagner was inspired to incorporate motifs more typical of the alphorn in his work. A notable instance can be heard in his herdsman's melody at the beginning of Act 3 of his opera *Tristan und Isolde*. Two experiences influenced this particular alphorn reference. In 1859 Wagner transcribed alphorn music that he heard on an excursion to the top of the Rigi above Lucerne where he stayed overnight in order to watch the sunrise. He wrote to his wife Minna of the source of the melody:

> At four in the morning we were woken by the guide with an Alphorn – I jumped up, and saw that it was raining, so went back to bed to try to sleep again; but the droll call went round and round in my head and out of it came a very cheerful melody which the herdsman now blows to call Isolde's ship, making a surprisingly merry and naïve effect.[64]

Wagner was so delighted with the phrases he heard that he wrote some of them thus in a telegram to Minna: gg gde cde gde cde gef df gfe de. However, the postal officer refused to accept the telegram, fearful that it was some secret code.

Some years later, Wagner's second wife Cosima recorded in her diary that Richard also enjoyed listening to an alphorn player in the market square in Lucerne. He likened the sound to the call of a wild goose. Wagner attempted to transcribe some of the music, but the player was too reticent to enter into conversation with him. A few years later, when Wagner returned to listen again, he learned that the player had died. Wagner commented that he would do the best he could for him in *Tristan*.

Wagner gave his herdsman's alphorn melody to the cor anglais, to be played offstage. His meticulous instructions in the score specify the following:

> The performance of the herdsman's dance on the cor anglais requires such an accomplished artist that it must be undertaken and played behind the scenes by the same musician who plays the cor anglais in the orchestra during the whole evening. As the cor anglais is not used again until Scene two, the player has enough time to resume his place in the orchestra by then…[65]

At the place in the score where the melody appears, Wagner comments that the cor anglais should resemble a very strong natural instrument, such as an alphorn. He suggests that the sound might be reinforced with other woodwinds if necessary, but also gives the alternative of using a natural instrument made of wood. However, although the melody draws upon alphorn calls for its inspiration, most of it is an elaboration of such motifs, using notes that could not be played on an alphorn. If an alphorn-like instrument were to be constructed to play the solo passage, it would need some mechanism to enable it to play the notes that are outside the harmonic series.

Fig. 5.35. Wagner, *Tristan und Isolde* Act 3, bars 48–100: herdsman's melody written for an offstage cor anglais, inspired by alphorn calls heard at the Rigikulm hotel and in the market square in Lucerne.[66]

Wagner's second extended stay in Switzerland, from 1866, was in a splendid villa at Tribschen outside Lucerne as a guest of its owner, King Ludwig II of Bavaria, who was Wagner's patron. He composed *Siegfried-Idyll* for thirteen solo players and conducted it on the stairwell of the villa on Christmas morning in 1870, Cosima's 33rd birthday, when their son Siegfried was a year old. The original title for the work was *Tribschener Idyll mit Fidi-Vogelsang und Orange-Sonnenaufgang, als Symphonischer Geburtstagsgruss* (Tribschen Idyll with Fidi's Birdsong and the orange Sunrise, Symphonic Birthday Greetings). Fidi was their nickname for one-year-old Siegfried, and the 'orange sunrise' is a reference to an orange-coloured bedroom wall that was lit up by the morning sun. Both bird calls and the morning calls of the alphorn are clearly represented in the music.

Fig. 5.36. The house at Tribschen where Wagner lived from 1866 to 1872.[67]

Three of the themes, including the horn call, also appear in the love duet at the end of Act 3 of the opera *Siegfried,* which Wagner was writing around the same time. Patterns of falling fourths and fifths played by the French horn settle into familiar turning arpeggio figurations so commonly played on the alphorn. Wagner sets them alongside bird-like calls played on the clarinet and the flute, over a still drone held by horn 2. Cosima loved the music so much that she immediately asked for the twenty-minute piece to be repeated. She wrote in her diary:

> I was awakened by sounds that reached my ears, that continually grew louder. I wasn't dreaming any more, music was being played, and what music! As the music played R. came to me with the five children and handed me the score of the symphonic birthday greetings, I was moved to tears; so was the whole household. R. had arranged his orchestra on the stairs and thus immortalised our Tribschen! The work is called the 'Tribschen Idyll' ... After we had breakfast, the orchestra re-assembled on the lower floor and played the Idyll again; to everyone's astonishment they also played Lohengrin's Bridal March and Beethoven's Septet; and to finish, the piece that we couldn't hear enough once more! Now I understood the work R. was doing at home, now also of the good Richter's trumpet (he played the Siegfried theme beautifully and had just learned the trumpet for that purpose).[68]

Fig. 5.37. Wagner, *Siegfried-Idyll*, bars 259–271.[69]

Johannes Brahms (1833–1897) was also inspired by visits to Switzerland to include alphorn motifs in his compositions. He grew up in Hamburg; thereafter he spent most of his professional life in Vienna, and his diaries mention his love of walking holidays with his father in the mountains.[70] His father was a horn player and Brahms's deep affinity with the instrument is apparent in all his horn writing. He did not write overtly descriptive music in his orchestral works; however, it is not unexpected that references to alphorn-like music are found in some of his compositions.

A particularly lovely example occurs in the final stages of the first movement of his dramatic Piano Concerto No. 1. This composition was conceived as a work for two pianos, sketched out in 1854. It was gradually expanded into a work on the scale of a full symphony, although Brahms worked on it in two-piano score for subsequent orchestration, since at that time he felt inexperienced in writing for the orchestra. Its final form as a piano concerto was realised in 1858.

The first movement is powerful and full of drama, of symphonic proportions. Documentation suggests that the work was a tribute to his close friend and mentor, Robert Schumann. At the start of Robert's final illness, Brahms pledged his ongoing support to Clara and her family. Following Robert's death at the end of July 1856, Brahms took Clara to Switzerland for a month, together with two of her sons, and his own sister. The turbulence of the opening movement of this Piano Concerto is eventually brought to rest with the calm reassurance of an alphorn-like horn solo: it may have reflected this period of recuperation in the Swiss Alps that followed the trauma of Robert's last years. The solo, with typical peaceful horn-call figurations, is marked *marcato, ma dolce*. It is set over quiet piano arpeggios while the rest of the orchestra is silent. Echoes are provided by the timpani.

Fig. 5.38. Alphorn-like horn solo in Brahms's Piano Concerto No. 1, bars 432–438.[71]

A second, more specific quotation of alphorn music by Brahms is widely documented. In 1868 he was again in Switzerland, taking a walking holiday in the Bernese Oberland with his father. He wrote to Clara on her wedding anniversary, 12 September, which was the day before her birthday, noting down a melody that he heard played on an alphorn in the valley of Lauterbrunnen.[72]

Fig. 5.39. Lauterbrunnen has long been a favoured tourist destination in Switzerland. The parallel limestone cliffs afford good echoes for an alphorn. Photo: Frances Jones.

Brahms wrote the accompanying text: '*Also blus das Alphorn heut: Hoch auf'm Berg, tief im Tal, grüß ich dich viel tausendmal!*' (Thus the alphorn blew today: from high in the mountains and deep in the valley, I send you many thousand greetings!).

The music that he transcribed bears only moderate similarity to the usual turning arpeggio motifs: this suggests that it is the music of a herdsman at work, in contrast to the more stylised phrases generally played for tourists. Significantly, it also incorporates the 'alphorn *fa*', thus it must have been played

on a horn of sufficient length to produce this note. This is the second note of
the second stave in Brahms's transcription:

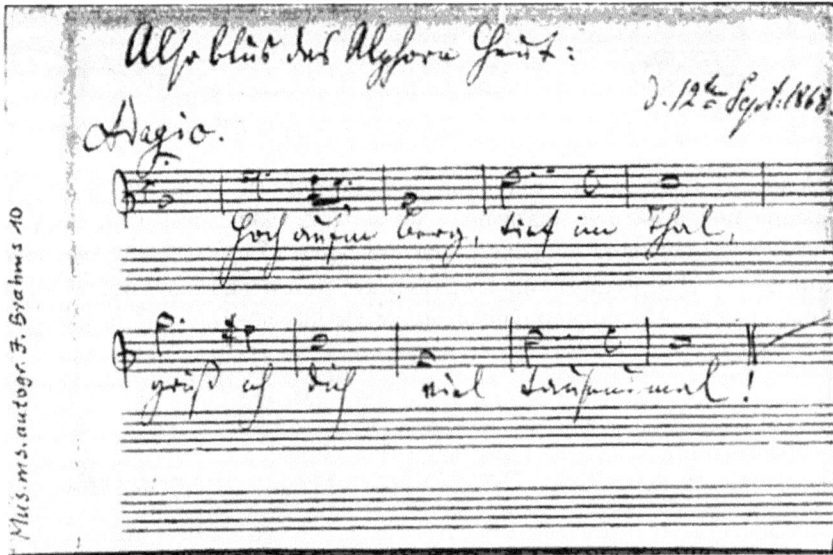

Fig. 5.40. Music sent by Brahms to Clara Schumann, an alphorn melody that he heard
in Lauterbrunnen.[73]

Two further features of alphorn playing can be seen in this transcription. It is
normal on an alphorn to play a 'warm-up' note before the commencement of a
melody. Brahms not only transcribes this note (the initial semibreve with a pause):
he also reproduces its faltering beginning, as an acciaccatura. Secondly, nowhere
else in the traditional repertoire is an alphorn motif found with a short note
(written here as the semiquaver D) in an otherwise straightforward arpeggio motif.
However, to mis-pitch an intended note is as common on the alphorn as it is on
the modern orchestral horn. Brahms includes this split note in his transcription.

Eight years later, Brahms uses the melody that he sent to Clara in the fourth
movement of his Symphony No. 1. There are several alterations: neither the first
semibreve nor its acciaccatura are included, and two times, the original rhythm
of a double dotted minim followed by a quaver is replaced with a dotted minim
followed by a crotchet. The theme appears directly after an intensely turbulent,
stormy movement, and here Brahms reproduces one of the vital functions of the
alphorn: to let the people in the village below know that all was well after a storm
in the mountains. He sets the melody over peaceful chords, a typical
accompaniment for an alphorn melody in a classical composition, to represent
the stillness of the mountain landscape. In the magnitude of this symphony, 21
years in gestation, the quotation of this melody here could represent a significant

point of resolution and relief after a long struggle towards his personal compositional voice. This work has also been called Brahms's 'Clara' Symphony, in which, with this peaceful alphorn theme, perhaps, the dark days of Robert's long illness are finally laid to rest.

Brahms sets the melody over peaceful string chords and gives the theme to horn 1; in addition, each semibreve is doubled by the second player. This is not only a practical consideration that allows the first player to take another full breath for each successive phrase with no break in the sound: the richness of two French horns in unison also gives an echo-like resonance to the sound, a subtle technique seen earlier in Schubert's 'Great' C major Symphony (Fig. 5.9). Although the accompaniment is *pianissimo*, the principal horn part is given the instruction *forte sempre* and *passionato*. This endows the phrases with an aura of majesty and grandeur, a perfect reminder of the magnificent mountain landscape in which Brahms heard the music.

Fig. 5.41. Brahms, Symphony No. 1, fourth movement, bars 28–43: introduction of the main theme on the horn. Brass parts, with horns in C on stave 1.[74]

Brahms's reference to the mountain melody here is not explicit: he does not supply a programmatic description of his intention to depict a mountain scenario, as his fellow composers were wont to do. His metaphor is more subtle. He knows that with this horn call, his audience will feel at ease and reassured by the strong tones of the alphorn melody, the same feeling of relief that one would experience after a storm in the mountains on a walking holiday. The atmosphere that Brahms creates here taps subliminally into the listener's own experience to lead them to a comfortable place.

The fame of this quotation is such that when in 1972 an East German five-mark nickel commemorative coin was issued 75 years after Brahms's death, the opening of this melody was chosen for the reverse side of the coin. Unfortunately, the quotation is incorrect: the third note reproduced on the coin is not the note that Brahms wrote, nor is it possible to play on an alphorn.

Fig. 5.42. East German five-mark commemorative coin with an erroneous quotation of Brahms's alphorn melody.[75]

The foremost Swiss composer of the nineteenth century was Joachim Raff (1822–1882). He was born and brought up beside Lake Zürich and became assistant to Franz Liszt at Weimar. Raff's stated intention as a composer was to combine programmatic elements with traditional genres and forms. Of his eleven symphonies, nine have descriptive titles: No. 1 is *An das Vaterland*, No. 3 is *Im Walde*, No. 7 *In den Alpen* and Nos. 8 to 11 are named after the four seasons.

Symphony No. 7, *In den Alpen*, was completed in 1875 when Raff was 53. He does not tell a narrative in this symphony, rather he creates atmospheres, describes landscapes and depicts Swiss scenes. He demonstrates his familiarity with 'tourist' alphorn motifs; the inclusion of such elements presupposes that Raff had some expectation that his audience would recognise this music as symbolic of the mountains. The first movement, entitled *Wanderung im Hochgebirge* (Excursion in the High Mountains), opens with a grandeur reminiscent of a broad mountain vista, but soon grows gentler in a second subject based on the sound of alphorns echoing across lakes and peaks, with turning arpeggio motifs introduced by the French horn and echoed on the oboe, set over a quiet backdrop provided by the strings. The alphorn motifs gradually become the main thematic material for the development section and indeed dominate the rest of the movement.

The second and third movements bear the titles *In der Herberge* (At the Inn) and *Am See* (On the Lake). The final movement, *Beim Schwingfest – Abschied* (At the Wrestling Contest – Farewell), recapitulates themes heard previously, including the alphorn music.

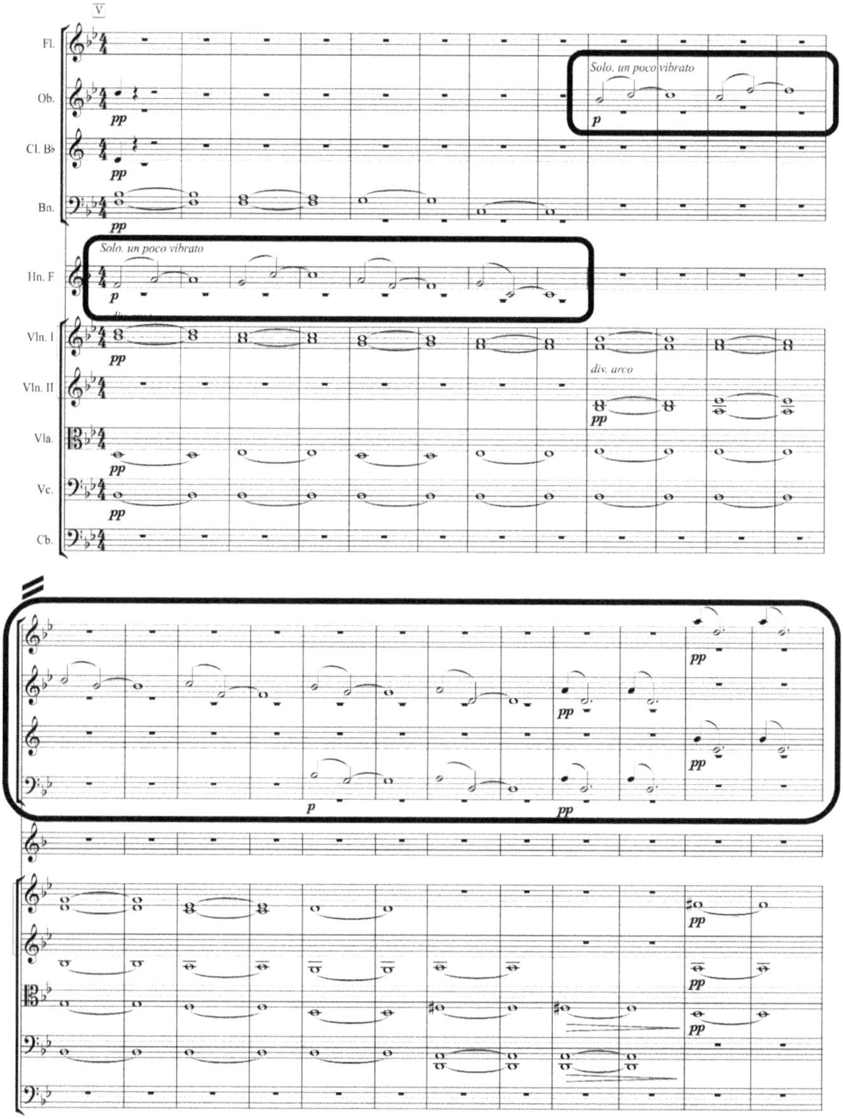

Fig. 5.43. Raff, Symphony No. 7: *In den Alpen*, first movement: *Wanderung im Hochgebirge*, bars 177–207, the first appearance of alphorn phrases.[76]

An Austrian composer who was greatly influenced by his natural surroundings was Gustav Mahler (1860–1911). Alphorn motifs feature in his music for voice and piano and also in his orchestral scores. His setting of the poem *Zu Strassburg auf der Schanz'* (In Strasbourg on the Ramparts) is a typical example of his use of alphorn music in his piano writing. Its text is found in *Des Knaben Wunderhorn* (The Youth's

Magic Horn), a collection of German folk poems edited by Achim von Arnim and Clemens Brentano, dedicated to Goethe and published in Heidelberg between 1805 and 1808. Most of the poems were drawn from oral tradition, although some were freely modified and transcribed into high German, and a few were specially written by the editors, both of whom were poets in their own right. The collection was a source of inspiration for many composers, including Brahms, Mahler, Mendelssohn, Schumann and Weber. Mahler was drawn to the collection throughout his life, and in 1888 he published a setting of 12 songs under the title *Lieder aus Des Knaben Wunderhorn*; altogether he wrote 24 settings of poems from the collection, including music that he was to use again in his Second, Third and Fourth Symphonies.

Both Brahms and Mahler set the poem *Zu Strassburg auf der Schanz'* for voice and piano. Its theme is the desperation of a homesick Swiss soldier who is about to be shot by firing squad for attempted desertion: he had been caught swimming across the Rhine after hearing a distant alphorn. Brahms's setting, WoO Posth. 37, No. 13, is in simple, homophonic, strophic form with no musical reference to the content of the lyrics. Mahler's setting, which dates from around 1880–83, is more sophisticated. As with the piano writing seen in the song settings of Berlioz and Liszt, Mahler's use of the piano resembles an orchestral score. He enhances the themes of the text with a haunting juxtaposition of music typical of the military bugle and the pastoral free-rhythm of the call of the alphorn. There is a recurring dichotomy between F major, which symbolises the mountains for which the soldier yearns, and F minor which

returns him to the distress of his present situation. The initial vocal phrase is in military style, with the instruction *In gemessenem Marschtempo* (in strict march tempo), while the mention of the alphorn is prepared with a slowing of the tempo (*ritardando*) and the music has the instruction *ein wenig zurückhaltend* (a little held back): this contrasts the military scene with the more tranquil world of the alphorn. Mahler gives the instruction that the sustain pedal should be in use throughout the alphorn motifs, to provide increased resonance in imitation of the sound of the alphorn as it reverberates in the mountains.

Fig. 5.44. The alphorn reverberates in the high mountains. Riffelberg, with the Matterhorn. The author. Photo: Martin Jones.

The text reads:

Zu Strassburg auf der Schanz',	In Strasburg on the ramparts,
da ging mein Trauern an;	there I was troubled;
das Alphorn hört' ich drüben wohl anstimmen,	I heard the distant alphorn calling,
ins Vaterland mußt ich hinüberschwimmen,	I had to swim to my homeland,
das ging ja nicht an.	that was not permitted.
Ein Stunde in der Nacht	One hour into the night
sie haben mich gebracht;	they caught me;
sie führten mich gleich vor des Hauptmanns Haus,	they took me directly to the Captain's house,
ach Gott, sie fischten mich im Strome auf,	ah God, they'd fished me out of the river,
mit mir ist's aus.	everything is over for me.
Frühmorgens um zehn Uhr	In the morning at ten o'clock
stellt man mich vor das Regiment;	they will put me before the regiment;
ich soll da bitten um Pardon,	I am supposed to beg for pardon,
und ich bekomm doch meinen Lohn,	and I will take what is due to me,
das weiß ich schon.	well do I know that.
Ihr Brüder allzumal,	You, all my brothers,
Heut' seht ihr mich zum letztenmal;	today you see me for the last time;
der Hirtenbub ist nur schuld daran.	the shepherd boy alone is to blame.
Das Alphorn hat mir's angetan,	The alphorn did this to me –
das klag ich an.	the blame belongs there.
Ihr Brüder alle drei,	You, my brothers, all three,
was ich euch bitt, erschießt mich gleich;	this I ask: shoot straight at me;
verschont mein junges Leben nicht,	do not spare my young life,
schießt zu, daß das Blut rausspritzt,	shoot so the blood splashes out:
das bitt ich euch.	this I beg you.
O Himmelskönig, Herr!	O King of heaven, Lord!
Nimm du meine arme Seele dahin,	Take my poor soul away,
nimm sie zu dir in den Himmel ein,	take it to you in Heaven,
laß sie ewig bei dir sein	let it be forever with you
und vergiß nicht mein!	and do not forget me!

Zu Straßburg auf der Schanz'

Aus „Des Knaben Wunderhorn"

Gustav Mahler

Fig. 5.45. Mahler's setting of *Zu Strassburg auf der Schanz'* from *Des Knaben Wunderhorn*, bars 1–8.[77]

The mountains were a substantial source of inspiration for Mahler. He spent the summer of 1893 in Steinbach on the Attersee near Salzburg and here he devised a routine that he was to follow for the rest of his life: to compose in the mountains in the summer and return to conducting and city duties for the rest of the year. He had a hut built where he could compose undisturbed: the windows afford uninterrupted views of the lake and the mountains beyond.

Mahler's writing for the French horn in his orchestral output is highly characterful: his awareness of the use of the horn in the countryside greatly influenced his use of the instrument in an orchestral context. His evocative writing displays many moods ranging from the deeply profound to the unrestrainedly joyous. In his depictions of the natural world and our relationship with it, the horn was fundamental to the fabric of his musical language. The First Symphony's exuberant whoops, the offstage echo effects in the Second, the posthorn calls in the Third, the haunting alphorn-like elegy for *obbligato* horn with the rest of the horns used as an echo in the Fifth and the extensive alphorn-style music in both of the *Nachtmusik* movements of his Seventh Symphony each demonstrate different facets of Mahler's use of the French horn as a metaphor in his symphonic writing.

Mahler draws on the heritage of the alphorn on several occasions: a classic example appears at the opening of his Fourth Symphony. He commented that this work formed a conclusion to his first three symphonies, all of which used motivic material from songs from *Des Knaben Wunderhorn*. In its simplicity and innocence, however, it was something of a reaction against the monumental scale of the Second and the persistent symbolism of the Third. With reference to this symphony he wrote in a letter to the soprano Anna von Mildenburg: 'Imagine such a mighty work that it reflects the entire world – one is, as it were, just an instrument, upon which the universe can play'.[78] When the conductor Bruno Walter visited Mahler at his composing hut in 1895 and stopped to admire the panoramic mountain views, Mahler said, 'You don't need to look: I have already composed all that'.[79] By bar 3 in the opening movement, Mahler has already introduced the jingling bells of horses' harnesses and alphorn calls:

Fig. 5.46. Mahler, Symphony No. 4. Cheerful alphorn calls appear by bar 3 of the opening of the first movement.[80]

Mahler's Seventh Symphony was completed in 1905. Both the second and the fourth movements bear the title *Nachtmusik* and between them is a waltz-like Scherzo marked *Schattenhaft* (Shadowy). The opening of Mahler's first *Nachtmusik* movement is reminiscent of alphorn calls and echoes, as he may have heard them in the mountains at evening time. A horn call, with an echo provided by a muted horn, establishes the scene before alphorn-like motifs played by many different woodwind instruments reverberate in the night air. This material is developed throughout the movement.

NACHTMUSIK

Fig. 5.47. Mahler, Symphony No. 7, second movement, *Nachtmusik*, bars 1–22: alphorn music, with echoes.[81]

A Bavarian composer who was also strongly influenced by both the mountains and the horn was Richard Strauss (1864–1949). As his father Franz Strauss was the foremost French horn player of the mid-nineteenth century, Richard was well-acquainted with the potential of the instrument in an orchestral context. He reproduced the sound of the alphorn in many of his compositions, even when the connection was tenuous. For example, he uses alphorn material in *Don Quixote*, sub-titled *Phantasische Variationen über ein Thema ritterlichen Charakters* (Fantasy variations on a Theme of Knightly Character) of 1897. This work contains vivid juxtapositions of profound emotion and delightful fantasy. Strauss uses repeating and overlapping alphorn calls with telling effect in one of the pastoral episodes, despite the fact that it is set in the Spanish countryside. As he depicts the Don's bizarre wanderings, Strauss includes echoing alphorn motifs mingled with the bleating of sheep, which are represented by *tremolo* notes for the strings, and trills and flutter tonguing for the woodwind and brass. Perhaps Strauss's awareness of the *pastorale* tradition led him to break into a gentle triple movement at this point.

Fig. 5.48. Strauss, *Don Quixote*, Variation 2, woodwind and horn parts, bars 227–231. Alphorn calls are given to a variety of woodwind instruments, with the accompaniment of trills and flutter tonguing.[82]

Strauss uses alphorn-inspired music in his extensive peaceful alphorn-style solo for the cor anglais, completed by the French horn, towards the end of his epic symphonic poem of 1899, *Ein Heldenleben* (A Hero's Life). He gave subheadings to the various sections of the work, although he later withdrew them. After agitated music that describes battles with critics, he originally wrote the heading *Des Helden Weltflucht und Vollendung* (The Hero's Retreat from the World and his Fulfilment) and the music depicts the hero's relaxation in peaceful retirement. Although the work is taken to be largely autobiographical, he was not at this time planning to retire (he was a healthy 35-year-old). Perhaps it represents his 77-year-old father, recently retired from his long—and at times turbulent—career as a horn player. 23 bars of calm alphorn-like melody are given to the cor anglais over quiet sustained chords in C major. This introduces a reflective coda in which the protagonist finally finds inner peace. It beautifully captures the atmosphere of serenity after turbulent times. Again Strauss introduces *pastorale* triplets for these gentle alphorn motifs.

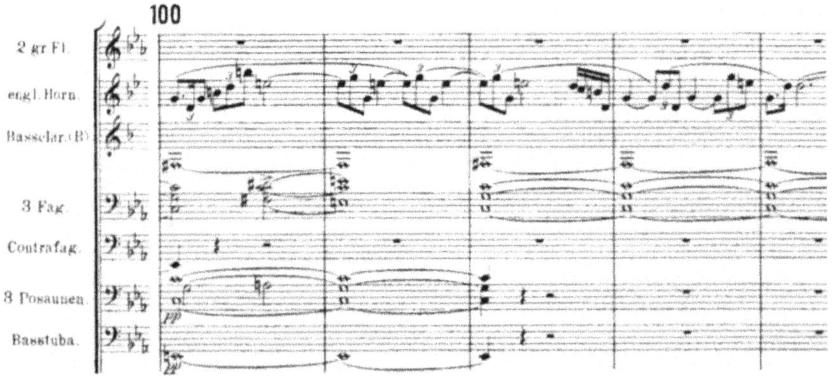

Fig. 5.49. Strauss, *Ein Heldenleben*, wind parts from rehearsal figure 100: part of the 23 bars reminiscent of the alphorn playing at twilight.[83]

In 1908 Strauss had a house built in Garmisch with panoramic views over the Bavarian Alps. Here he completed his evocative work *Eine Alpensinfonie* (An Alpine Symphony) in 1915, although he had written to his parents in 1900 of an idea formulating in his mind for a symphony that would open with a depiction of sunrise over the mountains. He had a lifelong affinity with the Alps, where he spent many summers with his family as a child. His sister Johanna recalled that from early childhood he had a deep love of nature: mountains, forests, meadows, flowers and animals. She tells of his desire to capture this delight in writing and in music.[84] In 1879, at the age of 15, Strauss wrote a detailed account in a letter to a school friend, Ludwig Thuille, of an excursion he had made around the Heimgarten, a dramatic peak not far from his childhood home in Munich. He describes the magnificent scenery and the adventures that the party experienced. These bear a striking resemblance to scenes that he depicts in *Eine Alpensinfonie* 36 years later. At the end of the letter, he tells Thuille that he wrote it all down at the piano, which indicates that even then, he strove to capture his experiences in sound:

> At 2am we rode in a hand-cart to the village that lies at the foot of the mountain. Then we set off by lantern light in total darkness and after 5 hours' climb we arrived at the summit. We had a wonderful view there. The lakes of Staffel (Murnau), Rieg, Ammer, Würm, Kochel and Walchen. Then the Isarthal with mountains around, the Ötzthal and Stubai glaciers, the Innsbruck mountains, Zugspitze, etc. Then we climbed round the other side, to Walchensee, although we lost our way and clambered around for 3 hours in the midday heat without finding a path. Walchensee is a beautiful lake, but it gives a feeling of sadness, surrounded by woods and high mountains. It has wonderful sparkling pale green water. Then we went above the lake to Uhrfelden, below the Herzogstand, a peak near the Heimgarten. From there an hour over the Kösselberg and an hour to Kochelsee (Kösselberg Inn). On the way there we had a terrible storm that

uprooted trees and tossed stones in our faces. As we reached the shelter the storm started. The Kochelsee is a very romantic, beautiful lake but the waves were so big that a crossing over to Schlehdorf, where our hand-cart was waiting, was out of the question. When the storm died down, we had no choice but to walk right round the whole of Kochelsee (2 hours). On the way it started to rain again and we walked briskly (without stopping for a minute), tired, wet through, to Schlehdorf where we stayed the night, and went on next morning much more comfortably in a cart to Murnau. The excursion was extremely interesting, different and original. The next day I wrote down the whole trip at the piano. Naturally it resembles Wagner's huge sound-painting rubbish.[85]

Strauss's composition *Eine Alpensinfonie* recalls many of the events of this teenage excursion. He provides headings in the score for each of the 23 sections. The work begins with a haunting representation of the stillness of night, followed by sunrise and an ascent up the mountain. The listener is taken through a forest that echoes with hunting horns, past a mountain torrent and a waterfall, and eventually reaches the high Alpine pastures, portrayed by cowbells and typical alphorn phrases introduced by the cor anglais, bassoons and bass clarinet. The alphorn motifs reverberate and echo some 36 times on a variety of wind instruments. There is a depiction of the mountaineer lost and in danger. After time spent at the summit where Strauss presents an apparition, there is a dramatic thunderstorm. A quick descent forms a recapitulation in which Strauss revisits themes from the ascent in reverse order. Finally there is sunset and stillness at the end of the day.

Fig. 5.50. View from the summit of Heimgarten, Bavaria. Photo: Frances Jones.

Although Strauss was to declare after the first rehearsal: '*Jetzt endlich habe ich zu instrumentieren gelernt*' (Now at last I have learnt to orchestrate), he described the creation of the work: '*Einmal so komponieren wollen, wie die Kuh die Milch gibt*' (I wanted for once to compose just as a cow gives milk) and stated that '*sittliche Reinigung aus eigener Kraft, Befreiung durch die Arbeit, Anbetung der ewigen herrlichen Natur*' (in this there is moral purification through one's own strength, deliverance through labour, and worship of nature, eternal and magnificent).[86] Strauss was deeply depressed by the ominous political events that were leading inevitably to the Great War and the destruction of the world as he knew it: this was a poignant portrayal of the joy of the natural world that might never be the same again. He described this symphony as a celebration of nature in contrast to faith, and initially echoed *Der Antichrist*, the title of a book by Nietzsche, in the title for this symphony, as *Der Antichrist: eine Alpensinfonie*, although he withdrew this reference before he published the work.

Despite his disillusionment with the concept of faith, Strauss does nevertheless betray a fundamental acceptance of religious practices on two occasions: it is notable that there is a substantial prayer-like section both when the mountaineer reaches the summit and also when the work draws to a close at the end of the day. He describes an other-worldly vision at the top of the mountain, with trills reminiscent of the fluttering of angels' wings, and he introduces the organ at this point. The epilogue, with its religious feel, is possibly a reference to the *Alpsegen* or evening prayer of thanksgiving for protection from dangers on the mountain: in this non-religious work, Strauss was nevertheless drawn to choose to colour this epilogue with an extended meditative organ solo. The presence of the organ here cannot be insignificant. It may be a deep realisation that whatever one's personal beliefs, the consecrated ground of the churchyard was in Strauss's day still one's ultimate resting place.

It is perhaps also significant that unlike in Haydn's *Die Jahreszeiten*, Beethoven's 'Pastoral' Symphony and Raff's *In den Alpen*, Strauss includes no interaction with the inhabitants of his landscape. Although hunters and herdsmen are encountered, this is not a shared celebration of life, but a solitary journey: it may reflect Strauss's own journey through the ultimate solitude of depression. Beethoven's work ends in celebration and joyful thanksgiving, while that of Strauss finishes in darkness and stillness.

His musical depictions of the 23 scenes in this narrative are extraordinarily graphic. He uses an orchestra of 150 players and includes cow-bells and a wind machine. His key structure is designed to give the French horns in the forest scene the normal key for the hunting horn, E flat, and it can be no coincidence that at the depiction of sunset, the orchestra plays long sustained background chords in the key of G flat, the natural key of the alphorn. He reserves recognisable alphorn calls for the scene when the mountaineer arrives at the open mountain pastures.

Auf der Alm.

Mäßig schnell (alla breve).

(gemächlich)

Kl.Fl.

I.II.
3 gr.Fl.
III.

2 Hob.

Engl. H.

Heckelph.

Es‑Clar.

2 B‑Clar.

3 Fag.
(unisono)

4 Hörner.
(Es)

Herden‑
geläute.

(leise, wie von Ferne)

(verschwindend)

Fig. 5.51. Strauss, *Eine Alpensinfonie*. Arrival at the high pastures (*Auf der Alm*), wind and cowbells parts. The beginning of the alphorn calls.[87]

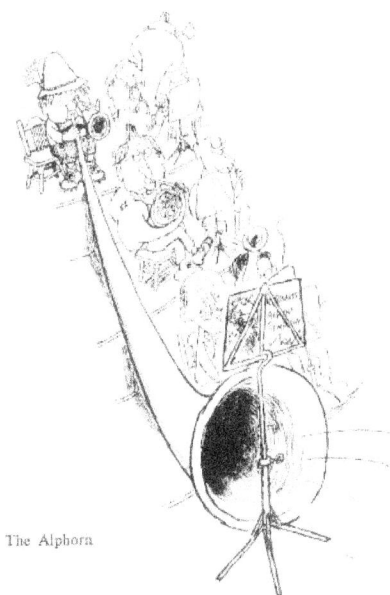

Strauss uses twenty French horns and four tenor horns (Wagner tubas) in this work, but although Gerard Hoffnung's cartoon of the work demonstrates that one might expect there to be an alphorn in the score, Strauss does not include one.

The Alphorn

Fig. 5.52. Drawing by Gerard Hoffnung: an alphorn player in Strauss's work *Eine Alpensinfonie*. Reproduced with kind permission of The Hoffnung Partnership, London.[88]

Richard Strauss and Richard Wagner (see p. 231) are the only two leading Romantic composers to include actual parts for alphorns in an orchestral score. Strauss wrote parts for three alphorns in his pastoral tragedy *Daphne*, subtitled *Bukolische Tragödie in einem Aufzug* (Bucolic Tragedy in one Act) completed in 1936. In this drama, he harks back to the world of the pastoral idylls of the ancient Greek dramatic tradition with a setting of a story from Ovid. Perhaps for Strauss this too was a form of escape from a troubled world, using nature as a setting for the unreal. *Daphne* is a story of love, longing and intrigue between shepherds, shepherdesses and gods. Strauss uses the sound of the alphorn to represent two different things. First, in the opening scene, he specifies that the stage should be set as a mythological mountain landscape with a herdsman playing an alphorn on stage as the curtain rises, while a short melody for an alphorn in G is written in the score.

> Stony river bank, picturesque groups of olive trees. Last sunshine. On the right the ground rises to the house of the fisherman Peneios. In the background is the impression of the river. The backdrop represents the formidable Mount Olympus. You can hear the movement of a large flock of sheep. Calls, running, shoving and pushing, dogs barking. Amid the noise the sound of a mighty alphorn can be heard. Curtain.[89]

This is a setting reminiscent of the scene that opened Grétry's opera *Guillaume Tell* of 1791. Strauss's alphorn phrase is repeated twice by offstage alphorns, once in A flat and then in A. After four bars the alphorn call is sounded again, in altered rhythm. Later in the scene, Strauss uses the alphorn to represent the powerful voice of the gods, when the herdsmen cry '*Furchtbar Getön! Eines Gottes Stimme!*' (Fearful sounds! The voice of a god!). Here Strauss adds in a footnote that the notes of the alphorn player onstage should be doubled by a pair of trombones, in the orchestra, for strength. The final call of the alphorn again represents the pastoral idyll as it accompanies the movement of a flock of sheep. It is intriguing, however, that Strauss has written phrases for the alphorns that are not playable on the instrument. No investigation for this study has revealed what lies behind this. The part is normally played on a trombone or a Wagner tuba.

Fig. 5.53. Alphorn part for Strauss's opera *Daphne*.[90]

The remaining six works to be examined in this chapter are by English composers. The alphorn as the voice of the Alps rarely represents a deep personal statement for the English, as the instrument does not belong to our world. We are guests in the Alps; the alphorn is generally experienced as part of this beautiful landscape, and its music is used as a metaphorical voice in the representation of this. The works chosen here demonstrate a variety of responses to the sound of the alphorn when heard by tourists, and do show a surprising range of different ways and contexts in which English composers have responded to the music of the alphorn.

For some years from 1893, Edward Elgar (1857–1934) took summer holidays in the Bavarian town of Garmisch. There he and his wife Alice met Richard Strauss and attended performances conducted by him. Elgar was inspired by these visits to compose six choral songs, *From the Bavarian Highlands*, Op. 27. Their melodies and words are based on traditional Bavarian folksongs; the English versions of the lyrics were provided by Alice. The set of songs is dedicated to the Slingsby-Bethell family, English proprietors of the guest house in Garmisch where the Elgars stayed. The work was originally scored for mixed chorus with piano accompaniment and was first performed by the Worcester Festival Choral Society under Elgar's direction in April 1896. That year Elgar orchestrated the accompaniment, and in 1897 he created a version for orchestra alone comprising the first, third and sixth songs, published under the title *Three Bavarian Dances*.

Each song is connected with the region around Garmisch. Although none of the melodies of the songs include alphorn or yodel motifs, Elgar includes alphorn phrases in the introduction to song No. 2, entitled *False Love*, in order to establish an appropriate mountain setting.

Fig. 5.54. Elgar, *From the Bavarian Highlands*, No. 2: *False Love*, bars 1–10. The piano introduction sets the scene with alphorn-like figurations.[91]

It is the first of the collection in a peaceful tempo, and the lyrics reflect the joyful sight of flower-strewn meadows in the springtime. It is not surprising that Elgar's alphorn motifs here are typical of those played to tourists. Alice's text begins:

Now we hear the Spring's sweet voice
Singing gladly through the world
Bidding all the earth rejoice.

All is merry in the field,
Flowers grow amidst the grass,
Blossoms blue, red, white they yield.

A near-contemporary of Elgar was Frederick Delius (1862–1934), from whose pen we are provided with one of the most evocative alphorn-derived passages of music in the English repertoire, in *A Mass of Life*. After a musical upbringing, Delius's desire to become a composer was eventually galvanised through listening to Afro-Caribbean musicians while working on an orange plantation in Florida. He subsequently studied composition in Leipzig before settling as a full-time composer in Paris. He remained in France for the rest of his life. Thomas Beecham promoted Delius's works in the UK and conducted the première of *A Mass of Life* in London in 1909. This work, scored for double chorus, soloists and orchestra, is based on Friedrich Nietzsche's influential philosophical novel *Also sprach Zarathustra* (Thus spoke Zarathustra), published in various sections between 1883 and 1885, which was also the inspiration for a tone poem by Richard Strauss of 1886, and works by Carl Orff and Arnold Bax.

The novel relates the travels and speeches of the protagonist. It forms a discussion of eternal recurrence, the timelessness of the universe irrespective of man, and man's will as the primary driving force of his actions. Nietzsche wrote that the concepts came to him while walking in the Swiss mountain region of Upper Engadine, as he contemplated the insignificance of man in this vast natural landscape.

For Delius, the term Mass here is interpreted as a period of self-exploration. He arranges extracts from Nietzsche's text in two parts: in Part 1, he examines laughter, dance and love, although the section descends into questions of doubt and downfall. Part 2 begins with a movement entitled *On the Mountains*, where Zarathustra is alone with his musings. The scenario inspires Delius to open with four minutes of evocative alphorn-like horn calls, with echoes, over a quiet backdrop of timpani and strings. In his hands, the symbolism is clear: the orchestral horns use the calls of the alphorn, which in turn represents its landscape.

The calls reverberate across the peaceful mountain scene in a timeless reflection of the insignificance of man and the magnificence, beauty and grandeur of nature. As the eye traces the wonder of the peaks all around, so the melody climbs and descends, lingering at the highest places:

Fig. 5.55. Delius, *A Mass of Life*, opening of Part II, alphorn-like overlapping horn-calls with echoes.

Arnold Bax (1883–1953) was another English composer inspired by Nietzsche's novel *Also sprach Zarathustra*. In the short score of his Symphony No. 3, he quotes the text: 'My wisdom became pregnant on lonely mountains; upon barren stones she brought forth her young'.[92] Bax opens his slow second movement with a haunting solo for unaccompanied French horn. With the choice of this instrument, in the context of this quotation the allusion is clear:

Fig. 5.56. Bax, Symphony No. 3, second movement, bars 1–7, for unaccompanied French horn.

William Walton (1902–1983) paid tribute to the Alps and the alphorn in *Façade*, in which he quotes the alphorn motifs from the overture to *Il Guglielmo Tell* by Rossini. *Façade* is an unusual work in that a narrative is declaimed while music, an integral part of the performance, is played.

The text is by Edith Sitwell. Her series of poems bearing the title *Façade* appeared in print from 1918 onwards in the literary magazine *Wheels*, an annual publication of the writings of Edith and her two brothers, Osbert and Sacheverell. Edith described her texts as 'abstract poems – that is, they are patterns in sound ... My experiments in *Façade* are in the nature of enquiries into the effect on rhythm, and on speed, of the use of rhymes, assonances and dissonances, placed outwardly and inwardly (at different places in the line) and in most elaborate patterns. There are experiments, also, in texture, in the subtle variations of thickness and thinness brought about by the changing of a consonant or labial, from word to word …'[93] Thus, although the meaning of the words follows a train of thought, deeper significance is not necessarily intended.

Walton was a close friend of the Sitwells and lodged with the family for a while. The *Façade* poems became the inspiration for an inventive set of musical accompaniments to many of the poems: in all, there are 43 different poems for which Walton wrote music. Some of the pieces were performed privately in the home of Edith's brother Osbert in 1922 and had their first public hearing in 1923. They received an unfavourable response from the critics. Many were first scored for flute, clarinet, trumpet, saxophone and cello, although Walton and others later gathered selections of the numbers into various Suites for full orchestra.

Walton responded not only to the abstract spoken sounds, but also to the meaning of the words. The poem *We bear velvet* inspired him to write *The Swiss Yodelling Song*, although no singing is actually intended. The Swiss connotation arose from the references in one stanza to William Tell and Mrs Cow and in others to chamois, edelweiss, mountain streams and cowbells. Yodel figurations open the piece; then in verse 3, which refers to the Swiss hero William Tell, Walton quotes eight bars of the famous *Ranz des Vaches* from Rossini's opera *Il Guglielmo Tell*. Walton included the quotation in homage to Rossini, a composer he revered throughout his life.[94] He gives the theme to the flute, with trills on each long note. In Walton's later version of *Façade* for full orchestra, his orchestration includes further subtle details: the oboe is given the theme, echoing the timbre of the tenoroon in Rossini's score, the piccolo adds sparkle, and the flute retains the decorative trills.

1.	We bear velvet cream Green and babyish, Small leaves seem; each stream Horses' tails that swish,		2.	And the chimes remind Us of sweet birds singing, Like the jangling bells On rose trees ringing.
3.	Man must say farewells To parents now, And to William Tell And Mrs. Cow.		4.	Man must say farewells To storks and Bettes, And to roses' bells And statuettes.
5.	Forests white and black In spring are blue With forget-me-nots, And to lovers true.		6.	Still the sweet bird begs And tries to cozen Them: "Buy angels' eggs Sold by the dozen."

7. Gone are clouds like inns
   On the gardens' brinks,
   And the mountain djinns, –
   Ganymede sells drinks;

8. While the days seem grey,
   And his heart of ice,
   Grey as chamois, or
   The edelweiss,

9. And the mountain streams
   Like cowbells sound –
   Tirra lirra, drowned
   In the water's dreams

10. Who has gone beyond
    The forest waves,
    While his true and fond
    Ones seek their graves.

Fig. 5.57. Orchestral version of Walton's *Façade: The Swiss Yodelling Song*, bars 9–15, quotation from Rossini's *Il Guglielmo Tell*, wind parts.[95]

A dramatic song-cycle by Benjamin Britten (1913–1976) includes alphorn material: his *Serenade for Tenor, Horn and Strings*, composed during the dark days of the Second World War in 1943. The *Serenade* is a setting of six poems about the night by different authors, in which the character of each of the poems is enhanced with evocative *obbligato* horn writing. The group of songs is framed with an instrumental Prologue and Epilogue. Britten demonstrates his awareness of the tradition of listening for the alphorn as night falls by writing the Prologue for the lone French horn; this music is repeated offstage at the end of the group of songs as an Epilogue, with calm and peaceful effect.

In the Prologue and Epilogue, Britten gives the French horn free-flowing music not constrained by pulse, with breath-length phrases each ending with a pause in the style of a *Kühreien*. He restricts the motifs to the open harmonic series. He not only specifies that the slightly 'out-of-tune' notes must be used ('to be played on natural harmonics'); he goes one step further: he includes the harmonic that is most different from equal temperament, the 11th harmonic, or 'alphorn *fa*'. It might be that these decisions derived from the intent that the music should not be wholly comfortable, that the listener should be unsettled by these unfamiliar sounds, as an invitation, in these horrific years of war, to face grim reality rather than hide in the picturesque.

The use of the natural harmonics and the 'alphorn *fa*' were the suggestion of Dennis Brain, for whom the horn part was written. It was an idea that Brain later regretted, as he found it a nuisance to repeatedly have to explain why his playing was out of tune. It was a radical decision, and the work provides a telling example of the effect of these notes on a public unaccustomed to them. Eleven years after the composition of the work, a review of a recording on the Decca label of a performance given by Peter Pears and Dennis Brain appeared in the quarterly music journal *Tempo* in autumn 1954,[96] which stated:

> The same artists [Pears and The New Symphony Orchestra under Eugene Goossens] but this time with Dennis Brain performing the Serenade. The only disappointments here lie in the opening and closing horn solos; a curiously faulty intonation is apparent here and there which jars the magic of both the Prologue and the Epilogue. Fortunately this disappears in the first song and from then on Dennis Brain's customary musicianship and brilliance are very much in evidence.
> Eric Thompson.

This prompted Britten to respond in the following issue:[97]

> Sir,
> Your review of the new Decca recording of my Serenade for Tenor, Horn and Strings has recently been shown to me. I should like, if you will allow me, to make a comment on it. In the Prologue and Epilogue the horn is directed to play on the natural harmonics of the instrument; this causes the apparent 'out-of-tuneness' of which your reviewer complains, and which is, in fact, exactly the effect I intend. In the many brilliant performances of his part that Dennis Brain has given he has always, I am sure, played it as I have marked it in the score. Anyone, therefore, who plays it 'in tune' is going directly against my wishes! If the critics do not like this effect they should blame me and not Mr. Brain.
> Yours etc.,
> Benjamin Britten

With this work, Britten and Brain shouldered the response feared by the *Eidgenössischer Jodlerverband* (Swiss Federal Yodel Association). This was an organisation set up in 1910 to promote yodelling and the alphorn as part of the Swiss image. It dictated that music played to tourists should be in a major key, uplifting and gently evocative of the pastoral idyll that it was intended to represent. In the interests of creating music that was both 'pleasing' and 'normal', the 'alphorn *fa*' was not permitted as to hear this note, when one is not familiar with the heritage of the alphorn, was likely to be interpreted as lack of skill on the part of the player: this was not in keeping with the image of their country that the Swiss wished to present.

It is not possible to gauge to what extent the general musical public is aware even today of the specific connection between Britten's choice to use the 11th harmonic and the alphorn. Horn players are sometimes aware: Barry Tuckwell writes that 'these out-of-tune harmonics create a mysterious pastoral atmosphere similar to that evoked by the Swiss Alphorn'.[98] David Matthews regards Britten's use of the natural harmonics here as a general rustic reference when he describes them as '... like a Mahlerian *Naturlaut*, a "sound of nature" ',[99] while Lloyd Moore describes the impact of the sound of natural harmonics on the trained musical ear: 'The Serenade opens with a Prologue for solo horn played on the instrument's 'natural' harmonics (causing some notes to sound deliberately out-of-tune), evoking an atmosphere of "natural," primeval innocence'.[100]

Closer investigation of the Prologue reveals not only Britten's use of the controversial 11th harmonic, the 'alphorn *fa*' (Fig. 5.58, the printed high F). A subtle use of the natural 7th harmonic, the written note B flat here, which sounds noticeably lower than it would in equal temperament, is particularly effective when used in the context of a minor third (bar 7). Although Britten had given the instruction 'to be played on the natural harmonics', he did not indicate whether the horn player should adjust the intonation where possible, to better conform with equal temperament. A recording of Brain playing the work at the London Promenade Concerts in 1953 displays a degree of subtle 'tempering' commonly achieved by horn players by alteration of the position of the hand in the bell of the horn, to fit more closely with equal temperament.

For the highest note, the written A in the third bar from the end, there is a choice of harmonics, no. 13 (too low) or no. 14 (too high). This has also been the subject of discussion. On the narrow bore French model horn that Brain used at this time, made by Raoux-Millereau, the 14th harmonic sounds lower than it does on modern instruments, thus this is probably the one Britten intended, closer to B flat, although he wrote an A in the score. Barry Tuckwell, who recorded the work with Britten and Pears, observes that the A is 'incorrectly notated and does not represent the composer's intention'.[101] The higher-pitched 14th harmonic is normally played today, although the score was never altered.

SERENADE

Horn in F

BENJAMIN BRITTEN
Op. 31

PROLOGUE

* *The Prologue to be played on natural harmonics.*

Fig. 5.58. Britten, *Serenade for Tenor, Horn and Strings*: Prologue, for unaccompanied French horn, 'to be played on natural harmonics'.[102]

As an epilogue to this selection of works that include alphorn-inspired material as a metaphor for its landscape, one more type of quotation will be cited. Benjamin Britten takes this journey of exploration from one extreme to the other: alongside the profoundly evocative use of alphorn material explored above, he also wrote the musical equivalent of the typical 'tourist' image of the alphorn, moments of pure, innocent Alpine cliché. In February 1955, now psychologically free from the dark shadow of the war years, Britten, Peter Pears, Mary Potter and some other friends took a skiing holiday in Zermatt. Mary Potter was a close friend of Britten and an artist who painted many portraits of him. They were neighbours in Aldeburgh. Mary sustained an injury on the first day of the holiday, so Britten composed a six-movement work entitled *Alpine Suite* for three recorders, to provide her with something to play while the rest of the party were out on the slopes. The work is dedicated to Mary, and the movements are *Arrival at Zermatt*, *Swiss Clock (Romance)*, *Nursery Slopes*, *Alpine Scene*, *Moto perpetuo: Down the Piste* and *Farewell to Zermatt*. In the fourth movement, *Alpine Scene*, Britten gives the instruction 'very slow' and chooses alphorn-like arpeggio calls for the second and third players, with a peaceful accompaniment, marked 'sustained'. Perhaps it was the relaxed atmosphere of a holiday in the Swiss mountains that drew from him a 'picture postcard' alphorn tune, with a touch of yodel too.

Fig. 5.59. Alpine scene: Zermatt, in winter, with the majestic Matterhorn rising behind.
Photo: Frances Jones.

4. Alpine Scene

Fig. 5.60. Britten, *Alpine Suite* for three recorders. Fourth movement, *Alpine Scene*, bars 1–8: both the second player and later the third player are given classic alphorn and yodel motifs.[103]

This selection of works that include musical material evocative of the alphorn shows the range of circumstances in which this has been used to bring the sound of the instrument into a formal performance space. In each example, the sound of the alphorn has had the function of a metaphor. On no occasion has an alphorn motif been found in a composed work without an obvious reason for it to have been used; on the contrary, allusions to the sound of the alphorn have been noted where an actual motif has not been included.

The sound of the alphorn has sometimes been used to represent nothing more subtle than the Swiss landscape or carefree enjoyment of a mountain scene; in contrast, it has been used with solemnity and as the voice of a heavenly presence. It has been used to signify many feelings, from unease to reassurance, from sorrow to joy. A substantial range of styles, moods and settings has been seen, from the beginning of the nineteenth century when Haydn's alphorn motifs accompanied the herdsman on his journey into the mountains, to the disturbance caused among critics by Britten's use of alphorn material that was too realistic for comfort.

The two great pillars of the orchestral repertoire that depict the natural landscape, Beethoven's 'Pastoral' Symphony and Strauss's *Eine Alpensinfonie*, both appear to have sprung from a profound fear that political forces were bringing cataclysmic changes to the world, one at the beginning of the nineteenth century and the other a century later. In both of these works the composer has attempted to capture in sound something permanent and unchanging, something beyond human destruction. For both Beethoven and Strauss a depiction of the natural landscape represented the unspoilt, the untainted, the timeless, not the work of man but something more fundamental. For both it also symbolised a place of personal quietude, where man could attempt to escape from the stresses and fears that were engulfing daily life; both through their music sought to bring this peace to their audiences. In both works, the quotation of an alphorn motif was the iconic metaphor for that natural world.

Within the arch of time that spans these two pillars, the mountain landscape has been depicted with an alphorn motif for many other reasons. Raff's Symphony *In den Alpen* which appeared during the middle part of the century does not convey feelings of angst or escapism. It is perhaps the most straightforward, innocent narrative examined here. There are no storms or 'dangerous moments': Raff enjoys his own landscape with his friends.

Thus a reference to the voice of the alphorn, whether by metaphor or by the inclusion of an actual instrument, is demonstrated to have had a deep resonance in the canon of classical music. The use of an alphorn motif by a composer had a powerful symbolic function. It has been an archetypal reference that a composer could use to refer to the Alps as a place; it could also be an evocation of freedom, of natural strength, of peace, of a simple life—of many different things that have been of importance to the composer and his audience.

Alongside the possibility that urban audiences had a memory of herding routines from their past rural heritage, now a significant factor reflected in the works examined above was the development in European transport systems and the improved access to the mountains that Switzerland provided for its visitors. Travel to and within the mountain wilderness, rare in the time of Beethoven, was much more feasible by the time of Strauss. Texts were widely available that contained eloquent descriptions of the effect of hearing the instrument in its mountain setting. With the assimilation of the sound of the instrument into the experience that was presented to visitors to Switzerland, the alphorn had become a known phenomenon again. Composers were able increasingly to assume that the inclusion of an alphorn motif would be recognised as a symbol of the mountains.

Britten and Brain, though, perhaps took the assumption too far: the subtlety of their allusions was not recognised. The confrontation between the 'alphorn *fa*' and the English musical establishment was, nevertheless, a landmark event. Two factors—a greater awareness of the idiosyncrasies of the alphorn and a general broadening of the spectrum of what is 'acceptable' in concert music in the twentieth century—have paved the way for the potential of the use of the instrument itself in more recent concert works. This subject will be considered in the concluding chapter of this book.

Notes

[1] Walter Scott, *Anne of Geierstein or the Maiden of the Mist* (Boston, MA: Sanborn, Carter and Bazin, 1855), 22.

[2] Thomas Roscoe, *The Tourist in Switzerland and Italy* (London: Jennings, 1830), 55–56.

[3] George Tarenne, *Recherches sur le Ranz des Vaches, ou sur les Chansons Pastorales des Bergers de la Suisse* (Paris: Louis, 1813), 16–17: *L'air du bergers du mont Pilate, dans le canton de Lucerne, également sans paroles, les pasteurs de cette contrée, peuplée des hommes les moins civilisés de toute la Suisse, ont coutume de le jouer sur la grande trompe des Alpes, nommée Alphorn, dont la courbure cissoïdale grossit et prolongu telement les sons, qu'on les entend quelquefois de plus de deux lieues. Cet air sert aussi de signal pour répeindre l'alarme contre les ennemis intérieurs et extérieurs. Il est extrèmement beau sur le cor pendant la nuit: ses modulations plaintives et languissantes vont jusqu'à l'âme.*

[4] George Gordon Byron, *Complete Works* (Paris: Baudry, 1837), 339.

[5] Percy Byssche Shelley, *The Poetical Works of Percy Bysshe Shelley* (Paris: Galiagni, 1841), 288.

[6] John Murray, *A Glance at some of the Beauties and Sublimities of Switzerland* (London: Murray, 1829), 81-82.

[7] Murray, *A Glance*, 218-9.

[8] John Murray, *A Hand-Book for Travellers in Switzerland, Savoy and Piedmont* (London: Murray, 1838), 36.

[9] 'On the National Songs and Music of Switzerland', *The New Monthly Magazine and Humorist*, Vol. 59 (1840), 367. No author given.

[10] Reproduced with kind permission of the ROTH-Stiftung, Burgdorf.

[11] Karl Baedeker, *Switzerland, with neighbouring Lakes of Northern Italy, Savoy, and the adjacent districts of Piedmont, Lombardy and the Tyrol. Handbook for Travellers* (Koblenz: Baedeker, 1863), Preface iii.

[12] John and Nelly Wood, 'An Autumn Tour of Switzerland', *The Graphic*, Issues 249-259 (September-November 1874).

[13] Murray, *Hand-Book*, 83.

[14] Murray, *Hand-Book*, 80.

[15] Reproduced with kind permission of the Swiss National Library, Prints and Drawings Department: Collection of Prints, Depictions and Folk Culture.

[16] Baedeker, *Switzerland*, 81.

[17] Displayed in the Heimatmuseum, Grindelwald. Reproduced with kind permission.

[18] Jemima Morrell, *Miss Jemima's Swiss Journal: The first conducted tour of Switzerland, 1863* (facsimile reprint, London: Routledge, 1998), 64.

[19] Reproduced with kind permission of the Victoria and Albert Museum, London.

[20] Max Maria von Weber, *Carl Maria von Weber, Ein Lebensbild*, Vol. 1 (Leipzig: Keil, 1864), 292: *Den 7. früh 3 Uhr auf und den Kulm besteigen ... Ich erstieg den Kulm in ¾ Stunden und kam höchst erhitzt oben an wo eine ziemliche Kälte herrschte so daß das vom Führer angemachte Feuer sehr erfreulich war. Um halb sechs Uhr erschien die Sonne in ihrem Glanze nachdem sie vorher die Spitzen der Gletscher vergoldet hatte und reichlich war ich für meine Mühe belohnt. Beschreiben muss man so etwas nicht.*

[21] Bernische Kunstgesellschaft, Aquarell auf Transparentpapier, 84.5 x 119cm. Reproduced with kind permission of the Kunstmuseum Bern.

[22] Alexandre Dumas, *Impressions de Voyage Suisse* (Paris: Charpentier, 1834), 549.

[23] Murray, *Hand-Book*, 49.

[24] Mark Twain, *A Tramp Abroad* (London: Chatto and Windus, 1880), 299–300. https://en.wikisource.org/wiki/A_Tramp_Abroad/XXVIII. Creative Commons Attribution-ShareAlike License.

[25] Baedeker, *Switzerland*, 74.

[26] Karl Baedeker, *Switzerland, and the adjacent districts of Italy, Savoy, and the Tyrol. Handbook for Travellers* (Leipzig: Baedeker, 1889), 88.

[27] Over 300 historic depictions of alphorns can be explored in my online Alphorn Artwork Archive, accessible through my website, www.AmazingAlphorn.com.

[28] Robert Schumann, *Gesammelte Schriften über Musik und Musiker*, Vol. 1 (Leipzig: Wigand, 1854), 464: *In Ihm findet sich auch eine Stelle, da, wo ein Horn wie aus der Ferne ruft, das scheint mir aus anderer Sphäre herabgekommen zu sein. Hier lauscht auch alles, als ob ein himmlischer Gast im Orchester herumschlichte.*

[29] Franz Schubert, *Symphony No. 7* [now No. 9] *Franz Schuberts Werke, Serie 1* (Leipzig: Breitkopf & Härtel, 1884), 48. https://imslp.org/wiki/Symphony_No.9,_D.944_(Schubert,_Franz).

[30] Josef Haydn, *Die Jahreszeiten* (Leipzig: Breitkopf & Härtel, 1802), 142. https://imslp.org/wiki/Die_Jahreszeiten,_Hob.XXI:3_(Haydn,_Joseph).

[31] Gino Pugnetti, *The Life and Times of Beethoven* (London: Hamlyn, 1967), 58–9. Extensive compilations of Beethoven's letters can be viewed on www.gutenberg.org.

[32] R. Larry Todd, *Mendelssohn: A Life in Music* (New York: Oxford University Press, 2003), 99; however in his book *Fanny Hensel: The Other Mendelssohn* (New York: Oxford University Press, 2009), 64, Larry Todd attributes this quotation to a letter written by Felix's sister Fanny.

[33] Felix Mendelssohn, *Reisebriefe von Felix Mendelssohn Bartholdy aus den Jahren 1830 bis 1832* ed. Paul Mendelssohn Bartholdy (Leipzig: Hermann Mendelssohn, 1861), 261: *Dafür ist der Rigi aber auch ganz offenbar unserer Familie zugethan, und hat mir aus Anhänglichkeit heut wieder einen so herrlichen, reinen Sonnenaufgang bescheert, wie damals. Der abnehmende Mond, das lustige Alphorn, die lange dauernde Morgenröthe, die sich erst um die kalten, schattigen Schneeberge legte, die weißen Wölkchen über dem Zuger See, die Klarheit und Schärfe der Zacken, die sich in allen Richtungen gegen einander neigen, das Licht, das sich nach und nach auf den Höhen zeigte, die trippelnden, frierenden Leute in ihren Bettdecken, die Mönche aus Maria zum Schnee, – nichts hat gefehlt. Ich konnte mich nicht von dem Anblick trennen, und blieb noch sechs Stunden fortwährend auf der Spitze, und sah den Bergen zu. Ich dachte mir, wenn wir uns einmal wiedersehen, so müßte doch manches anders geworden sein, und wollte mir gern den Anblick so recht fest einprägen.*

[34] Felix Mendelssohn, *Sinfonie, No. 9* (Leipzig: Deutscher Verlag für Musik, 1967), 25. https://imslp.org/wiki/String_Symphony_No.9_in_C_major,_MWV_N_9_(Mendelssohn,_Felix).

[35] https://commons.wikimedia.org/wiki/File:Ansicht_von_Luzern_-_Aquarell_Mendelsohn_1847.jpg. Creative Commons CC0 License.

[36] Kuhn, ed. *Sammlung von Schweizer Kühreihen und alten Volkliedern, nach ihren bekannten Melodien in Musik gesetzt* (Bern: Burgdorfer, 1812), frontispiece. Universitätsbibliothek Basel. https://www.e-rara.ch/bau_1/doi/10.3931/e-rara-50794. Public Domain Mark 1.0.

[37] Franz Schubert, *Schuberts Werke, Serie XX, Band 10, Anhang* (Leipzig: Breitkopf & Härtel, 1895), 75. https://imslp.org/wiki/Der_Hirt_auf_dem_Felsen,_D.965_(Schubert,_Franz).

[38] translation by John South Shedlock and Frances Jones.

[39] Friedrich von Schiller, *Wilhelm Tell* (London: Macmillan, 1898), 5–6.

[40] Gioachino Rossini, *Guillaume Tell* (Paris: E. Troupenas, c.1829), 21. https://imslp.org/wiki/Guillaume_Tell_(Rossini,_Gioacchino).

[41] Hector Berlioz, *The Memoirs of Hector Berlioz*, trans. David Cairns (London: Gollancz, 1969), 125–6.

[42] Hector Berlioz, *Hector Berlioz Werke, Serie 1, Band 1* (Leipzig: Breitkopf & Härtel, 1900), 60. https://imslp.org/wiki/Symphonie_fantastique,_H_48_(Berlioz,_Hector): *Un soir d'été à la campagne, il entend deux pâtres qui dialoguent un Ranz des Vaches; ce duo pastoral, le lieu de la scène, le léger bruissement des arbres doucement agités par le vent, quelques motifs d'espoir qu'il a conçus depuis peu, tout concourt a render à son coeur un calme inaccoutumé, à donner à ses idées une couleur plus riante; mais elle apparait de nouveau, son coeur se serre, des douloureux pressentiments l'agitent, si elle le trompait ... L'un des pâtres reprend sa naïve mélodie, l'autre ne répond plus. Le soleil se couche ... bruit éloigné du tonnerre ... solitude ... silence ...*

[43] Hector Berlioz, *Grand Traité d'Instrumentation et d'Orchestration Modernes* (Paris: Schonenberger, 1843), 124: *Dans l'Adagio d'une de mes Symphonies, le Cor anglais, après avoir répète à l'octave Basse les phrases d'un hautbois, comme ferait dans un dialogue pastoral la voix d'un adolescent répondant a celle d'une jeune fille, en redit les fragments (à la fin du morceau) avec un sourd accompagnement de quatre timbales, pendant le silence de tout le reste de l'orchestre. Les sentiments d'absence, d'oubli, d'isolement douloureux qui naissent dans l'aime de certains auditeurs à l'évocation de cette mélodie abandonee, n'auraient pas le quart de leur force si elle était chantée par un autre instrument que le cor Anglais.*

[44] Berlioz, *Hector Berlioz Werke*, 60.

[45] Jessica Wiskus, *The Rhythm of Thought: Art, Literature and Music after Merleau-Ponty* (Chicago: University of Chicago Press, 2013), 39–40.

[46] Hector Berlioz, *Le Jeune Pâtre Breton*, Op. 13, No. 4 (Leipzig: Breitkopf & Härtel, c.1903), 3.

[47] Karin Pendle, 'The Transformation of a Libretto: Goethe's 'Jery und Bätely' ', *Music and Letters*, Vol. 55, No. 1 (January 1974), 77–78. The extracts from Goethe's letters are quoted in English, with no translator acknowledged.

[48] Gaetano Donizetti, *Betly, o La Capanna Svizzera*, ms c.1840, 31. https://imslp.org/wiki/Betly_(Donizetti,_Gaetano).

[49] https://commons.wikimedia.org/wiki/File:Joseph_Mallord_William_Turner_-_Tell's_Chapel,_Lake_Lucerne_-_Google_Art_Project.jpg. Creative Commons CC0 License.

[50] Liszt, *Pianofortewerke*, Vol. 4, 62. Franz Liszt, *Pianofortewerke*, Vol. 4 (Leipzig: Breitkopf & Härtel, 1916). https://imslp.org/wiki/Album_d'un_voyageur,_S.156_(Liszt,_Franz).

[51] Liszt, *Pianofortewerke*, Vol. 4, 134.

[52] Liszt, *Pianofortewerke*, Vol. 4, 114.

[53] J. B. Glück, *Les Délices de la Suisse* (Basel: Knop, 1835), 25. Reproduced with kind permission of the University of Basel, item reference Sign. kk VII 649.

[54] Liszt, *Pianofortewerke*, Vol. 4, 70.

[55] Franz Liszt, *Musikalischwerke* Series 7, Vol. 1 (Leipzig: Breitkopf & Härtel, 1917), 13. https://imslp.org/wiki/3_Lieder_aus_Schillers_'Wilhelm_Tell',_S.292_(Liszt,_Franz).

[56] Franz Liszt, *Symphonische Dichtungen für grosses Orchester, Band 1* (Leipzig: Breitkopf & Härtel, c.1885), 309. https://imslp.org/wiki/Les_préludes,_S.97_(Liszt,_Franz).

[57] Andrew Rutherford, *Byron: A Critical Study* (Redwood City, CA: Stanford University Press, 1961), 76.

[58] Laura Tunbridge, 'Schumann as Manfred', *The Musical Quarterly*, Vol. 87 (2004), 557.

[59] Robert Schumann, *Manfred* (Leipzig: Breitkopf & Härtel, c.1862), 71. https://imslp.org/wiki/Manfred,_Op.115_(Schumann,_Robert).

[60] Ibid.

[61] Robert Schumann, *Des Knaben Berglied, Sämtliche Lieder*, Vol. 2 (Leipzig: Peters, c.1900), 189. https://imslp.org/wiki/Liederalbum_für_die_Jugend,_Op.79_(Schumann,_Robert).

[62] Ibid., 202.

[63] Robert Schumann, *Robert Schumanns Werke, Serie XIII* (Leipzig: Breitkopf & Härtel, 1887), 6. https://imslp.org/wiki/6_Gedichte_von_N._Lenau_und_Requiem,_Op.90_ (Schumann,_Robert).

[64] Letter reproduced in Edwin Lindner, *Richard Wagner über Tristan und Isolde* (Leipzig: Breitkopf & Härtel, 1912), 101–2: *Früh um 4 Uhr weckte der Knecht mit dem Alphorn. Ich fuhr auf, sah, daß es regnete und bleib liegen um weiter zu schlafen. Doch ging mir das drollige Geblase im Kopf herum, und daraus entstand eine sehr lustige Melodie, die jetzt der Hirt aussen bläat, wenn er Isoldes Schiff ankündigt, was eine überrachend heiterer und naïve Wirkung macht.*

[65] Richard Wagner, *Tristan und Isolde* (Leipzig: Peters, 1912), Vorwort, 6: *Der Vortrag des Hirtenreigens auf dem Englischen Horn erfordert einen so vollendeten Künstler, daßer jedenfalls von deselbsen Bläser übernommen und hinter der Szene ausgeführt muß, welcher im Verlaufe des ganzen Abends das Englische Horn im Orchester bläst. Da das Englische Horn erst für die zweite Szene wieder im Orchester angewandt ist, wird der Bläser genügige Zeit haben bis dahin seinen Platz daselbst wieder einzunehmen* ... https://imslp.org/wiki/Tristan_und_Isolde,_WWV_90_(Wagner,_Richard).

[66] Ibid., Act 3, 306.

[67] Copyright Richard Wagner Museum, Luzern. Reproduced with kind permission.

[68] Cosima Wagner, *Cosima Wagner's Diaries: an abridgement*, Geoffrey Skelton, ed. (London: Random, 1994), 84: *Wie ich aufwachte, vernahm mein Ohr einen Klang, immer voller schwoll er an, nicht mehr im Traum durfte ich mich wähnen, Musik erschallte, und welche Musik! Als sie verklungen, trat R. mit den fünf Kindern zu mir ein und überreichte mir die Partitur des 'Symphonischen Geburtstagsgrusses', in Tränen war ich, aber auch das ganze Haus. Auf der Treppe hatte R. sein Orchester gestellt und so unser Tribschen auf ewig geweiht! Die 'Tribscher Idylle' so heisst das Werk ... Nach dem Frühstück stellte das Orchester sich wieder ein, und in der unteren Wohnung ertönte nun die Idylle wieder, zu unserer aller Erschütterung, darauf Lohengrin's Brautzug, das Septett von Beethoven, und zum Schluss noch einmal die nie genug Gehörte! Nun begriff ich R.'s heimliches Arbeiten, nun auch des guten Richter's Trompete (er schmetterte das Siegfried-Thema prachtvoll und hatte eigens dazu Trompete gelernte).*

⁶⁹ Richard Wagner, *Siegfried-Idyll* (Leipzig: Breitkopf & Härtel, c.1900), 13. https://imslp.org/wiki/Siegfried-Idyll,_WWV_103_(Wagner,_Richard).

⁷⁰ Johannes Brahms, *Johannes Brahms: Life and Letters*, ed. Styra Avins (Oxford: Oxford University Press, 1997), 350, 400.

⁷¹ Johannes Brahms, *Johannes Brahms Sämtliche Werke, Band 6* (Leipzig: Breitkopf & Härtel, 1926–27), 39. https://imslp.org/wiki/Piano_Concerto_No.1,_Op.15_(Brahms,_Johannes).

⁷² Mention of this manuscript occurs in most texts that refer in detail to this symphony. Many erroneously state that it is on a card, e.g. Malcolm MacDonald, *Brahms* (New York: Schirmer, 1990), 246; or a postcard, e.g. David Lee Brodbeck, *Brahms: Symphony No. 1* (Cambridge: Cambridge University Press 1997), 15, and Bachmann-Geiser, *Das Alphorn*, 111. Styra Avins, in *Johannes Brahms: Life and Letters* (Oxford: Oxford University Press, 1997), 225, even states that the 'postcard' was sent to Clara 'in a painted box from Switzerland'. Enquiry at the Staatsbibliothek, Berlin where it is now kept reveals that there is no knowledge of a box and it is not a postcard but part of a sheet of paper, blank on the reverse. It was donated to the library by Clara's youngest daughter Eugenie in 1936, before which it had been kept in a picture frame (email from curator, Roland Schmidt-Hensel, July 2012). Many sources also state that it was sent from the Rigi, however Brahms's accompanying text does not describe the open landscape of that area. Residents of Lauterbrunnen are familiar with the details of Brahms's holidays in this popular walkers' destination and this visit to the valley and the quotation are recorded in a book about Lauterbrunnen: Ernst Gertsch, *Der Schönste Platz der Welt* (Interlaken: Schaefli, 1997), 31.

⁷³ Reproduced with kind permission of the Staatsbibliothek, Berlin, Musikabteilung mit Mendelssohn-Archiv: Mus.ms.autogr. J. Brahms: 10.

⁷⁴ Johannes Brahms, *Symphony No. 1* (Berlin: Simrock, 1877), 49–50. https://imslp.org/wiki/Symphony_No.1,_Op.68_(Brahms,_Johannes).

⁷⁵ Author's collection.

⁷⁶ Joachim Raff, *Symphony No. 7* (Leipzig: Seitz, 1876), 38.

⁷⁷ Gustav Mahler, *Lieder und Gesänge* (Mainz: B. Schott's Söhne, c.1892), Vol. 3, 2. https://imslp.org/wiki/Lieder_und_Gesänge_aus_der_Jugendzeit_(Mahler,_Gustav).

⁷⁸ Paul Bekker, *Gustav Mahlers Sinfonien* (Berlin: Schuster & Loeffler, 1921), 108: *Nun aber denke Dir so ein großes Werk, in welchem sich in der Tat die ganze Welt spiegelt – man ist, sozusagen, selbst nur ein Instrument, auf dem das Universum spielt.*

⁷⁹ Arved Mark Ashby, *Absolute Music, Mechanical Reproduction* (Oakland, CA: University of California Press, 2010), 222: *Sie brauchen gar nicht mehr hinzusehen – Das habe ich schon alles wegkomponiert.*

⁸⁰ Gustav Mahler, *Symphony No. 4* (Vienna: Universal Edition, c.1905), 1. https://imslp.org/wiki/Symphony_No.4_(Mahler,_Gustav).

⁸¹ Gustav Mahler, *Symphony No. 7* (Leipzig: Eulenburg, 1909), 81. https://imslp.org/wiki/Symphony_No.7_(Mahler,_Gustav).

⁸² Richard Strauss, *Don Quixote* (Munich: Jos. Aibl Verlag, 1898), 25. https://imslp.org/wiki/Don_Quixote,_Op.35_(Strauss,_Richard).

⁸³ Richard Strauss, *Ein Heldenleben* (Leipzig: Leuckart, 1899), 304. https://imslp.org/wiki/Ein_Heldenleben,_Op.40_(Strauss,_Richard).

⁸⁴ Peter Höyng, 'Leaving the Summit Behind' in *Heights of Reflection: Mountains in the German Imagination from the Middle Ages to the Twenty-first Century* ed. Sean Moore Ireton and Caroline Schaumann (Elizabethtown, NY: Camden, 2012), 233.

[85] Alfons Ott, 'Richard Strauss und Ludwig Thuille: Briefe der Freundschaft 1877–1907', *Münchener Musikgeschichte*, Vol. 4 (1969), 185–6: *Nachts 2 Uhr fuhren wir auf einem Leiterwagen nach dem Dorfe, welches am Fuße des Berges liegt. Sodann steigen wir bei Laternenschein in stockfinsterer Nacht auf u. kamen nach 5 stündigen Marsche am Gipfel an. Dort hat man eine herrliche Aussicht. Staffelsee (Murnau) Rieg-, Ammer-, Würm-, Kochel-, Walchensee. Dann das Isarthal mit Gebirge, Ötzthaler- u. Stubaierferner, Innsbrucker Berge, Zugspitze, pp. Dann steigen wir auf der anderen Seite hinab, um nach Walchensee zu kommen, versteigen uns jedoch u. mußten in der Mittagshitze 3 Stunden ohne Weg herumklettern. Der Walchensee ist ein schöner See, macht einem jedoch melancolischen Eindruck, denn er ist rings von Wäldern u. hohen Bergen eingefaßt. Er hat herrliches, kristallhelles u. hellgrünes Wasser. Sodann fuhren wir über den See nach Uhrfelden, wo am Fuße des neben dem Heimgarten liegenden Herzogstand liegt. Von da eine Stunde über den Kösselberg eine Stunde an den Kochelsee (Wirtshaus Kösselberg). Schon auf dem Wege daher hatte uns ein furchtbarer Sturm überfallen, der Bäume entwurzelte u. uns Steine ins Gesicht warf. Kaum in Trockenen, ging der Sturm los. Der Kochelsee ein sehr romantischer, schöner See warf ungeheure Wellen, so daß eine Überfahrt nach dem gegenüber liegenden Schlehdorf, wo uns der Leiterwagen erwartete, nicht zu denken war. Nachdem der Sturm sich gelegt, mußten wir uns, ob wir wollten oder nicht dazu bequemen, um den ganzen Kochelsee (2 Stunden) herumzulaufen. Auf dem Wege kam wieder Regen u. so kamen wir endlich nach rasendschnellem Marsche (wir setzten nicht eine Minute aus) ermüdet, durchnäßt bis auf die Haut, in Schlehdorf an, wo wir übernachteten, u. fuhren dann am nächsten Morgen in aller Gemütsruhe auf dem Leiterwagen nach Murnau. Die Partie war bis zum höchsten Grad interessant, apart u. originell. Am nächsten Tage habe ich die ganze Partie auf dem Klavier dargestellt. Natürlich riesige Tonmalereien u. Schmarrn (nach Wagner).*

[86] Michael Kennedy, *Richard Strauss* (London: Dent, 1976), 140.

[87] Richard Strauss, *Eine Alpensinfonie* (Leipzig: Leuckart, 1915), 56.

[88] Gerard Hoffnung, *The Hoffnung Symphony Orchestra* (London: Dobson, 1955), 46. Copyright: The Hoffnung Partnership.

[89] Richard Strauss, *Daphne* (Vienna: self-published, 1938), 7: *Steiniges Flußufer, dichte Ölbaumgruppen. Letzte Sonne. Rechts steigt die Landschaft zum Hause des Fischers Peneios auf. Im Hintergrund ist der Fluß zu denken. Den Abschluß bildet das gewaltige Massiv des Olymp. Man hört die Bewegung großer Schafherden. Zurufe, Geläute, Schieben, Drängen, Hundegebell. Mitten hinein der Laut eines mächtigen Alphorns. Vorhang.*

[90] Reproduced with kind permission of Boosey & Hawkes Music Publishers Ltd and Schott Music Limited. All rights reserved.

[91] Edward Elgar, *From the Bavarian Highlands* (London: Stainer and Bell, 1901), 13. https://imslp.org/wiki/From_the_Bavarian_Highlands,_Op.27_(Elgar,_Edward).

[92] Arnold Bax, *Symphony No. 3* (London: Murdoch, Murdoch & Co., 1931).

[93] Edith Sitwell's text on a record sleeve for *Façade*, Decca Eclipse ECS560, 1970.

[94] Susana Walton, *William Walton: Behind the Façade* (Oxford: Oxford University Press, 1988), 60.

[95] William Walton, *Façade* Suite No. 1: 3. *The Swiss Yodelling Song* (Oxford: Oxford University Press, 1936), 33. Copyright Oxford University Press. Reproduced with permission.

[96] *Tempo*, Vol. 33 (Autumn 1954), 40.

[97] *Tempo*, Vol. 34 (Winter 1954/55), 39.

[98] Barry Tuckwell, *Horn* (New York: Schirmer, 1983), 113.

[99] David Matthews, *Britten, Life and Times* (London: Haus Publishing, 2003), 72.

[100] Stephen Gamble and William C. Lynch, *Dennis Brain: A Life in Music* (Denton, TX: University of North Texas Press, 2011), 158.

[101] Barry Tuckwell, *Horn* (New York: Schirmer, 1983), 112.

[102] Benjamin Britten, *Serenade for Tenor, Horn and Strings*, Op. 31 (London: Boosey & Hawkes, 1944), 1. Copyright Boosey & Hawkes. Reproduced with permission.

[103] Benjamin Britten, *Alpine Suite* (London: Boosey & Hawkes, 1956), 6. Copyright Boosey & Hawkes. Reproduced with permission.

Chapter 6

The Alphorn for the Modern Composer

This final chapter presents an exploration of different facets of the use of the alphorn today. Influence can be seen in two directions: this folk instrument is increasingly used by the modern composer, and classical music has also had an impact on the music that is now played on the alphorn in Switzerland. With the use of the alphorn in popular genres, film music, rock and jazz, the boundaries around various categories of music are becoming blurred.

There are now thousands of alphorn players, mostly in Switzerland but also outside its borders. Through the summer months there are annual courses, festivals, competitions or just gatherings for alphorn playing, primarily in Switzerland but also in Austria and Germany, in Canada, the United States and Japan.

Fig. 6.1. Männlichen Alphorntreffen, 2016. The author plays alongside 120 alphorn players, on a high ridge at the foot of the Eiger.

The seminal collection of classic melodies used by alphorn players is Alfred Leonz Gassmann's *s'Alphornbüechli* (The Little Alphorn Book) which has remained in print in its original form, including the text in old German script, since its initial publication in 1938. Gassmann initially quotes many of the old *Kühreien* transcripts, thereafter the main body of music comprises 90 'tourist'-type melodies that he has both assembled and composed himself in this style.

Fig. 6.2. Gassmann, *s'Alphornbüechli*, 1938. The cover shows an alphorn player on Kleine Scheidegg, in the Bernese Oberland.[1]

Two examples of pieces from this collection show the alphorn 'tradition' as it stands today: *Am Brienzersee* (Beside Lake Brienz), Fig. 6.3, and *De Neu Melchthaler* (The New Melody from Melchtal), Fig. 6.4. These demonstrate the way in which the notes of the harmonic series are used, the breath-length phrases that end with a paused note, the freedom from strict pulse or rhythm, the repeating motifs, the contrasting slower and faster sections and the use of the echo. The written instructions also reiterate the stylistic requirements with such comments in *Am Brienzersee* as *Kräftig und bestimmt* (strong and clear), *steigernd* (crescendo), *etwas bewegter* (somewhat moving forward), *echo, rit.,* and *ten.*, many pauses, commas, copious dynamic markings and the comment below the music: '*Wärend der I. und III. Teil in majestätischer Größe erstehen, soll der II. Teil leicht beschwingt erklingen*' (While the first and third sections should rise in great majesty, the second part should have a light, swinging sound). In *De Neu Melchthaler* the instructions *In voller Rundung* (full and round), *Langsam, getragen* (slow, held back) and *etwas schneller* (somewhat faster) are given.

There is also no shortage of new music to play: many alphorn enthusiasts compose, producing collections of 'typical' alphorn pieces for solo, duo, trio or quartet. Surprisingly, considering the restrictions of the notes available (and approved) and what is considered 'normal' with regard to rhythms, shapes, tonality and phrase structure, all are unique. Many pieces have a place name as a title and herein lies a potential clue to the individual characteristics of each composition: the mountain skyline as viewed from the place in the title is often used as the shape of the melody. Thus a melody is rooted in its location and connected to its landscape in a unique way which reinforces the feeling of nostalgia that can result from hearing a piece named after one's home village.

Fig. 6.3. Gassmann, *s'Alphornbüechli*: *Am Brienzersee*. © 1938 by Hug Musikverlage, Zürich (Walter Wild Musikverlag GmBH).

Fig. 6.4. Gassmann, *s'Alphornbüechli*: *De Neu Melchthaler*. © 1938 by Hug Musikverlage, Zürich (Walter Wild Musikverlag GmBH).

There is, however, a deep division among Swiss alphorn players between those who believe that stereotypical music as it is still played for tourists today should not be diluted, and those who wish to explore the full potential of the instrument. This is a complex situation. In 1977 the song *Swiss Lady*, composed by Peter Reber and performed by the Pepe Lienhard Band, was awarded sixth place in the Eurovision Song Contest, the highest position ever achieved by a Swiss entry. The 'lady' in the lyrics is the alphorn and a 'cheesy-pop' refrain is played on the instrument. It was immediately very popular in Switzerland, but the traditional alphorn establishment was rocked.

In 1980 it was challenged again when renowned Swiss alphorn specialist Hans-Jürg Sommer composed an atmospheric piece for two alphorns named *Moos-Ruef* (Call over the Moorland). Instead of using harmonic no. 4 as its tonic, upon which the major arpeggio is built with the addition of harmonics no. 5 and no. 6, the tonic of this piece is the 6th harmonic. This produces a minor triad when harmonics no. 7 (a rather flat minor 3rd above) and no. 9 (the dominant) are added. The resulting intonation is extraordinary, as the low tuning of harmonic no. 7 emphasises its minor character and produces a haunting quality that is unavailable in equal temperament. Sommer also used harmonic no. 11, the 'alphorn *fa*' in this melody (written as F in Fig. 6.5), which sounds a quarter-tone above the note written. The melody of the first section makes prominent use of the 'alphorn *fa*', the second section is reminiscent of the traditional evening prayer or *Betruf*, and the third is a mischievous *Tanz der Geister* (Dance of the Ghosts). Sommer and a colleague played *Moos-Ruef* in a Swiss Federal Yodel Association alphorn competition in 1980. The performance was disqualified. Comments were made by the adjudicators that the playing of such pieces is 'provocative' and marks are not awarded.

It is easier as an outsider from the UK to take an overview of the situation. Without doubt, the 'postcard' melodies are beautiful and symbolise the idyll of a mountain landscape, in accordance with the guidelines of the Swiss Federal Yodel Association. With engagements to play for a Swiss person's wedding or another Swiss-related event either in the UK or abroad, this style of playing is what is expected, and the joy that such music brings particularly to Swiss living abroad is immeasurable. It is equally understandable, however, that players and composers should wish to explore different facets of the instrument and demonstrate that the alphorn has more to offer than this. Its unique sonority does not need to be tied to this role: there is a vast range of possibility of different types of music and sounds that can be played on this instrument.

Swiss Lady and *Moos-ruef* are examples of new approaches to the instrument, that have now taken root in Switzerland. Young female performers such as Eliana Burki and Lisa Stoll popularise the instrument in the world of jazz, rock and other related idioms, and many beautiful works have been written in the wake of *Moos-ruef* that use the minor tonality and the 'alphorn *fa*'.

Fig. 6.5. Hans-Jürg Sommer, *Moos-Ruef*, 1980.[2]

Two further new styles are now found within Switzerland. Much of the music of Balthasar Streiff is exploratory: he uses multiphonics, didgeridoo techniques, vocalisation and electronic loop effects to create innovative, powerful music, often atmospheric and even mystical. Another direction arises from the situation that many who now take up the alphorn are already proficient players of the trumpet, French horn, euphonium or trombone. The enforced relaxation of attitudes in Swiss alphorn competitions has now progressed to the stage that the use of advanced techniques from the repertoire of these instruments, such as flutter tonguing, lip trills or the playing of chords,[3] is something that is now not only allowed: performers of works that include such techniques can win a Swiss alphorn competition. As an example, the winner of the solo performance category at the international alphorn festival in Nendaz in the canton of Valais in 2009, Frenchman Olivier Brisville, played a haunting work of his own composition that includes some of these techniques: a lip trill in bar 19, and chords in the final two bars. Thus the tables have finally turned: classical music now influences the development of alphorn playing in Switzerland.

Fig. 6.6. Olivier Brisville, *Solo No. 1*, 2009. The piece includes a lip trill and chords.[4]

Fig. 6.7. A group entertains guests at the international alphorn festival in Nendaz, 2009.
Photo: Frances Jones.

A unique situation has led to the use of bitonality in Swiss alphorn music. As noted earlier, the instrument played in Switzerland today uses the harmonic series of F sharp (or G flat), which, it is agreed among Swiss players, is the alphorn's most resonant length. In other countries, however, there is an increasing amount of repertoire composed for an instrument a little longer, of 12ft in length, which produces harmonics based on F, because in this key it can more easily be accompanied by a keyboard, strings or winds. Many players nowadays, therefore, have the facility to play either in F sharp or in F, and there are now a few fascinating and often beautiful works that combine these two tonalities.[5] An example is *Firnfern 1* (Distant Horizon 1), composed by Balthasar Streiff in 1997, an evocative piece in which the melody is shared between the two instruments. Often the F alphorn is given a phrase and the F sharp instrument, labelled as *Ges* (G flat) on the part, responds with the echo a semitone higher (see Fig. 6.8).

The alphorn itself is now found to an increasing degree in the concert hall. There are many significant works that have been composed for the instrument for both formal and semi-formal performance. There are twentieth-century concertos for alphorn and strings or alphorn with full orchestra, there are works for alphorn and concert band, and also a large number of smaller-scale works for alphorn with organ, alphorn with choir, alphorn with piano and other combinations of instruments. As the key of F sharp is not an ideal key for interaction with other instruments, the carbon-fibre instrument has been developed with interchangeable sections, to facilitate playing in a range of different keys, from alphorn in G descending chromatically to alphorn in D.

Firnfern 1

Balthasar Streiff

Fig. 6.8. Balthasar Streiff, *Firnfern 1*, 1997. The notes on stave 1 sound a semitone higher than the notes on stave 2.[6]

Fig. 6.9. The author performs on a carbon-fibre alphorn set up in E flat. Aberystwyth Musicfest. 2006. Photo: Martin Jones.

Issues of intonation arise when the alphorn is played alongside other instruments fixed in equal temperament, such as an organ or a piano, or indeed, with an orchestra. Many works written within the alphorn community for alphorn and organ, or alphorn and piano, do not resolve the 'out of tune' issue, and the resultant clashes of tuning unfortunately reinforce the perception that the alphorn is to be dismissed in 'serious' music circles because it cannot be played in tune. While the octaves and fifths of a well-made modern instrument now sit perfectly with equal temperament, the 'alphorn *fa*' and the flat 7th harmonic need sensitive use and when used in an appropriate context, without simultaneous sounding of equally tempered neighbours, are haunting and atmospheric.

When a work for alphorn is written by a composer in response to a commission from a French horn player who also plays the alphorn, the result is either a mix of genres, or indeed no reference to the heritage of the alphorn at all. Unlike all the quotations seen in the previous chapter, where the symbolism of the alphorn as a metaphor for the Alps has been fundamental to the relevance of the instrument, here the approach to the alphorn is often that of a fascinating and unusual sound, rather than as a representation of the Alps.

Hungarian French horn player Jozef Molnar settled in Lausanne, Switzerland and is a leading ambassador for the alphorn: he has commissioned many works to be written for the instrument. Fellow Hungarian Ferenc Farkas (1905–2000) wrote a *Concertino Rustico* for alphorn and strings for him in 1977. The short three-movement work opens with an extended passage of atmospheric unaccompanied horn calls, with echoes, although there are no typical alphorn motifs. The main material for the first movement comprises lively rhythmic music that utilises the full range of the alphorn. The second movement also begins with unaccompanied alphorn calls and the strings later join with a gentle, peaceful backdrop. Hungarian harmony and tonality pervade the soundscape, the 'alphorn *fa*' accommodated alongside the scale with the raised fourth that is familiar from Hungarian-style music of Brahms or Kodály. The lively dance-like final movement is remarkable for its range of tonality and key, despite the restrictions placed on the work by the harmonic series of the alphorn.

Another of Molnar's commissions was from Swiss composer Jean Daetwyler (1907–1994). His *Dialogue avec la nature*, for alphorn, piccolo and orchestra, is a descriptive work, a series of reflections of Switzerland's natural landscape, although not with the images with which the alphorn is usually associated. While other composers celebrate the beauty of the alpine landscape with the beautiful sounds of the alphorn call, Daetwyler chooses here to do the opposite. The first movement depicts the insignificance of man in the world of nature and the isolation of the herdsman alone in the mountains, with a forbidding backdrop of emptiness, of snowfields and glaciers. Herdsman's calls are interspersed with shimmering, unsettling music that creates pictures of intimidating open spaces and jagged, dangerous icefalls.

Fig. 6.10. Postcard, c.1930: alphorn player by icefalls of the Rhone glacier. These icefalls no longer exist, as the glacier has now retreated to reveal just the scoured bedrock beneath.[7]

In the second movement, the alphorn player is less a soloist, more a participant in a surreal, spooky dance, as if spirits and skeletons are cavorting and celebrating the transience of man. The third movement sets up a mysterious and ominous atmosphere, with lonely bird calls on flute, piccolo and oboe. Traditional alphorn calls eventually grow into a solemn rendition of the celebrated *Ranz des Vaches* in the version familiar from the festivals in Vevey. The fourth movement is a grotesque and driving Dance of Death with a central funereal procession. The relationship of the alphorn with the Swiss landscape in this work has no connection with communication of the beauty of an idyllic holiday destination. There are no carefree tourist alphorn motifs here.

A third work, for alphorn and piano, was written for Molnar by French horn player Ifor James, a leading player in England: *Alphorn Memory*. It was written in 1998 after James had settled in Freiburg in southern Germany.

Fig. 6.11. Ifor James, *Alphorn Memory*, 1998.[8]

This is a beautiful work, and although it begins and ends with atmospheric unaccompanied horn calls, again the music has no motivic connection with Swiss alphorn music: rather it resembles the style of writing found in the Prologue of Britten's *Serenade for Horn and Strings*; indeed the publication offers performance on a normal French horn as an alternative option. A gentle echo resonance effect is created by the alphorn bell placed under the grand piano while the sustain pedal is held down; this effect would be achieved with a French horn by holding the bell near the strings. The alternative specification for organ instead of piano does not accommodate this.

Alarum for a Warmer World was written for me by my husband, Martin Jones, for performance at the opening of the first World Conference on Climate Change in Exeter, UK, in 2005. There were several reasons for the choice of the alphorn for this *Alarum* (*quasi*-Shakespeare). It signified a wake-up call to scientists who had gathered from across the globe and a warning of the potential dangers in store if we do not address what we might be doing to our planet. Documents record the use of the alphorn in the Alps as early as 1212 as a call to arms and to sound the alarm in times of conflict.[9] The alphorn was also an appropriate choice of instrument because of its simplicity, its strength and its position as a symbol of the landscape, particularly that of Switzerland, a country so visibly affected by climate change with the dramatic retreat of its glaciers (see Fig. 6.10). Certain features found in Swiss alphorn music are apparent: echo effects, freedom from regular pulse, breath-length phrases that end with paused notes and repeating short motifs. It is restricted to the notes of the harmonic series. Nevertheless, *Alarum for a Warmer World* is not 'typical' Swiss music: there is little to connect it with such melodies in its motifs, effect or character. There is an effective use of the unique intonation of the alphorn's natural harmonics in this work, with interplay between the tonic major and the dominant minor as chord centres. As in *Moos-Ruef* and other works that use the 7th harmonic to supply a particularly flat rendition of a minor third, this feature adds depth to the colour of the tonality.

The music opens with an arresting call, followed by its echo. It proceeds with many motivic statements, perhaps questioning, perhaps answers or comments, in a multi-sectioned Shakespearian declamatory monologue. The call to action returns as a final reprise: a plan to protect the planet must be established before the close of the conference. The composer uses modern quarter-tone notation to indicate the flat 7th harmonic (written B) and the high 11th harmonic, the 'alphorn *fa*' (written F).

Fig. 6.12. Martin Jones, *Alarum for a Warmer World*, 2005.[10]

An Englyn for Frances by Welsh composer Gareth Peredur Churchill was written for a concert of new music at the University of Aberystwyth, Wales, in 2005. An *englyn* is a form of Welsh poetry. There are at least 11 different types of *englyn*, each with a specific syntax, number of lines, number of syllables in each line and an individual rhyming pattern. Thus, this piece follows a pre-determined formal literary structure: it is in the form named *unodl union*. Musical features include freedom from pulse, breath-length phrases, contrasting sections and an echo, but similarities with Swiss alphorn music go no further. As with *Moos-Ruef,* the work centres around the minor triad produced from harmonics nos. 6, 7 and 9. It has no bar lines and is a meticulously written score with extremes of dynamic range, detailed articulation, grace notes and glissandi. Based on the minor tonality, it is a piece that reflects the gentle, misty Welsh landscape.

Fig. 6.13. Gareth Peredur Churchill, *An Englyn for Frances,* 2005.[11]

The sound of the natural harmonics, the rich tone and the freedom from rhythm give the work a primeval, timeless atmosphere. Thus, this alphorn work is also a reflection of a landscape, but one very different from that of Switzerland. It is extraordinary that a Welsh composer chose the voice of the alphorn to represent his own natural world and that he has been able to convey an equally haunting impression with this instrument, although it is a world so different from the landscape of the Alps.

Fig. 6.14. *An Englyn for Frances* drifts over the gentle Welsh countryside at sunset. The author, Moel Famau, North Wales.

Tree of Light was the result of a commission from the London 2012 Olympic Committee for a composition by Orlando Gough to be performed on three occasions at ceremonies to welcome the arrival of the Olympic torch on its journey around the UK in July 2012. The torch-bearer lit a fire in a cauldron where the flame remained overnight in 70 places and *Tree of Light* was written for the ceremonies in three locations before its return to London: in Oxford, Henley-on-Thames and in Reading's Madejski Football Stadium. Each performance was to include 1,000 local schoolchildren, a local choir of 200 and a group of disabled adults who played percussion instruments. The professional band comprised saxophones, French horn, oboe, steel pans, bass guitar, drums and alphorn. *Tree of Light* is a multi-media work that describes our interaction with the environment, mistakes made, and lessons learned. The work consists of 14 musical numbers that follow the life-story of a tree in the forest. It tells of its growth and of the habitat it provides for animal life, the use of the forest for timber, its depletion, plunder and burning, its rebirth and finally its conservation. Each performance was in the open air and began at dusk: the increasing darkness was an integral part of the setting. The children, dressed in white, danced in front of the forest backdrop in vast formations that represented trees, different types of animals, men felling the forest and other scenes in the course of the narrative.

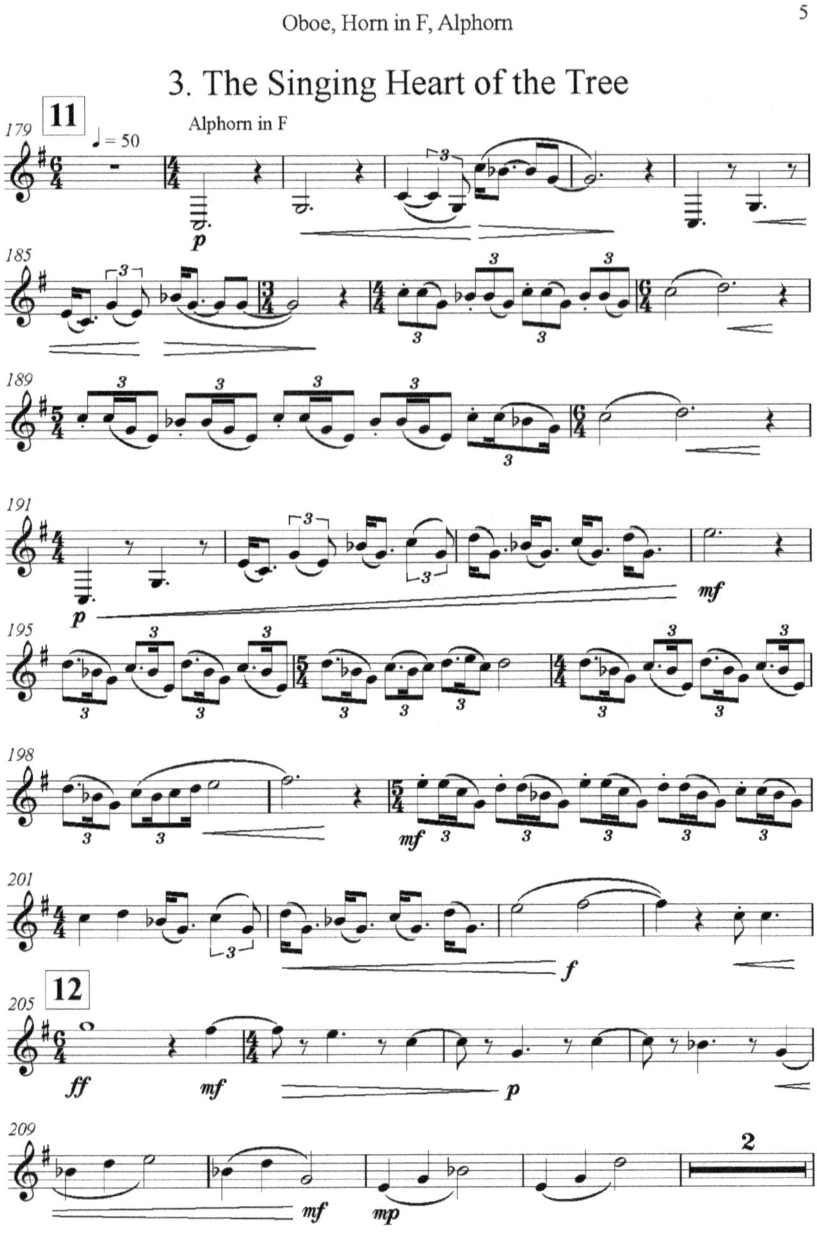
5
Oboe, Horn in F, Alphorn
3. The Singing Heart of the Tree
11
Alphorn in F
= 50
12

Fig. 6.15. Orlando Gough, first alphorn solo from *Tree of Light*, 2012.[12]

The alphorn is the voice of the tree: the spokesman for the forest. It has substantial solos at three points during the 45-minute production. It is rare to find the alphorn used not because it is Swiss, but because it is a tree. Gough's music for the alphorn is primeval and powerful, majestic and proud. In the first solo, 'The Singing Heart of the Tree', the accompaniment for the first 16 bars is a low tremolo played on the bass guitar which is gradually joined by rolls on steel pans from bar 196 to enhance the impact of the crescendo. From bar 200, a soprano saxophone sometimes echoes the alphorn line and sometimes plays a third above it. Gradually the accompaniment dies away as the number comes to a close, the thousand children standing still; each child slowly waving a long stick with an LED light at the tip, to create pre-arranged patterns in the darkness like fireflies.

A new direction in composition for the alphorn was encountered in the film score for *The Grand Budapest Hotel.* The composer of the scores for *The King's Speech* and some of the *Harry Potter* films, Alexandre Desplat, recorded the soundtrack for his next film, *The Grand Budapest Hotel*, in May 2013. The hotel is set in an imaginary mountainous region of Eastern Europe, reached by a funicular railway. There are snow scenes, cable car rides, a chase on skis and sledges and a 'cliff-hanger' scene over the end of a glacier. The score includes music for yodel quartet and a part for alphorn, and the soundtrack won a BAFTA award for Best Original Film Music. It is a new and fascinating phenomenon, however, that a composer can encounter the timbre of an 'alphorn' on a computer-generated sound palette and incorporate that sound into a film score unconstrained by the fact that an alphorn can only play the notes of the harmonic series. Thus here, throughout the score, the alphorn has been given melodies that cannot be played on one instrument.

The solution for the recording was to use a mixture of wooden and carbon-fibre alphorns that were set up at a variety of different lengths as required for each number. There were four alphorns, four microphones, three alphorn players and a spacious recording studio. I marked up a separate copy of the part for each player for each number with the notes colour-coded to indicate on which instrument each note would be played, while a chart showed which player should play which instrument or instruments in each number. Notation raised interesting questions, but I advised that the part should be written as if for a French horn in F and that we would make the further transpositions as required. Melodic flow and shape posed a challenge, as was the balance between the timbre of the different instruments and the tone of each player.

ALPINE HORN   **THE GRAND BUDAPEST HOTEL**

E♭ F F♯ G

THEME 1 & 2

Theme 1

Freely

♩ = 58

Theme 2

Freely ♩ = 138

	needed	Marc	Jossy	Frances
p.1 Theme 1	F, F♯, G	F	F♯	G
p.1 Theme 2	E♭, F, F♯, G	F	F♯	E♭, G

Fig. 6.16. Alexandre Desplat, extract from the score for the film *The Grand Budapest Hotel* and chart devised to play the extract. © 2014 Copyright Galilea Music.[13]

Epilogue

These examples show a selection of the types of music now being composed for the alphorn, both in Switzerland and beyond its borders. They demonstrate a blurring of the boundaries between art music and other genres. Whereas in the eighteenth-century, Czech composers incorporated the herdsman's horn played by musically literate herdsmen in formal performances, nowadays music is written to be played by musicians trained on other instruments.

Viewed from a purely historical perspective, this exploration has revealed an extraordinary journey unique in the development of a musical genre. We find that the humble herdsman's horn was a well-established piece of equipment for use in animal management and farming routines by the time of the Romans. Because of this background, an idiosyncratic repertoire evolved that is unlike that of any other instrument. Once the alphorn was discovered by the world of art music, we begin to see the instrument and its music through the eyes of the composer, upon whom the haunting beauty of its world made a powerful impression: a world then reflected back to an audience with profound understanding and deep affection.

The instrument was invited into the performance space to portray shepherds in the annual retelling of the Christmas story in many Czech villages in the eighteenth century. We find that an unsophisticated work by Leopold Mozart is not a strange anomaly but belongs to a genre not uncommon at the time of its composition. As composers were becoming aware of the instrument and its traditional Swiss repertoire, we find that simple alphorn calls from the Swiss canton of Appenzell were known in many parts of Europe by the eighteenth century and were to become not only the basis for the favourite Swiss song, still much loved today, but were also transformed into the popular song *Home, sweet home.* We see how a large number of nineteenth- and twentieth-century composers were moved by the sound of the alphorn to incorporate its motifs into their works at significant moments, and that the instrument has enjoyed a considerable revival in recent times.

This voyage of discovery has also revealed many unexpected things. The opportunity to get to know what may have been the motifs played by eighteenth-century Czech herdsmen is remarkable. Examination of the material used in a seven-minute work by Leopold Mozart in relation to its cultural context has shed light on the use of a repertoire of musical references to the *pastorella* tradition that are not generally recognised by audiences of today. That so many nineteenth-century composers used alphorn motifs that they heard in the Alps is an indication of the impact made on them by the sound of the instrument then, an impact that is still felt by visitors to the mountains today.

A nineteenth-century composer included an alphorn motif in a work in the expectation that it would be recognised by his audience. This indicates the degree to which awareness of the sound of the alphorn was assumed even then. This awareness has evolved and changed. Audiences of the eighteenth century may still have been familiar with the use of the horn by a local herdsman; audiences of the nineteenth century may have become aware of the instrument through literature, whereas contemporary audiences are more normally aware of the alphorn because of visits to the Alps, Swiss events or through the media.

Ground-breaking compositions that used the natural harmonics, such as Britten's *Serenade for Tenor, Horn and Strings,* or on a smaller platform Sommer's *Moos-ruef,* created shock-waves at the time but both in their way have opened people's eyes and prepared the way for progress, new understandings and new concepts.

Looking back, it is interesting that from the time of Haydn until the present day, composers rarely included the instrument itself in the formal performance space; instead, they were able to refer to it using its motifs as a metaphor. The power of just a simple alphorn figuration to represent the natural world in works for formal performance is a remarkable phenomenon.

Whereas in the Czech examples, where villagers were musically literate and parts for the herdsman were included in the works written for the community's Christmas celebrations, in the nineteenth century, alphorn players rarely entered the world of the professional composer and the formal performance. More recently, however, the circle has become complete: not only is there a substantial body of works written for the concert platform that use the alphorn; in addition, many experienced brass players play the instrument, and sophisticated brass instrument techniques are used in alphorn repertoire.

Nowadays, the instrument itself is increasingly incorporated into the music of diverse styles. The restrictions placed on the music that was acceptable to the Swiss Federal Yodel Association have been loosened, and the instrument is emancipated, its repertoire free to grow in a multitude of different directions. Works such as *Moos-ruef* and *Firnfern 1*, once seen as a threat to the image of the instrument, are now much-loved contributions to the repertoire for the alphorn, not only because they are evocative and beautiful, but also because such music is unique to the alphorn. Nevertheless, it is clear that the carefully contrived image of the alphorn as the ambassador of the Alps remains as strong today as it was in the nineteenth century, deeply ingrained as it is in the hearts of the Swiss and those who visit the Alps. The two worlds not only coexist: the potential for a new sort of alphorn music using experimental techniques adds considerably to the exploration of the unique potential and beauty of the instrument. Even the world of popular music has embraced the special voice of the alphorn and its sound is replicated on synthesizers, so that its timbre can be enjoyed without the constraints of the harmonic series.

More people than ever play the instrument; more people than ever come into contact with the instrument during holidays in Switzerland as travel has become increasingly easier. Not only do enthusiastic players from all over the world congregate in their hundreds at numerous alphorn festivals held every summer in Switzerland; many thousands of visitors also come and enjoy the events too.

Although the alphorn is no longer used in the Alps as a herding instrument, its connection to the Swiss landscape is maintained in other ways, by the composition of pieces based on particular skylines. The association of the instrument with landscape has now been extended to places and contexts outside the Alps: in works such as *Alarum for a Warmer World*, *An Englyn for Frances* and *Tree of Light* the alphorn represents the natural world in places quite different from picturesque mountains of Switzerland. The alphorn is, after all, a hollowed-out tree. It retains the form of a tree; furthermore, it also retains its purity in that it has none of the man-made additions or alterations that are found on all other musical instruments. The use of the natural harmonic series reinforces its status as an unsophisticated, natural instrument, while its size and the strength of its tone emphasise its earthy character.

This book celebrates the impact that the alphorn has had on the musical world, on many levels of society, for many centuries. It is Switzerland's chosen national icon. Beyond the symbolism of its sound, even stripped of its aural presence, it is embraced as the voice of their mountains. An image of an alphorn features on countless Swiss souvenirs, as enthusiastically today as it has done since the beginnings of tourism. We find it depicted on Swiss postcards and stamps, chocolate boxes and musical boxes, milk cartons and sugar wrappers, calendars and place-mats, key rings and pen-knives. For the tourist, the depiction represents the sound, which represents the mountains, which represents an idyllic holiday experience. For the Swiss, it is the voice of their rural heritage, even when only in a picture. No other instrument has this power. The underlying strength of this imagery is the haunting sound of the alphorn, that all these depictions recall. It is fundamentally its aural impact that has communicated with us across the centuries, an effect that shows no sign of waning. The outstanding beauty and unique voice of the instrument will undoubtedly ensure that it will continue to be enjoyed long into the future.

Notes

[1] Alfred Leonz Gassmann, *s'Alphornbüechli*, (Zürich: Hug, 1938). Copyright Hug Musikverlage. Reproduced with permission, and the following two music extracts.

[2] Hans-Jürg Sommer, *Moos-Ruef*, (Oensingen: Sommer, 1980). Reproduced with kind permission of Hans-Jürg Sommer.

[3] If a player, while playing a low note, also sings a higher note, for example the tenth above or the twelfth above, not only are the two notes heard, but intermediate harmonics also resonate to make a three or four part chord. It is a technique found in Weber's *Concertino* for horn, Op. 45, written in 1815.

[4] Olivier Brisville, *Solo No. 1*, unpublished (2009). Reproduced with kind permission of Olivier Brisville.

[5] This is achieved in one of four ways: a pair of instruments, an alternative longer upper section (most alphorns are made in three sections), a short additional section that can be inserted at the first joint, or use of a carbon-fibre instrument that can be set up in six different lengths, to provide a range of harmonic series from G down to D.

[6] Balthasar Streiff, *Firnfern 1*, unpublished (1997). Reproduced with kind permission of Balthasar Streiff.

[7] Photo-Edition: O. Süssli-Jenny, Thalwil-Zürich.

⁸ Ifor James, *Alphorn Memory*, (Crans-Montana: Reift, 1998). Reproduced with kind permission of Marc Reift.

⁹ Alois Lütolf, *Sagen, Bräuche und Legenden aus den fünf Orten Luzern, Schwyz, Unterwalden und Zug* (Luzern: Schiffmann, 1815), 413.

¹⁰ Martin Jones, *Alarum for a Warmer World*, unpublished (2005). Reproduced with kind permission of Martin Jones.

¹¹ Gareth Peredur Churchill, *An Englyn for Frances*, unpublished (2005). Reproduced with kind permission of Gareth Peredur Churchill.

¹² Orlando Gough, *Tree of Light*, unpublished (2012). Reproduced with kind permission of Orlando Gough.

¹³ Alexandre Desplat, *The Grand Budapest Hotel*, (Wisconsin: Hal Leonard, 2014), opening number. Printed by kind permission of Hal Leonard Europe Limited.© 2014 Copyright Galilea Music.

Appendix
Works that include Alphorn Motifs

This Appendix is a comprehensive list of published works that I have found that include a quotation of a motif reminiscent of material played on an alphorn. However, several factors prevent it from being a complete list:

1. it is not possible to locate every piece that has a quotation of an alphorn motif; indeed new works will continue to be written,
2. it is not always possible to be certain that a composer has used an alphorn motif in a composition: this is a personal interpretation,
3. material written for the alphorn is not included.

Bach, Johann Sebastian. *Pastorale* BWV 590, in *Bach-Gesellschaft Ausgabe* Vol. 38. Organ. Leipzig: Breitkopf & Härtel, 1891.

Battmann, Jacques Louis de. *Le Cor des Alpes (de H. Proch), Fantasia pour le Piano*, Op. 253. Bordeaux: Ikelmer, 1868.

Bax, Arnold. *Symphony No. 3*. Los Angeles: Warner Chappell Music, 1929.

Becker, Constantin Julius. *The Alphorn*. Voice, horn and piano. London: Ewer, 1844.

Beethoven, Ludwig van. *Symphony No. 6*. Leipzig: Breitkopf & Härtel, c.1826.

Bergancini, Joseph. *Le Ranz des Vaches avec Six Variations*. Piano. Paris: Bergancini, c.1810.

Berlioz, Hector. *Le Jeune Pâtre Breton*. Voice, horn and piano. Leipzig: Breitkopf & Härtel, c.1903.

Berlioz, Hector. *Symphonie fantastique*. Paris: Schlesinger, 1845.

Bishop, Henry Rowley. *Clari, or the Maid of Milan*. London: Goulding, D'Almaine, Potter & Co, 1823.

Bishop, Henry Rowley. *Home Sweet Home*. Voice and piano. London: Goulding, D'Almaine, Potter & Co, c.1825.

Bishop, Henry Rowley. *Melodies of Various Nations*. Voice and piano. London: Goulding, D'Almaine, Potter & Co, 1921.

Brahms, Johannes. *Piano Concerto No. 1*. Winterthur: Rieter-Biedermann, 1861.

Brahms, Johannes. *Symphony No. 1*. Berlin: Simrock, 1877.

Britten, Benjamin. *Alpine Suite*. 3 recorders. London: Boosey & Hawkes, 1956.

Britten, Benjamin. *Fanfare for St. Edmundsbury*. 3 trumpets. London: Boosey & Hawkes, 1969.

Britten, Benjamin. *Serenade for Tenor, Horn & Strings*. London: Boosey & Hawkes, 1944.

Carpentier, Adolph Clair le. *Divertissement du Salon sur le Cor des Alpes, mélodie de Proch*, Op. 49. Piano. Paris: Meissonnier, 1840.

Clementi, Muzio. *Six Sonatinas*, Op. 36. Piano. Vienna: Artaria, 1788.

Copland, Aaron. *Four Dance Episodes from Rodeo*. Orchestra. London: Boosey & Hawkes, 1946.

Crusell, Bernhard. *Clarinet Concerto No. 2*, Op. 5. Hamburg: Sikorski, 1962. First published 1818.

Daetwyler, Jean. *Dialogue avec la nature*, for alphorn, piccolo and orchestra. Crans-Montana: Reift, 1971.

Debussy, Claude. *Prélude à l'Après-Midi d'un Faune.* Orchestra. Paris: Fromont, c.1895.

Delius, Frederick. *A Mass of Life.* London: Boosey & Hawkes, 1905.

Dohler, Theodore. *Fantasie Brillante pour le Piano sur l'air favori Le Cor des Alpes de H. Proch*, Op. 18. Paris: Blanchet, c.1835.

Dohler, Theodore. *Grande Fantasie et Variations sur des thèmes favoris de l'opéra Guillaume Tell de Rossini pour piano*, Op. 28. Paris: Schott, 1860.

Dohler, Theodore. *Caprice brilliant et une Valse Suisse sur le Ranz des Vaches, pour Piano*, Op. 40. Paris: Schonenberger, 1842.

Donizetti, Gaetano. *Betly, o La Capanna Svizzera.* Operetta. Milan: Ricordi, 1854.

Doppler, Franz. *Souvenir du Rigi*, Op. 34. Flute, horn and piano, with optional cow bell in C. Mainz: Schott, 1876.

Doret, Gustave. *Les Armaillis.* Opera. Paris: Choudens, 1906.

Dvořák, Antonín. *Symphony No. 4.* London: Novello, 1892.

Elgar, Edward. *From the Bavarian Highlands.* Voice and piano. London: Stainer & Bell, 1901.

Gerdessen, Johannes. *Alphornklänge, Salonstück für Pianoforte*, Op. 20. Leipzig: Grude, 1893.

Gossec, François-Joseph. *Le Triomphe de la République, ou Le Camp de Grand Pré.* Opera. Paris: Huguet, 1794.

Grétry, André. *Guillaume Tell.* Opera. Paris: Huguet, 1791.

Grétry, André. *Lisbeth.* Opera. Paris: Frey, 1797.

Grieg, Edvard. *Seven Children's Songs*, Op. 61, No. 3: *Farmyard Song.* Piano. Oslo: Christiania, 1895.

Grieg, Edvard. *Two Nordic Melodies*, Op. 63, No. 2: *Kuhreigen.* Orchestra. Leipzig: Peters, 1896.

Haydn, Josef. *Die Jahreszeiten.* Oratorio. Leipzig: Breitkopf & Härtel, 1802.

Haydn, Joseph. *Die Schöpfung.* Oratorio. Leipzig: Breitkopf & Härtel, 1820.

Holst, Gustavus von. *Fantasia Tirolese.* Harp. London: Holst, c.1826.

Hünten, François. *Le Cor des Alpes. Variations for Piano*, Op. 113, No. 3. Paris: Hünten, c.1860.

Kienzl, Wilhelm. *Der Kuhreigen*, Op. 85. Opera. Leipzig: Weinberger, 1911.

Leduc, Alphonse. *Le Cor des Alpes, 2e Fantaisie Gracieuse*, Op. 103. Piano. Paris: Leduc, c.1845.

Liszt, Franz. *Drei Lieder aus Schillers Wilhelm Tell*, No. 2: *Der Hirt.* Voice and piano. Leipzig: Breitkopf & Härtel, 1917.

Liszt, Franz. *Les Préludes.* Orchestra. Leipzig: Breitkopf & Härtel, 1885.

Liszt, Franz. *Tagebuch eines Wanderers: Eindrücke und Poesien No. 5: Die Tellskapelle; No. 11: Ein Abend in den Bergen; Melodieenblüten von den Alpen No. 1 and No. 6; Paraphrasen No. 1: Kuhreigen. Aufzug auf die Alp.* Leipzig: Breitkopf & Härtel, 1916.

Mahler, Gustav. *Symphony No. 4.* Wien: Doblinger, 1902.

Mahler, Gustav. *Symphony No. 7.* Leipzig: Eulenburg, 1909.

Mahler, Gustav. *Zu Strassburg auf der Schanz'.* Voice and piano. Mainz: Schott, 1892.

Mendelssohn, Felix. *Sinfonie No. 9.* String orchestra. Leipzig: Deutscher Verlag für Musik, 1967.

Meyerbeer, Giacomo. *Chanson Suisse: Fais Sonner la Clochette: Ranz des Vaches d'Appenzell.* Voice and piano. Paris: Brandus, 1849.

Meyerbeer, Giacomo. *Des Schäfers Lied.* Voice, clarinet (or harmonium) and piano. Paris, 1842.

Meyerbeer, Giacomo. *Dinorah: Sui prati il fior.* Opera. London: Boosey & Hawkes, no date.

Meyerbeer, Giacomo. *Rondino sur le Ranz des Vaches.* Piano. Paris: Schlesinger. no date.

Niedermeyer, Louis. *Fantaisie sur le Ranz des Vaches*, Op. 94. Piano. Paris: Pacini, c.1826.

Nielsen, Carl. *Helios Overture*, Op. 17. Copenhagen: Hansen, 1905.

Proch, Heinrich. *Das Alpenhorn*, Op. 18. Voice and piano. Wien: Diabelli, 1836.

Raff, Joachim. *Symphony No. 7.* Leipzig: Seitz, 1876.

Rossini, Gioachino. *Il Guglielmo Tell.* Opera. Paris: Troupenas, 1829.

Rummel, Joseph. *Le Cor des Alpes.* Piano. Paris: Lemoine, c.1860.

Schubert, Franz. *Der Hirt auf dem Felsen.* Voice, clarinet and piano. Berlin: Lienau, c.1960. First published 1830.

Schumann, Robert. *Liederalbum für die Jugend* Op. 79, No. 9: *Des Knaben Berglied.* Voice and piano. Leipzig: Peters, c.1900. First published 1849.

Schumann, Robert. *Liederalbum für die Jugend* Op. 79, No. 23: *Des Sennen Abschied.* Voice and piano. Leipzig: Peters, c.1900. First published 1849.

Schumann, Robert. *6 Gedichte von N. Lenau und Requiem* Op. 90, No. 4: *Die Sennin.* Voice and piano. Leipzig: Peters, c.1900. First published 1850.

Schumann, Robert. *Manfred.* Leipzig: Breitkopf & Härtel, c.1862.

Schütz, Heinrich. *Weinachtshistorie.* Oratorio. Basel: Barenreiter, 1955. First published 1664.

Strauss, Richard. *Alphorn*, Op. 29. Voice, horn and piano. Mainz: Schott, 1995. First published 1819.

Strauss, Richard. *Don Quixote.* Munich: Aibl, 1898.

Strauss, Richard. *Eine Alpensinfonie*, Op. 64. Orchestra. London: Eulenburg, 1996. First published 1915.

Strauss, Richard. *Ein Heldenleben*, Op. 40. Orchestra. London: Eulenburg, 1958. First published 1899.

Strauss, Richard. *Sinfonia Domestica*, Op. 53. Orchestra. Berlin: Bote & Bock, 1904.

Sweelinck, Jan Pieterszoon. *Fantasia*, in The Fitzwilliam Virginal Book. Organ. Compiled 1609–1619. First published 1899.

Verroust, Stanislas. *Le Ranz des Vaches, suivi d'un Air suisse favori varié.* Oboe and piano, Op. 40. Paris: Richault, c.1845.

Viotti, Giovanni Battista. *Concerto for Violin and Orchestra No. 9.* Arrangement for string sextet and piano by Theodore Latour. London: Bland & Weller, 1784.

Viotti, Giovanni Battista. *Serenade for piano with violin obbligato and cello.* Theme quoted in Chappell White, *Viotti, Thematic Catalogue.* New York: Pendragon, 1985.

Wachs, Frédéric. *40 Mignardises pour Piano,* No. 4: *Le Cor des Alpes.* Paris: Aine, c.1860.

Wagner, Richard, *Tristan und Isolde,* WWV 90. Opera. Leipzig: Breitkopf & Härtel, 1860.

Wagner, Richard. *Die Meistersinger von Nürnberg,* WWV 96. Opera. Mainz: Schott, c.1903.

Wagner, Richard. *Siegfried-Idyll,* WWV 103. Orchestra. Mainz: Schott, c.1878.

Walton, William. *Façade: The Swiss Yodelling Song.* Orchestra and voice. Oxford: Oxford University Press, 1936.

Weigl, Joseph. *Die Schweizerfamilie.* Operetta. Vienna: Weigl, c.1810.

Bibliography

Books and Journal Articles

Ashby, Arved Mark. *Absolute Music, Mechanical Reproduction.* Oakland, CA: University of California Press, 2010.

Avins, Styra. *Johannes Brahms: Life and Letters.* Oxford: Oxford University Press, 1997.

Bachmann-Geiser, Brigitte. *Das Alphorn vom Lock- zum Rockinstrument.* Bern: Haupt, 1999.

Baedeker, Karl. *Switzerland, and the adjacent districts of Italy, Savoy, and the Tyrol. Handbook for Travellers.* Leipzig: Baedeker, 1889.

Baedeker, Karl. *Switzerland, with neighbouring Lakes of Northern Italy, Savoy, and the adjacent districts of Piedmont, Lombardy and the Tyrol. Handbook for Travellers.* Koblenz: Baedeker, 1863.

Bartók, Béla. *The Relationship of Folk Song to the Development of the Art Music of our Time, Béla Bartók Essays,* ed. Benjamin Suchof. London: Faber, 1992.

Baumann, Max Peter. *Musikfolklore und Musikfolklorismus.* Winterthur: Amadeus, 1976.

Bekker, Paul. *Gustav Mahlers Sinfonien.* Berlin: Schuster & Loeffler, 1921.

Berkovec, Jiří. *České Pastorely.* Prague: Supraphon, 1987.

Berlioz, Hector. *Grand Traité d'Instrumentation et d'Orchestration Modernes.* Paris: Schonenberger, 1843.

Berlioz, Hector. *The Memoirs of Hector Berlioz,* trans. David Cairns. London: Gollancz, 1969.

Boswell, James. *Life of Samuel Johnson.* Dublin: Cross, 1792.

Bridel, Louis and Philippe-Sirice. *Conservateur Suisse ou Recueil Complet des Étrennes Helvétiennes.* Lausanne: Knab, 1813.

Britten, Benjamin. Letters in *Tempo* Vol. 33 (Autumn 1954), 40, and Vol. 34 (Winter 1954/55), 34.

Brodbeck, David Lee. *Brahms: Symphony No. 1.* Cambridge: Cambridge University Press, 1997.

Burney, Charles. *The Present State of Music in Germany, the Netherlands and the United Provinces.* London: Becket, 1773.

Byron, George Gordon. *The Works of Lord Byron,* ed. Thomas Moore. London: Murray, 1832.

Capeler, Moritz. *Pilati Montis Historia.* Basel: Rodolphi, 1767.

Carmichael, Alexander. *Carmina Gadelica, Hymns and Incantations collected in the Highlands of Scotland in the Last Century.* 1899. Reprint, Edinburgh: Floris, 1994.

Chateaubriand, François-René. *Memoires d'Outre-tombe.* 1849. No publisher given.

Cooper, James Fenimore. *Le Bourreau de Berne, ou L'Abbaye des Vignerons.* Paris: Gosselin, 1839.

Description de la Fête des Vignerons Célébrée à Vevey, le 5 août 1819. Vevey: Loertscher, 1819. No author given.

Duncan, Barbara. 'Home Sweet Home', *University of Rochester Bulletin* Vol. 4, No. 2 (Winter 1949). Reprint, no page numbers.

Dumas, Alexandre. *Impressions de Voyage Suisse.* Paris: Charpentier, 1834.

Ebel, Johann Gottfried. *Schilderung der Gebirgsvölker in der Schweitz* Vol. 1. Leipzig: Wolf, 1798.

Erbsen, Wayne. *Rousing Songs and True Tales of the Civil War.* Asheville, NC: Native Ground Books, 1999.

Finno, Jacobus. *Piae Cantiones ecclesiasticae et scholasticae veterum episcoporum.* Greifswald: Ferberum, 1582.

Gamble, Stephen and William C. Lynch. *Dennis Brain: A Life in Music.* Denton, TX: University of North Texas Press, 2011.

Geiser, Brigitte. *Das Alphorn in der Schweiz.* Bern: Haupt, 1976.

Gertsch, Ernst. *Der Schönste Platz der Welt.* Interlaken: Schlaefli, 1997.

Gesner, Conrad. *De raris et admirandis herbis.* Zurich: Gesnarum, 1555.

Goethe, Johann Wolfgang von. *Faust, eine Tragödie.* Stuttgart: Cotta'schen, 1834.

Grove, George, ed. *A Dictionary of Music and Musicians.* London: Macmillan, 1889.

Guarini, Battista. *Il Pastor Fido.* Venice: Bonfadino, 1590.

Haller, Albrecht von. *Die Alpen.* Bern: Haller, 1729.

Hoffnung, Gerard. *The Hoffnung Symphony Orchestra.* London: Dobson, 1955.

Hornbostel. Erich Moritz von and Curt Sachs. *Zeitschrift für Ethnologie* Vol. 46 (1914), 553–90.

Höyng, Peter. 'Leaving the Summit Behind' in *Heights of Reflection: Mountains in the German Imagination from the Middle Ages to the Twenty-first Century* ed. Sean Moore Ireton and Caroline Schaumann. Elizabethtown, NY: Camden, 2012.

Huet, Félix. *Étude sur les différentes écoles se violon depuis Corelli jusqu'à Baillot.* Châlons-sur-Marne: Thouille, 1880.

Jones, Frances. 'The influence of the Christmas Pastorella on Beethoven's *Pastoral Symphony*', *The Consort* Vol. 72 (Summer 2016), 90–108.

Kennedy, Michael. *Richard Strauss.* London: Dent, 1976.

Kyburz, Abraham. *Theologia Naturalis.* Bern, 1754. No publisher given.

Laborde, Benjamin. *L'essai sur la Musique Ancienne et Moderne.* Paris: Pierre, 1780.

Lindner, Edwin. *Richard Wagner über Tristan und Isolde.* Leipzig: Breitkopf & Härtel, 1912.

Lütolf, Alois. *Sagen, Bräuche und Legenden aus den fünf Orten Luzern, Schwyz, Unterwalden und Zug.* Luzern: Schiffmann, 1815.

MacDonald, Malcolm. *Brahms.* New York: Schirmer, 1990.

Mannlich, Joseph Christian von. 'Gluck à Paris en 1774: Memoires sur la musique à Paris à fin du règne de Louis XV', *La Revue musicale* Vol. 15 (1934), 260.

Matthews, David. *Britten, Life and Times.* London: Haus, 2003.

Mendelssohn, Felix. *Reisebriefe von Felix Mendelssohn Bartholdy aus den Jahren 1830 bis 1832*, ed. Paul Mendelssohn Bartholdy. Leipzig: Hermann Mendelssohn, 1861.

Morrell, Jemima. *Miss Jemima's Swiss Journal: The first conducted tour of Switzerland,* 1863. Facsimile reprint, London: Routledge, 1998.

Murray, John. *A Glance at some of the Beauties and Sublimities of Switzerland.* London: Murray, 1829.

Murray, John. *A Hand-Book for Travellers in Switzerland, Savoy and Piedmont.* London: Murray, 1838.

Nietzsche, Friedrich. *Also Sprach Zarathustra.* Leipzig: Fritzsch, 1886.

'On the National Songs and Music of Switzerland', *The New Monthly Magazine and Humorist* Vol. 59 (1840), 362–84. No author given.

'On the Ranz des Vaches', *Harmonicon* Vol. 2 (1824), 37–39. No author given.

Ott, Alfons. 'Richard Strauss und Ludwig Thuille: Briefe der Freundschaft 1877–1907', *Münchener Musikgeschichte* Vol. 4 (1969), 185–6.

Pendle, Karin. 'The Transformation of a Libretto: Goethe's "Jery und Bätely" ', *Music and Letters* Vol. 55, No. 1 (January 1974), 77–88.

Polybius, *Histories,* trans. Evelyn Shuckburgh. London: Loeb Classical Library, 1927.

Praetorius, Michael. *Syntagma Musicum.* Wittenberg: Wolfenbüttel, 1619.

Pugnetti, Gino. *The Life and Times of Beethoven.* London: Hamlyn, 1967.

'Ranz des Vaches', *The Music Box* Vol. 4, No. 1 (1969), 53–58. No author given.

Rawson, Robert. 'Gottfried Finger's Christmas Pastorellas', *Early Music* Vol. 33, No. 4 (2005), 591–606.

Roscoe, Thomas. *The Tourist in Switzerland and Italy.* London: Jennings, 1830.

Rousseau, Jean-Jacques. *Dictionnaire de Musique.* Paris: Duchesne, 1768.

Rutherford, Andrew. *Byron: A Critical Study.* Redwood City, CA: Stanford University Press, 1961.

Schiller, Friedrich von. *Wilhelm Tell,* 1804. Reprint, New York: Macmillan, 1898.

Scholes, Percy. *Oxford Companion to Music.* Oxford: Oxford University Press, 1960.

Schumann, Robert. *Gesammelte Schriften über Musik und Musiker.* Leipzig: Wigand, 1854.

Scott, Walter. *Anne of Geierstein or the Maiden of the Mist.* Boston, MA: Sanborn, Carter and Bazin, 1855.

Shakespeare, William. *King Lear.* London: Butter, 1608.

Shelley, Percy Bysshe. *The Poetical Works of Percy Bysshe Shelley.* Paris: Galiagni, 1841.

Silber, Irwin. *Songs of the Civil War.* New York: Columbia University Press, 1960.

Szadrowsky, Heinrich. 'Die Musik und die tonerzeugenden Instrumente der Alpenbewohner', *Jahrbuch des Schweizer Alpenclubs* Vol. 4 (1867/8), 313.

Tarenne, George. *Recherches sur le Ranz des Vaches, ou sur les Chansons Pastorales des Bergers de la Suisse.* Paris: Louis, 1813.

Thornton, Robert John. *Philosophy of Medicine, or Medical Extracts on the Nature of Health.* London: Johnson, 1797.

Thumb, Tom. *The Famous Tommy Thumb's Little Story-book.* London: Crowder, 1760.

Todd, R. Larry. *Fanny Hensel: The Other Mendelssohn.* New York: Oxford University Press, 2009.

Todd, R. Larry. *Mendelssohn: A Life in Music.* New York: Oxford University Press, 2003.

Tuckwell, Barry. *Horn.* New York: Schirmer, 1983.

Tunbridge, Laura. 'Schumann as Manfred', *The Musical Quarterly* Vol. 87 (2004), 557.

Twain, Mark. *A Tramp Abroad.* London: Chatto & Windus, 1880.

Varro. *De Rerum Rusticum* (c.90–27 BC). Reprint, trans. W. D. Hooper, London: Loeb Classical Library, 1934.

Viotti, Giovanni Battista. Letter, 26 June 1792, in Collection of papers of or relating to Giovanni Battista Viotti. ms. 4118, Royal College of Music Library, London.

Virgil, *Aeneid*, trans. H. Rushton Fairclough, revised G. P. Goold. Loeb Classical Library. MA: Harvard University Press, 1918.

Wagner, Cosima. *Cosima Wagner's Diaries: an abridgement*, ed. Geoffrey Skelton. London: Random House, 1994.

Walton, Susana. *William Walton: Behind the Façade.* Oxford: Oxford University Press, 1988.

Walton, William. *Façade.* Edith Sitwell, Peter Pears, The English Opera Group Ensemble. Anthony Collins. LP Decca Eclipse ECS560. 1970, sleeve notes.

Weber, Max Maria von. *Carl Maria von Weber, ein Lebensbild.* Leipzig: Keil, 1864.

White, Chappell. *Viotti, Thematic Catalogue.* New York: Pendragon Press, 1985.

Wiskus, Jessica. *The Rhythm of Thought: Art, Literature and Music after Merleau-Ponty.* Chicago: University of Chicago Press, 2013.

Wood, John and Nelly. 'An Autumn Tour of Switzerland', *The Graphic* issues 249–259 (September–November 1874).

Wordsworth, William. *Memorials of a Tour on the Continent.* London: Longman, 1822.

Zwinger, Theodorus. *Dissertationem Medicarum Selectorum.* Basel: Koenig, 1710.

Scores

Bach, Johann Sebastian. *Pastorale* in F major, BWV 590, in *Bach-Gesellschaft Ausgabe* Vol. 38. Leipzig: Breitkopf & Härtel, 1891.

Bach, Johann Sebastian. *Weihnachts-Oratorium.* London: Eulenburg, 1961.

Bax, Arnold. *Symphony No. 3.* Los Angeles: Warner Chappell Music, 1929.

Beethoven, Ludwig van. *Symphony No. 6.* Leipzig: Breitkopf & Härtel, c.1826.

Berlioz, Hector. *Le Jeune Pâtre Breton.* Leipzig: Breitkopf & Härtel, c.1903.

Berlioz, Hector. *Symphonie fantastique.* Paris: Schlesinger, 1845.

Bishop, Henry Rowley. *Clari, or the Maid of Milan.* London: Goulding, D'Almaine, Potter & Co, 1823.

Bishop, Henry Rowley. *Melodies of Various Nations.* London: Goulding, D'Almaine, Potter & Co, 1821.

Brahms, Johannes. *Piano Concerto No. 1.* Winterthur: Rieter-Biedermann, 1861.

Brahms, Johannes. *Symphony No. 1.* Berlin: Simrock, 1877.

Brisville, Olivier. *Solo No. 1.* unpublished, 2009.

Britten, Benjamin. *Alpine Suite.* London: Boosey & Hawkes, 1956.

Britten, Benjamin. *Serenade for Tenor, Horn & Strings.* London: Boosey & Hawkes, 1944.

Brogerin, Maria Josepha Barbara. *Liederbüchlein,* 1730. ms. Rootuus, Gonten, Zentrum für Appenzeller und Toggenburger Volksmusik.

Churchill, Gareth Peredur. *An Englyn for Frances.* Unpublished, 2005.

Clementi, Muzio. *Six Sonatinas,* Op. 36. Piano. Vienna: Artaria, 1788.

Corelli, Arcangelo. *Concerto Grosso in G minor 'Fatto per la Notte di Natale',* Op. 6, No. 8. Leipzig: Kahnt, 1913.

Czerni, Dominico. *Offertorium Pastorale,* 1759. ms. MXXVIIIF242, České Muzeum Hudby, Prague.

Daetwyler, Jean. *Dialogue avec la nature,* for alphorn, piccolo and orchestra. Crans-Montana: Reift, 1971.

Daubrawský, Ferdinand. *Pastorella Czeska.* ms. MVIIID110, České Muzeum Hudby, Prague.

Daubrawský, Ferdinand. *Pastorella Czeska.* ms. MVIIID111, České Muzeum Hudby, Prague.

Daubrawský, Ferdinand. *Pastorella Czeska.* ms. MVIIID130, České Muzeum Hudby, Prague.

Debussy, Claude. *Prélude à l'Après-Midi d'un Faune.* Paris: Fromont, c.1895.

Delius, Frederick. *A Mass of Life.* London: Boosey & Hawkes, 1905.

Desplat, Alexandre. *The Grand Budapest Hotel.* Wisconsin: Hal Leonard, 2014.

Donizetti, Gaetano. *Betly, o La Capanna Svizzera.* Milan: Ricordi, 1854.

Duschek, ?František. *Pastorella.* ms. MVIIIF23, České Muzeum Hudby, Prague.

Elgar, Edward. *From the Bavarian Highlands.* London: Stainer & Bell, 1901.

Farkas, Ferenc. *Concertino Rustico* for alphorn and string orchestra. Budapest: Universal, 1977.

Fibiger, Jan Augustin. *Pro Nativitate Domini.* ms. MXXIXD249, České Muzeum Hudby, Prague.

Gassmann, Alfred Leonz. *s'Alphornbüechli.* Zurich: Hug, 1938.

Glück, J. B. *Les Délices de la Suisse.* Basel: Knop, 1835.

Gossec, François-Joseph. *Le Triomphe de la République, ou Le Camp de Grand Pré.* Paris: Huguet, 1794.

Gough, Orlando. *Tree of Light.* Unpublished, 2012.

Grétry, André. *Guillaume Tell.* Paris: Huguet, 1791.

Habermann, František Václav. *Motetto pastoralni II.* ms. MXIF8, České Muzeum Hudby, Prague.

Handel, Georg Frideric. *Il Pastor Fido* in *Collected Works* Vol. 30. Edited by Friedrich Chrysander. Leipzig: Breitkopf & Härtel, 1892.

Handel, Georg Frideric. *Messiah.* Facsimile reprint. Edited by Friedrich Chrysander. Hamburg: Strumper, 1892.

Haydn, Josef. *Die Jahreszeiten.* Leipzig: Breitkopf & Härtel, 1802.

Holetschek. *Pastorella.* ms. MXXB282, České Muzeum Hudby, Prague.

Holst, Gustavus von. *Fantasia Tirolese.* London: Holst, c.1826.

James, Ifor. *Alphorn Memory.* Crans-Montana: Reift, 1998.

Jech, František Václav. *Mottetto.* ms. MXF198, České Muzeum Hudby, Prague.

Jones, Martin. *Alarum for a Warmer World.* unpublished, 2005.

Kautník, Tomáš Norbert. *Offertorium Pastorale*. ms. MXXIXB187, České Muzeum Hudby, Prague.

Kollovrátek, Tomáš. *2do Pastorella*. ms. MXID42, České Muzeum Hudby, Prague.

Kollovrátek, Tomáš. *Offertorium Pastorale*, 1810. ms. MXID54, České Muzeum Hudby, Prague.

Kollovrátek, Tomáš. *Offertorium pro Festis Natalitijs*. ms. MXID94, České Muzeum Hudby, Prague.

Kuhn, Gottlieb Jakob, ed. *Sammlung von Schweizer Kühreihen und alten Volkliedern*, 2nd ed. Bern: Burgdorfer, 1812.

Kuhn, Gottlieb Jakob, ed. *Sammlung von Schweizer Kühreihen und alten Volkliedern*, 3rd ed. Bern: Burgdorfer, 1818.

Linek, Jiři Ignác. *Pastorella*. ms. MVIB155, České Muzeum Hudby, Prague.

Linek, Jiři Ignác. *Pastorella*. ms. MXVF342, České Muzeum Hudby, Prague.

Liszt, Franz. *Drei Lieder aus Schillers Wilhelm Tell*, in *Musikalischwerke* Series 7, Vol. 1. Leipzig: Breitkopf & Härtel, 1917.

Liszt, Franz. *Les Préludes*. Leipzig: Breitkopf & Härtel, 1885.

Liszt, Franz. *Tagebuch eines Wanderers*, in *Pianofortewerke* Vol. 4. Leipzig: Breitkopf & Härtel, 1916.

Mahler, Gustav. *Zu Strassburg auf der Schanz'.* Mainz: Schott, 1892.

Mahler, Gustav. *Symphony No. 4*. Wien: Doblinger, 1902.

Mahler, Gustav. *Symphony No. 7*. Leipzig: Eulenburg, 1909.

Matiegka. *Pastorala*, 1833. ms. MXIIE151, České Muzeum Hudby, Prague.

Mendelssohn, Felix. *Sinfonie No. 9*. Leipzig: Deutscher Verlag für Musik, 1967.

Meyerbeer, Giacomo. *Ranz des Vaches d'Appenzell. 40 Mélodies à une et plusiers voix*. Paris: Brandus, c.1849.

Mozart, Leopold. *Denkmäler Deutscher Tonkunst* Vol. 2: *Leopold Mozart Ausgewählte Werke*. Edited by Max Sieffert. Leipzig: Breitkopf & Härtel, 1908.

Mozart, Leopold. *Der Morgen und der Abend der Innwohnern der hochfürstl. Residenz-Stadt Salzburg melodisch und harmonisch angekündigt. Oder: Zwölf Musikstücke für das Clavier, davon eine täglich in der Vestung Hohensalzburg auf dem sogenannten Hornnwerke Morgens und Abends gespielt wird*. Augsburg: Lotter, 1759.

Mozart, Leopold. *Divertimento Sinfonia Pastorale*. Mus. ms. 15328, Preußischer Kulturbesitz, Staatsbibliothek, Berlin.

Mozart, Leopold. *Pastorale für Streichquartett und Corno Pastoriccio*. ms. XI29298(H26029), Archiv der Gesellschaft der Musikfreunde, Wien.

Mozart, Leopold. *Sinfonia Pastorale*. ms. Ba 120 Bü 161, Fürst zu Hohenlohe-Bartensteinisches Archiv, Schloss Neuenstein, Staatsarchiv, Ludwigsburg.

Mozart, Leopold. *Sinfonia Pastorale ex G*. ms. D-HR/III41/24/o, Fürstlich Öttingen-Wallersteinischen Bibliothek, University of Augsburg.

Mozart, Leopold. *Sinfonia Pastorale ex G*. Mus. ms. 6218D-R,540, Bayerische Staatsbibliothek, München.

Mozart, Leopold. *Sinfonia Pastorella*. ms. MGII42, Chor-Stift Lambach, Stadtbibliothek, Augsburg.

Mozart, Leopold. *Sinfonia Concerto for Alphorn and Strings.* Edited by Marvin McCoy. Minneapolis: McCoy, 1978.

Mozart, Leopold. *Sinfonia Pastorale.* Edited by Kurt Janetzky. Zürich: Kunzelmann, 1979.

Mozart, Leopold. *Sinfonia Pastorale.* Edited by Christian Broy. Augsburg: Wißner, 2001.

Mozart, Leopold. *Sinfonia Pastorella for Alphorn and Strings.* Edited by Frances Jones. Oxford: Edition HH, 2014.

Mozart, Wolfgang Amadeus. *Galimathias Musicum,* in *Wolfgang Amadeus Mozarts Werke* Series 24, Supplemente Vol. 1. Leipzig: Breitkopf & Härtel, 1886.

Mozart, Wolfgang Amadeus. *Symphony No. 19,* in *Wolfgang Amadeus Mozarts Werke* Series 8, *Sinfonien* Vol. 1. Leipzig: Breitkopf & Härtel, 1880.

Niedermeyer, Louis. *Fantaisie sur le Ranz des Vaches.* Paris: Pacini, c. 1826.

Nowotný, Josef Ondřej. *Offertorium Pastorale.* ms. MXLA157, České Muzeum Hudby, Prague.

Orff, Carl. *Carmina Burana.* Mainz: Schott, 1937.

Petipeský, Tadeáš. *Motteto de nativitate pro Sacro die Certatio pastoralis,* 1761. ms. MIIIA146, České Muzeum Hudby, Prague.

Raff, Joachim. *Symphony No. 7.* Leipzig: Seitz, 1876.

Reber, Peter. *Swiss Lady.* Kronach: Geiger, 1977.

Rhaw (or Rhau), Georg. *Symphoniae Iucundae.* Wittenberg: Rhaw, 1538.

Rhaw (or Rhau), Georg. *Bicinia Gallica, Latina, Germanica et Quaedam Fugae.* Wittenberg: Rhaw, 1545.

Rossini, Gioachino. *Guillaume Tell.* Paris: Troupenas, 1829.

Ryba, Jakub Jan. *Pastoral Offertorium.* ms. MXIVG79, České Muzeum Hudby, Prague.

Schubert, Franz. *Der Hirt auf dem Felsen.* Berlin: Lienau, c.1960.

Schubert, Franz. *Symphony No. 7* [now No. 9] in *Franz Schuberts Werke* Series 1. Leipzig: Breitkopf & Härtel, 1884.

Schumann, Robert. *Sämtliche Lieder,* Vol. 2. Leipzig: Peters, c.1900.

Schumann, Robert. *Robert Schumanns Werke* Series 8. Leipzig: Breitkopf & Härtel, 1887.

Schumann, Robert. *Manfred.* Leipzig: Breitkopf & Härtel, c.1862.

Štietina, Josepho. *Pastorella Nativitate D[omini] N[ostri] J[esu] Christi.* ms. MXVA202, České Muzeum Hudby, Prague.

Strauss, Richard. *Alphorn.* Mainz: Schott, 1995.

Strauss, Richard. *Daphne.* Vienna: Strauss, 1938.

Strauss, Richard. *Don Quixote.* Munich: Aibl, 1898.

Strauss, Richard. *Eine Alpensinfonie.* Leipzig: Leuckart, 1915.

Strauss, Richard. *Ein Heldenleben.* Leipzig: Leuckart, 1899.

Streiff, Balthasar. *Firnfern 1.* unpublished, 1997.

Viotti, Giovanni Battista. *Concerto for Violin and Orchestra No. 9.* Arrangement for string sextet and piano by Theodore Latour. London: Bland & Weller, 1784.

Viotti, Giovanni Battista. *Serenade for piano with violin obbligato and cello.* Theme quoted in Chappell White, *Viotti, Thematic Catalogue.* New York: Pendragon Press, 1985.

Vivaldi, Antonio (?Nicolas Chédeville). *Six Sonatas: Il Pastor Fido.* Op. 13. Paris: Boivin, c.1737.

Vivaldi, Antonio. Concerto in D *La Pastorella.* Edited by Gian Francesco Malipiero. Milan: Ricordi, 1953.

Vivaldi, Antonio. *Le quattro stagioni: da Il cimento dell'armonia e dell'inventione,* Op. 8. Edited by Paul Everett and Michael Talbot. Milan: Ricordi, 2010.

Vogt, Gustav. *Hom sweet Hom!* 1865. ms. 14098, Bibliothèque nationale, Paris.

Wagner, Richard. *La Descente de la Courtille.* Mainz: Schott, 2014.

Wagner, Richard. *Tristan und Isolde.* Leipzig: Peters, 1860.

Wagner, Richard. *Siegfried-Idyll.* Leipzig: Breitkopf & Härtel, c.1878.

Wagner, Sigismund von. *Acht Schweizer-Kühreihen, mit Musik und Text.* Bern: Haller, 1805.

Walton, William. *Façade* Suite No. 1. Oxford: Oxford University Press, 1936.

Wyss, Johann Rudolf, ed. *Sammlung von Schweizer Kühreihen und Volksliedern,* 4th ed. Bern: Burgdorfer, 1826.

Index

Weber, Carl Maria von, 195, 242,
   266, 293
William Tell, 160, 204, 211, 220,
   225, 227, 257
Wordsworth, William, 149, 156,
   181

Y

yodel, 20, 21, 190, 202, 209, 213,
   214, 254, 257, 261, 263, 289

Z

zampogna, 108
Zanetti, Roger, 7
Želiv, 32, 78
Zwinger, Theodor, 144, 145, 146,
   148, 180
Zwingli, Ulrich, 148

www.ingramcontent.com/pod-product-compliance
Lightning Source LLC
Chambersburg PA
CBHW070902080426

R18103500001B/R181035PG41932CBX00011B/1

9 781648 892462